POSTCARD HISTORY SERIES

Ritchie County

IN VINTAGE POSTCARDS

POSTCARD HISTORY SERIES

Ritchie County

IN VINTAGE POSTCARDS

Rock S. Wilson

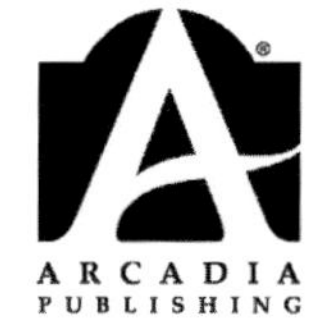

ISBN 978-0-7385-1710-0

Published by Arcadia Publishing
Charleston, South Carolina

Printed in the United States of America

Library of Congress Catalog Card Number: 2004108735

For all general information contact Arcadia Publishing at:
Telephone 843-853-2070
Fax 843-853-0044
E-mail sales@arcadiapublishing.com
For customer service and orders:
Toll-Free 1-888-313-2665

Visit us on the Internet at www.arcadiapublishing.com

Contents

Introduction

The writing of this book has truly been a labor of love.

My deep affinity for the county stems from the fact that my family has a long history here. My great-great-grandfather Archibald Blackburn Wilson of Pennsboro (Lynn Camp) was the first county surveyor in Ritchie County and was responsible for surveying many of the lines that separated the new Ritchie County from the counties from which it was formed. He also represented Ritchie County in the convention that framed the first constitution for the state of West Virginia in December of 1861. He was very instrumental in the formation of the United Brethern (UB) Church in Pennsboro and occupied the first grave in the cemetery when he died in 1866. His son, my great-grandfather Bazil Wilson, lived in the Goffs area all of his life and is buried in the Bethany Cemetery. Bazil Wilson's son, my grandfather Hank Wilson of Smithville and later Harrisville, worked for "the Hope" and also lived in Ritchie County all of his life. He is buried in the Independent Order of Odd Fellows (IOOF) Cemetery in Harrisville. My father lived in Ritchie County until his late 40s, when he moved to Parkersburg in order to be closer to work. However, he still lives in Ritchie County in his heart. My roots indeed grow deep here—150 years deep.

I have been collecting Ritchie County postcards for many years in anticipation of eventually writing this book. I was amazed at the vast amount of postcards of Ritchie County, especially those that date to around the first decade of the 20th century. I did not have quite enough to fill this book in the way I desired, so I began to inquire of others if they might have postcards I could borrow. I went first to David Scott of the Ritchie County Historical Society. He was kind enough to read this entire publication prior to print to assist with accuracy. I then went to Dean Six, who is certainly one of the most knowledgeable individuals alive regarding the history of the county and the owner of quite a vast collection of postcards. He also reviewed captions for me in order to assure additional accuracy. It was not until someone told me of Ella Lilly that I hit the "mother lode." I was told that she had been collecting Ritchie County postcards for many years, and that I should see her. When I called, she readily agreed to allow me to see her collection. By this time, I was sure that I had acquired most of the cards that were ever made of Ritchie County. I could not have been more wrong. She had an incredible collection, including more than 100 cards that I had never seen anywhere in publication. It brought new excitement to this project and probably moved this mission from interesting to historically important. With bated breath, I inquired about her willingness to allow them to be used in my publication. She acquiesced, and I could not be more appreciative for her generosity. Her help has led me to print nearly 200 of the best cards of the lot and to consider a second publication in the future. The hunt continues, and you just may see another volume in this series when I have found what I believe to be 200 more images worthy of print. In this vein, I ask readers to inform me of any cards not seen in this book that they may own or be aware of, to let me know of any additional information known about a particular card, or to correct any caption that may have incorrect information, in hopes of setting the record straight in the sequel. There are indications that there may be several hundred Ritchie County postcards in total, and we have just hit the tip of the iceberg. We shall see.

I do not profess to be a great scholar of Ritchie County history. This project, particularly through research of the captions, has taught me a great deal. However, most of the cards speak for themselves and show a very interesting perspective of Ritchie County history. Keep in mind that all the pictures shown are actual postcards, mostly with divided backs and made for mailing. They are not photographs; that's what makes them interesting. Postcards are images that have been created from already existing photographs. By taking enough interest in an image to turn it into a postcard, the image instantly takes on significance. It is no longer just a photograph, but a photograph that someone thought was interesting enough to make a permanent record of in the form of a postcard. Postcards provide great historical significance to us today because we know they had importance at the time of their making. Much of my information for captions came from the Minnie Kendall Lowther history and the many publications printed by the Ritchie County Historical Society.

I would like to thank my lovely wife, Valerie, for putting up with these postcards lying all over our home for the many weeks it took to organize this project, for supporting me in all things, and for her many prayers. I would also like to send a thank you to the most wonderful child I have ever known, Timber Cheyenne, age 2, for not tromping all over or destroying Daddy's postcard collection.

Many of the cards in this publication are very personal. One card shows the First Apostolic Church of Harrisville where I attended church most of my life. Another card depicts Court House Cave near where I lived and played endlessly as a youth. Other cards in this book depict the Safe Insurance Building in Harrisville that I owned for many years as well as the interior of the R.C. Marshall Hardware in Cairo, a store that I assisted manually in the restoration of and now share ownership in. Still more cards show the building where my office is now located in Pennsboro as well as the courthouse where I now spend a great deal of my life. The United Brethern Church in Pennsboro, where my great-great-grandfather was laid to rest, is depicted in yet another card in this book. My life is all over many of these cards. I believe many of you will have this same experience as you peruse these marvelous postcards, and I have high hopes they will take you down a wonderful, memorable path of the history of your life and of Ritchie County. Enjoy . . . .

Rock S. Wilson

One

Harrisville

Harrisville was established as the county seat of Ritchie County in 1843 and remains the county seat today. Harrisville's advantage in business was its place as the county seat. However, Harrisville had a disadvantage by not being on the Baltimore & Ohio (B&O) main line as were its business rivals Pennsboro, Ellenboro, and Cairo. Connector lines to Cornwallis and Pennsboro from the main line helped to get products to market but never really provided an established business environment equal to that of Cairo and Pennsboro in the early part of the 20th century. Nevertheless, Harrisville thrived. The following postcards depict many businesses found there, as well as numerous other points of interest.

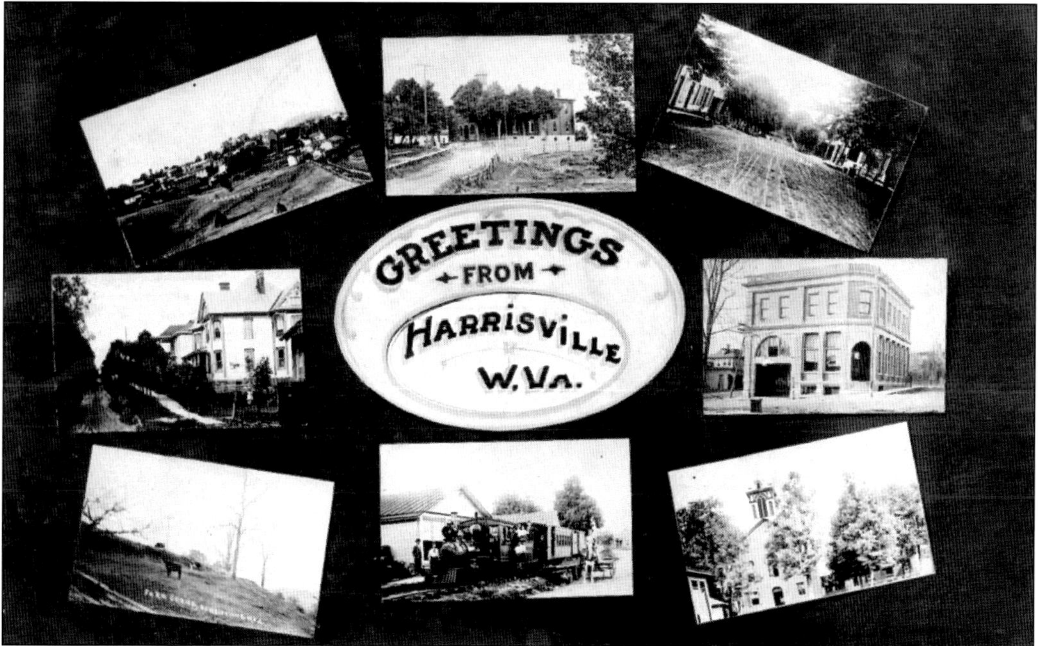

Many postcard companies offered a series of postcards. Shown here is a card with eight different views of Harrisville on one card. Each of these views was also featured on individual cards, almost all of which are included in this publication. Each view shown on this particular card, which was postmarked in 1909, can thus be dated to the same era.

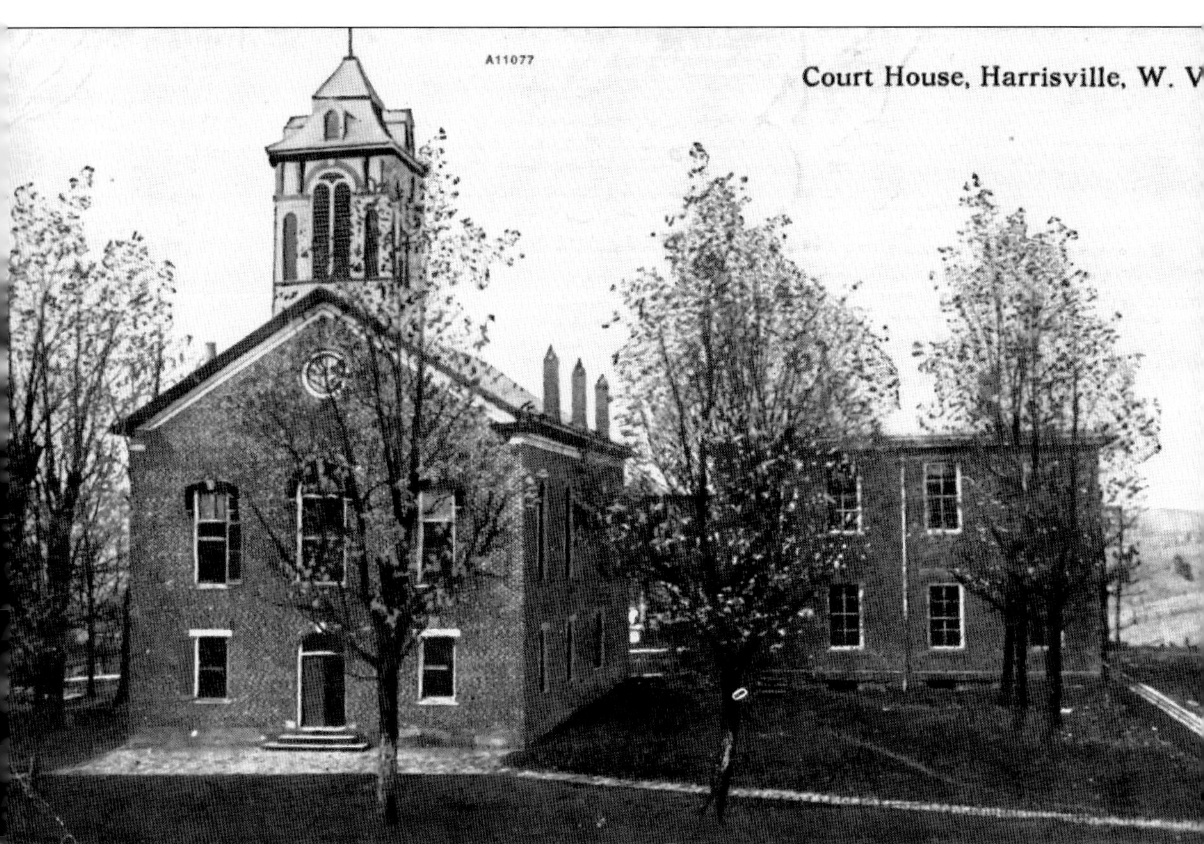

The cards on these pages depict three separate views of the second Ritchie County Courthouse, which was built in 1874. The main building of this structure was attached to the annex to the right via a second-story walkway, which can vaguely be seen behind the tree. The present courthouse was built in 1923 around this structure.

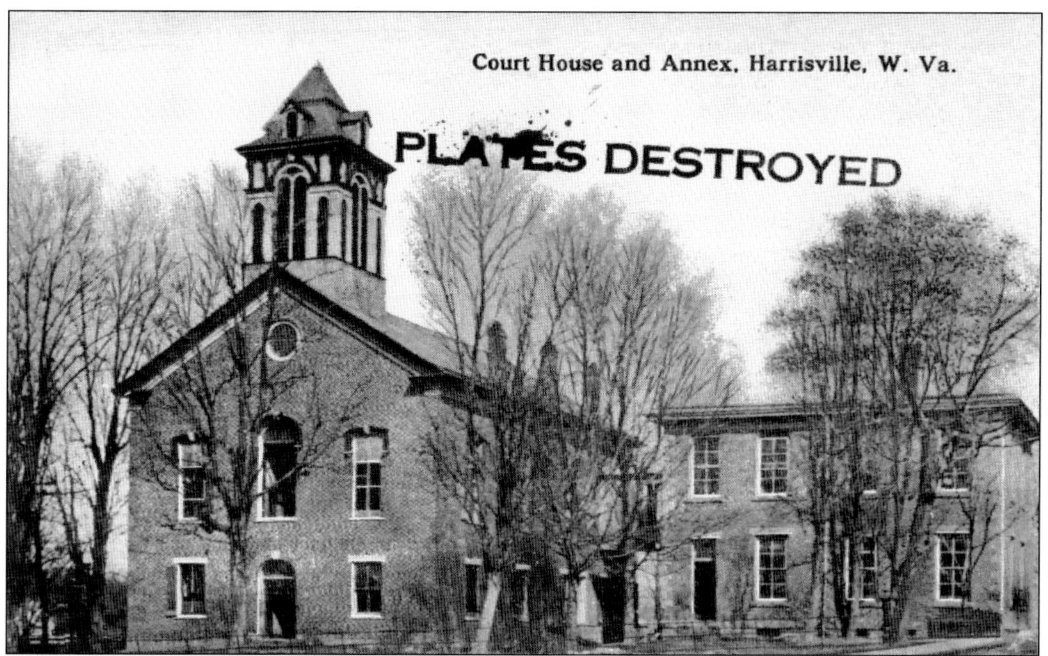

The card to the left on page 10 was postmarked in 1913. The card above is *c.* 1915, and the card below is *c.* 1905.

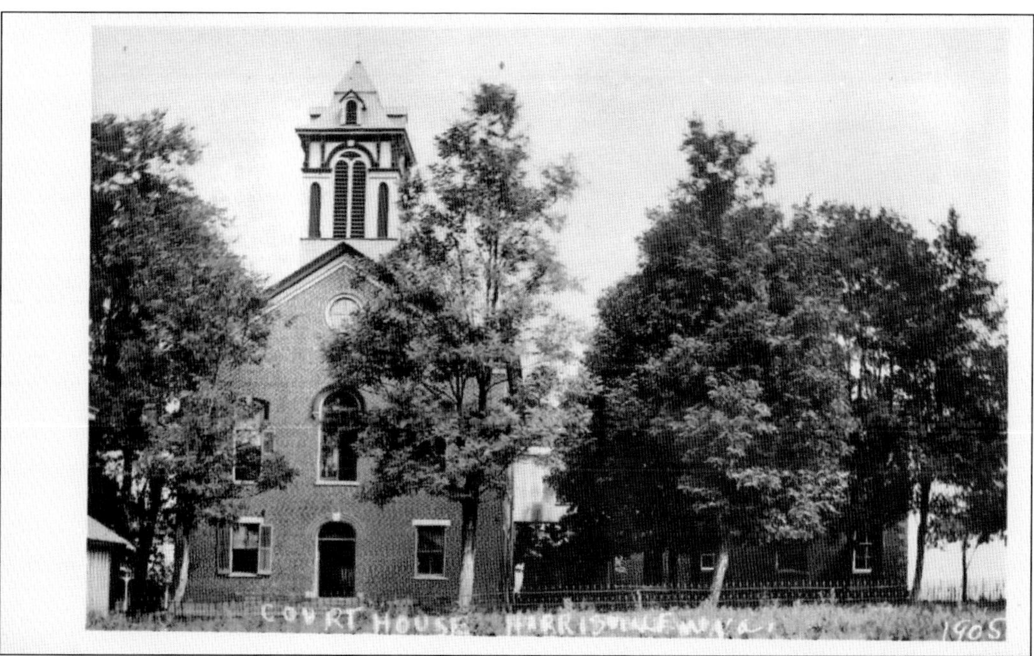

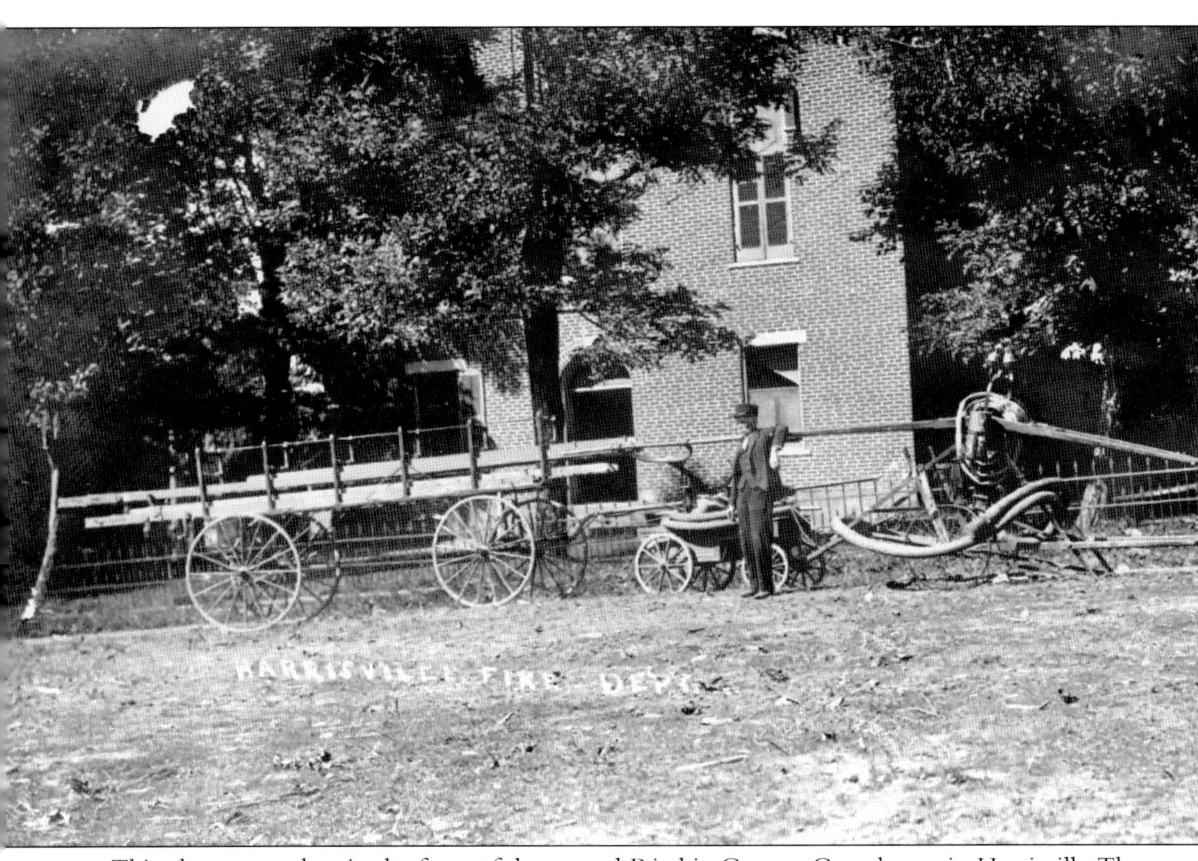

This photo was taken in the front of the second Ritchie County Courthouse in Harrisville. The front of the *c.* 1905 card reads "Harrisville Fire Dept."

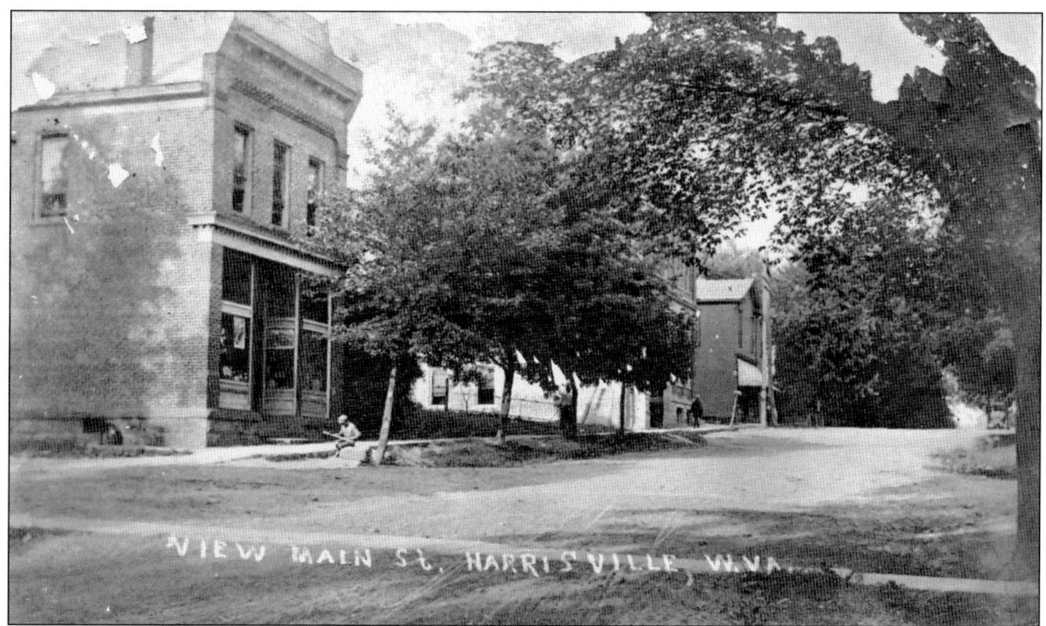

Shown here are two different cards with views of Main Street in Harrisville. They depict the difference in real photo postcards and those enhanced by color or other touch-ups. Above is a real photo card showing the boy sitting on the corner of Main and Court Streets with a bat, but the one below has been enhanced. Look closely at the top of the building in the forefront and at the crisp lines in the postcard on the bottom. The top card was postmarked in 1910.

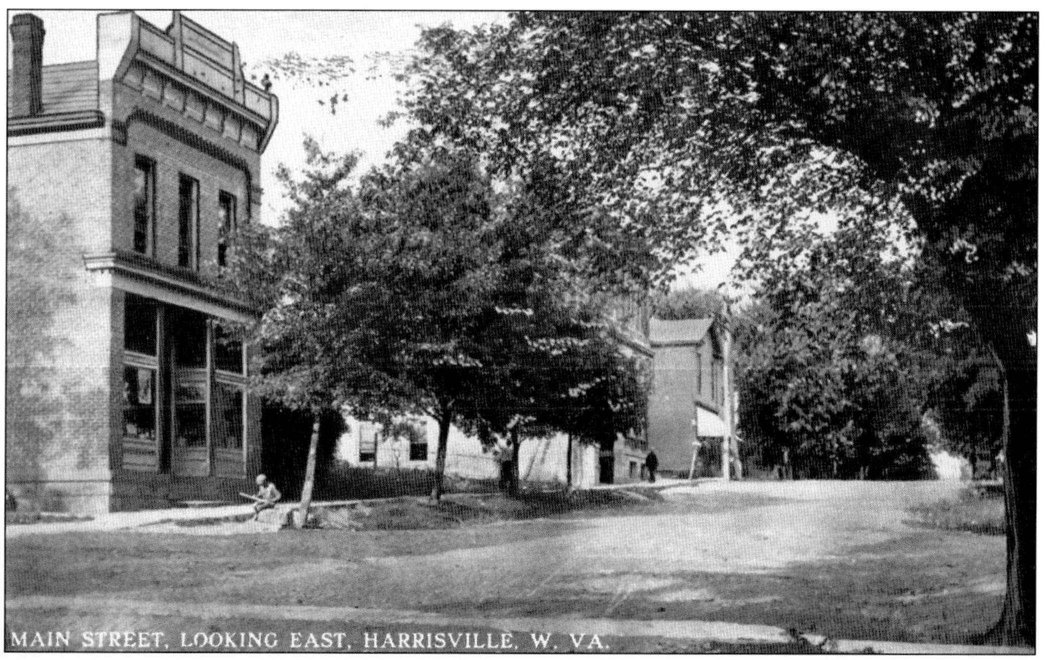

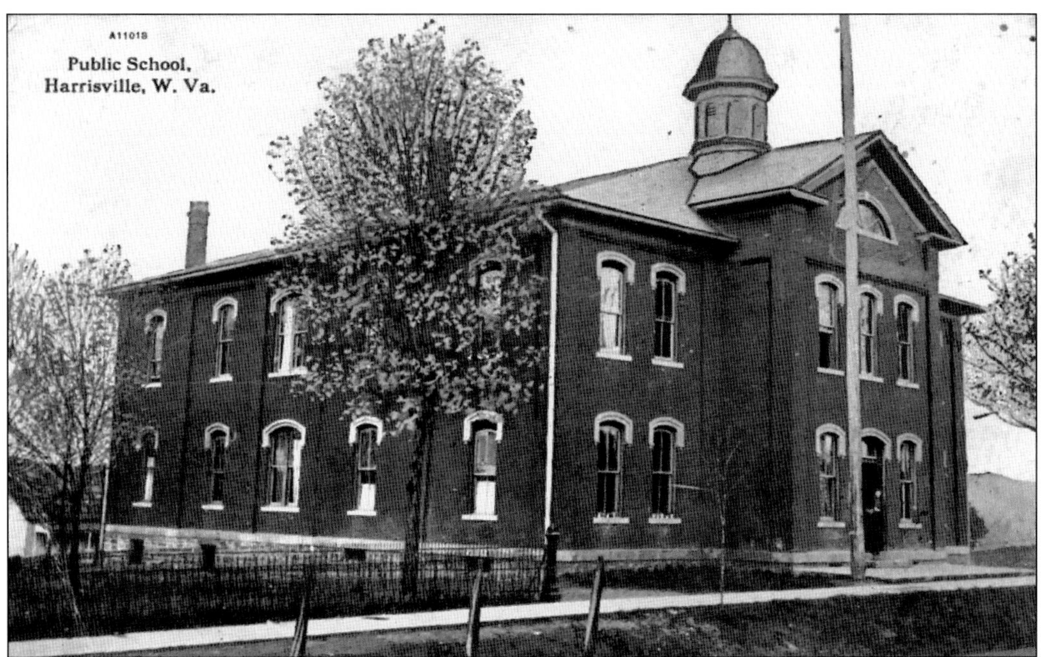

Depicted here are two views of the grade school in Harrisville, now home to the General Thomas M. Harris Museum at 127 West Main Street. The original building was constructed in 1878 and enlarged in 1904 when the back was added on. It served as the Harrisville Grade School and later as the grade school until 1924. Still later, the building housed the Ritchie County Board of Education for many years. In the bottom card, one can see the Baptist church just beyond the grade school prior to the construction of its parsonage, which sat between the two buildings. The top card was postmarked in 1913, and the bottom card was postmarked in 1908.

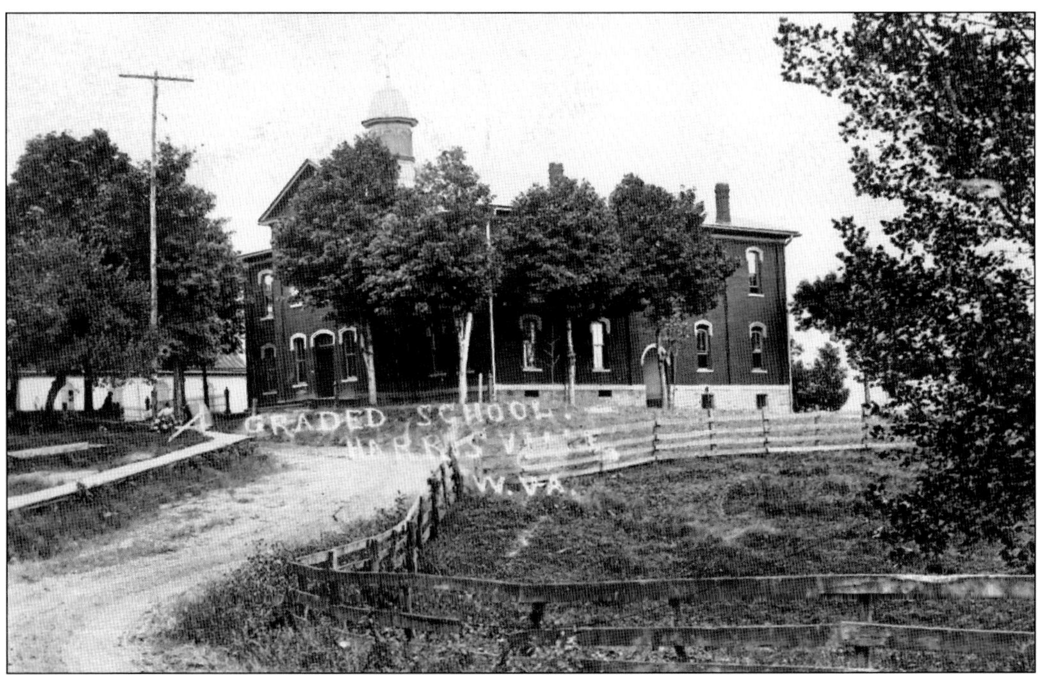

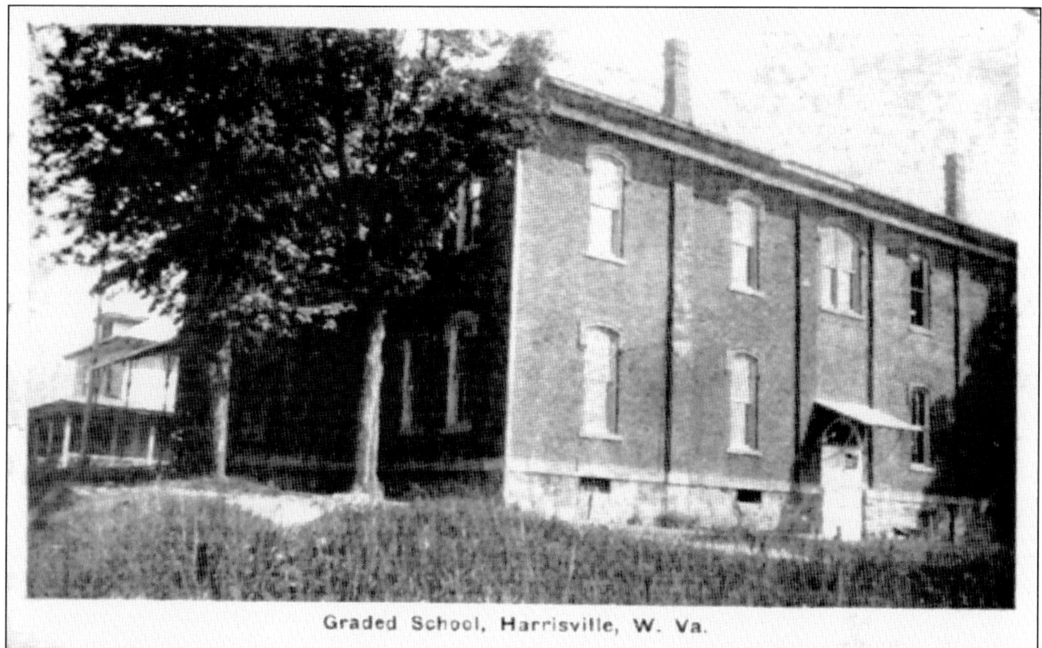

Here is another view of the grade school with the Baptist church parsonage just beyond it. This undated card was published by the Auburn Greeting Card Company in Auburn, Indiana.

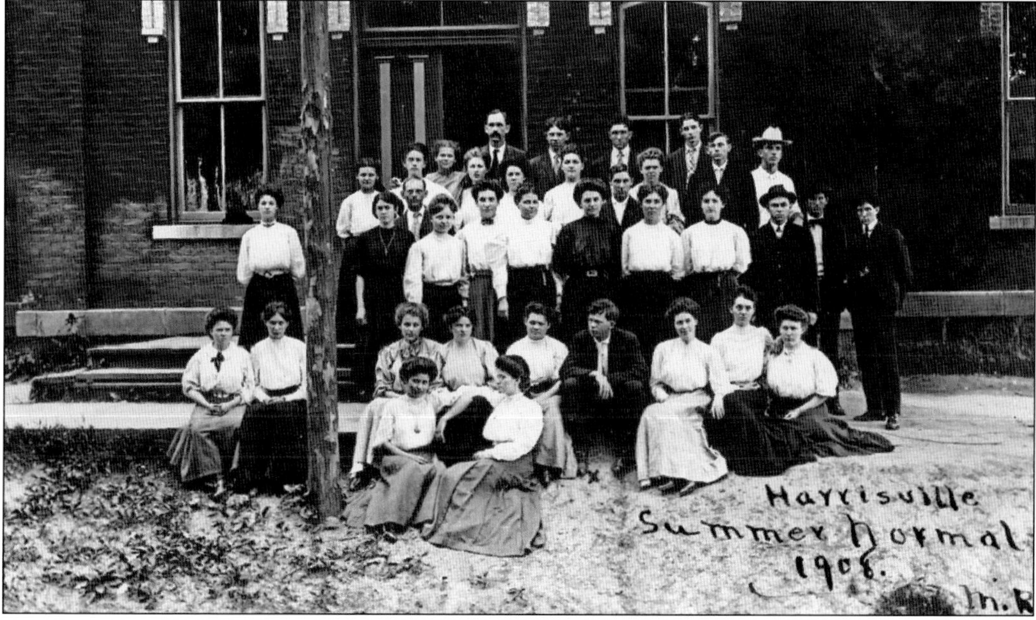

Harrisville Summer Normal School is shown outside of the Harrisville Grade School. Summer Normal Schools were implemented for teacher training courses in schools around West Virginia in the summer months. This message on the back of this 1908 card is from M.R. (purportedly one of the young ladies pictured) and reads, "Here are our 'mugs.' What do you think of them. Especially the one marked with an X. He is a friend of mine. Ha Ha. One of the teachers sons. That is not his best though, he is a beaut." The card was sent to Miss Rae Bee of Pennsboro.

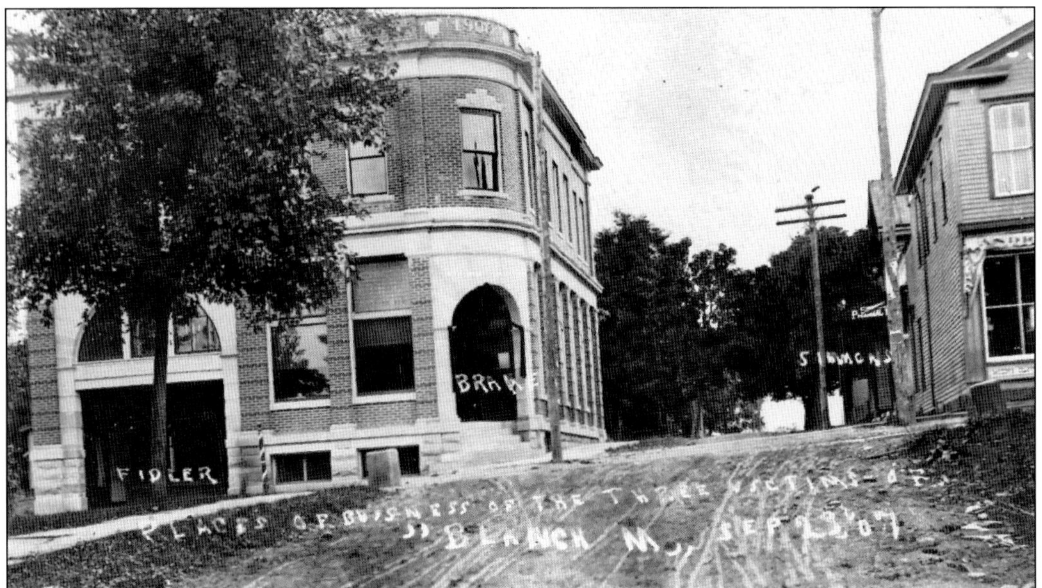

The First National Bank building is located on the corner of Main and Spring Streets. This *c.* 1907 card indicates that these are the places of business of the three victims of the *Blanche M.* (a boat disaster near Pt. Pleasant, West Virginia) on September 23, 1907. Fidler, Brake, and Simmons are noted on the front of the card. The Simmons Pharmacy sign can be seen on the right just above the Simmons notation.

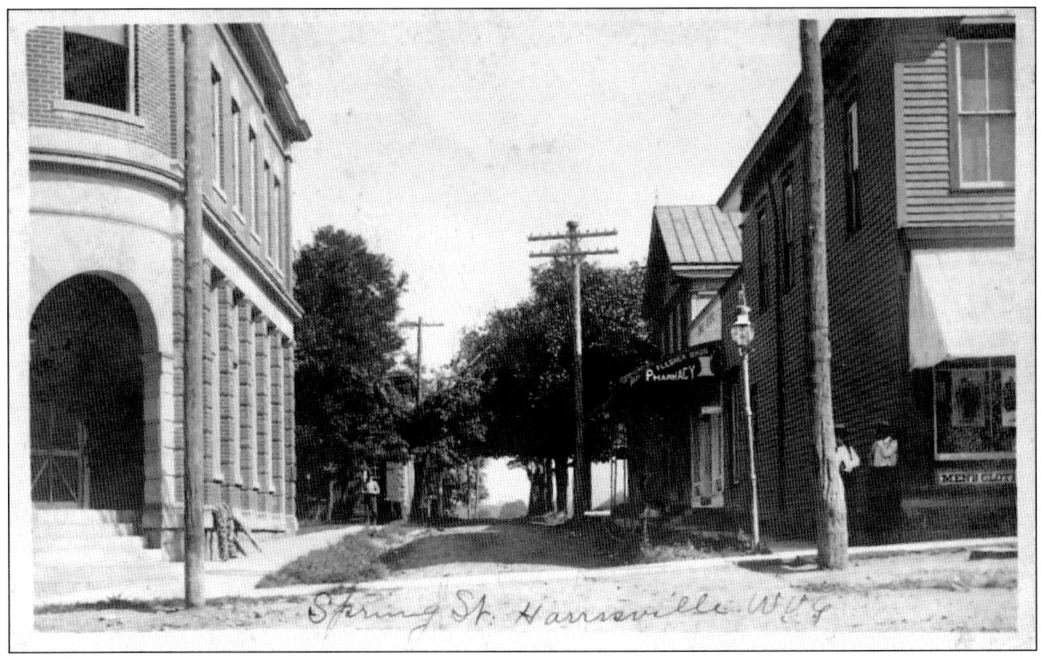

Looking up Spring Street from Main Street, this card provides another view of the First National Bank building on the left and the pharmacy on the right. Can you find the difference between the picture at the top and this one? This card, postmarked in 1909, shows that between 1907 and 1909, Simmons Pharmacy became Flesher's Pharmacy.

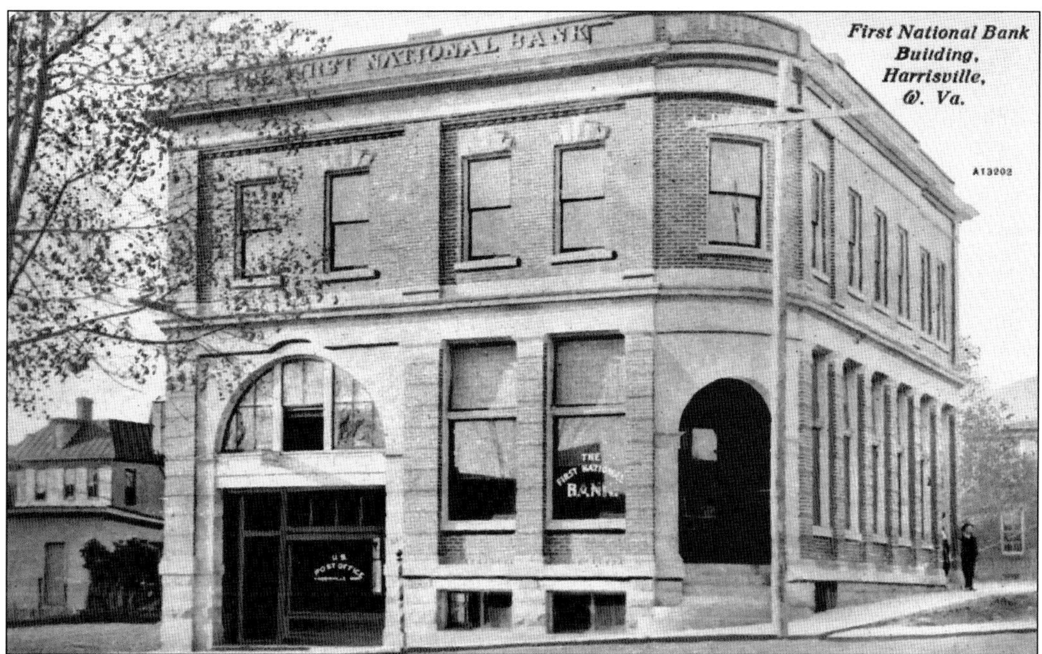

Here are some additional views of the First National Bank building on the corner of Main and Spring Streets. The building was originally constructed in 1906 and housed the First National Bank and the U.S. Post Office. The building was later home to Safe Insurance for many years and now houses Carolyn's Sandwich Shop and the *Pennsboro News*. Originally two stories, the building received a third story and an addition to its back by the 1950s. Note that the images are identical aside from enhancements that were added to the bottom card, including the presence of the car. One can tell it is the same view by the presence of the man on the sidewalk in both images. The top card was postmarked in 1911.

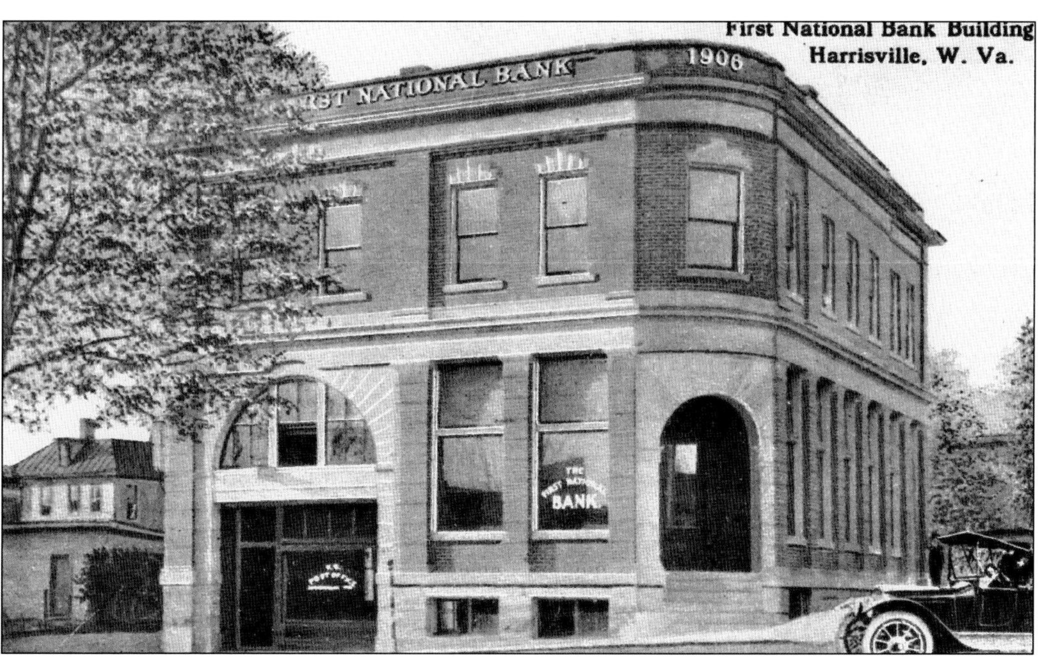

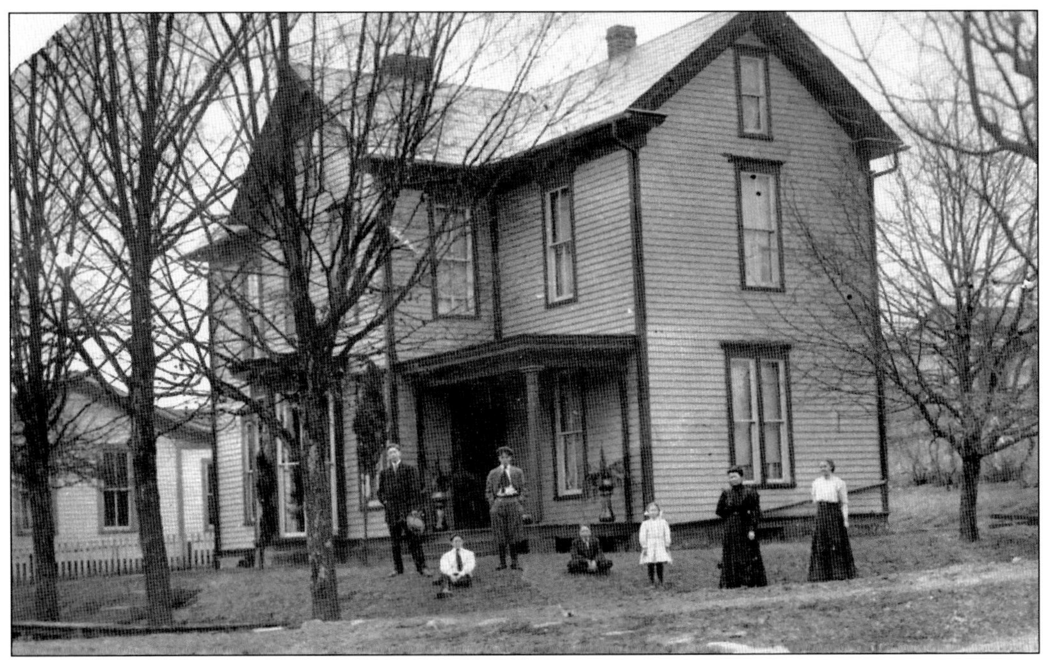

This *c.* 1907 card depicts one of the many distinct homes of Ritchie County, which was located at the corner of E. South and Cross Streets. The family shown here is most likely the Fidler family, as they were the owners of the property at the time this card was created. This home was torn down in 2001.

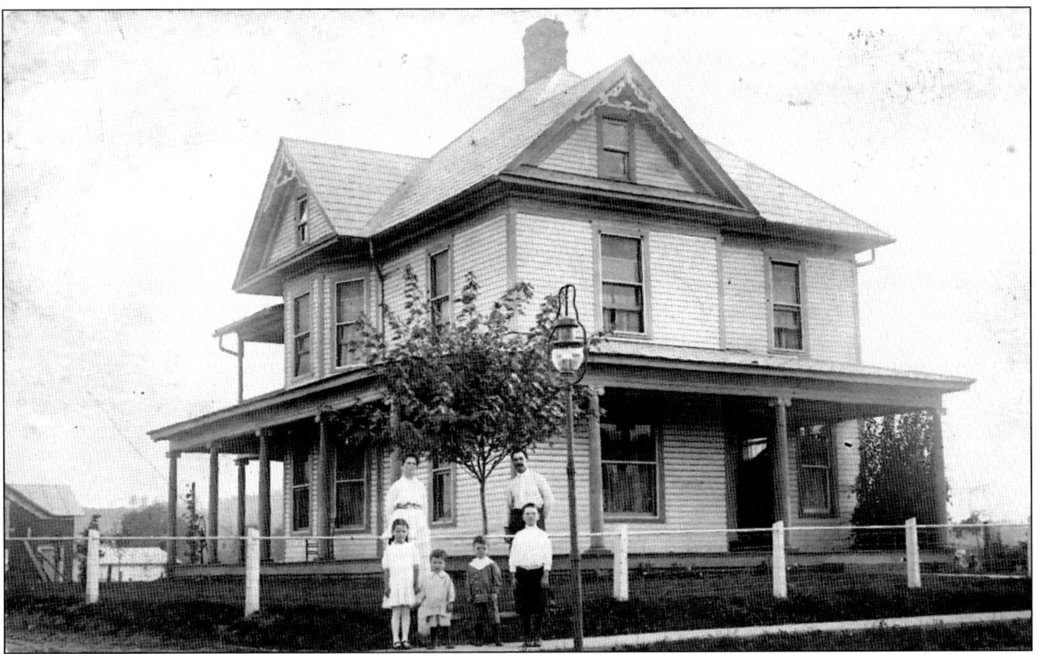

The current home of John "Shorty" Bumgardner is situated on the corner of E. South and Stout Street. The family depicted in this *c.* 1910 card is most likely that of Dr. A. Hayes Elliott and his wife, June, the previous owners of this home. This home was built in 1910.

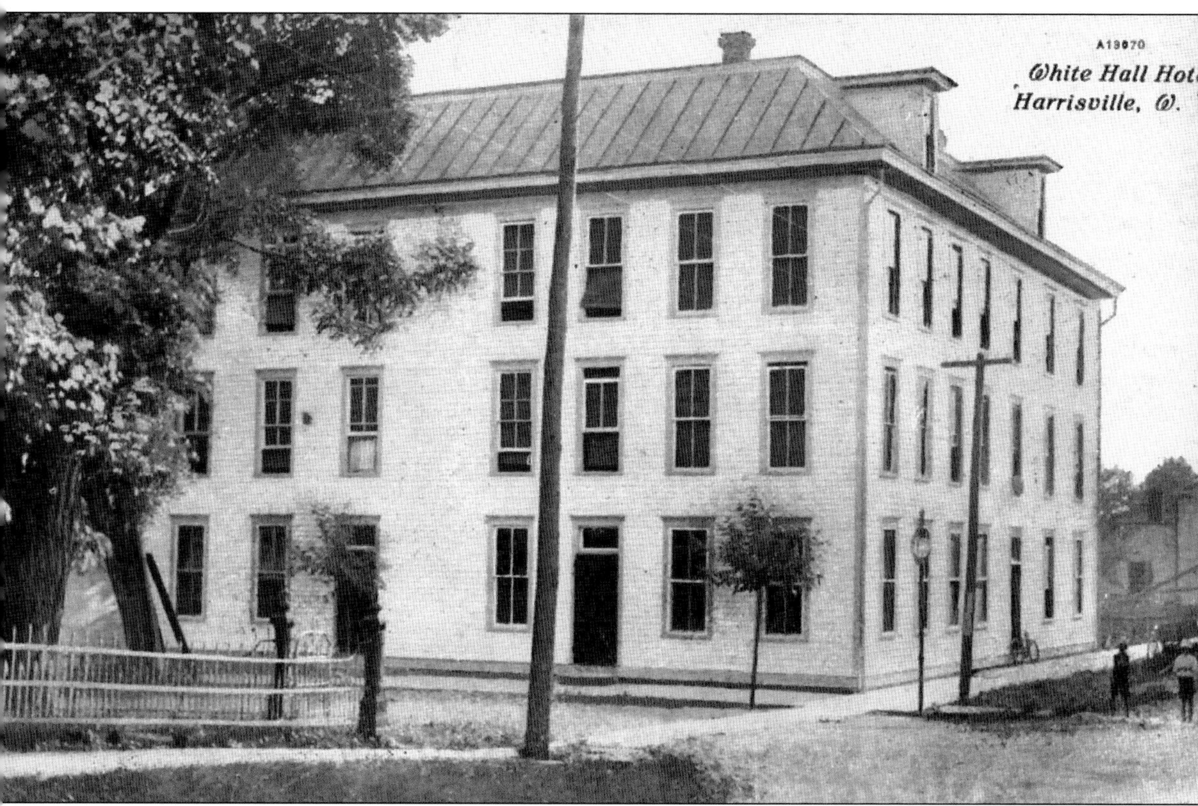

The White Hall Hotel was located in Harrisville on the corner of Court and High Street on what is now the parking lot for Huntington National Bank. This structure was built in 1893 after the original hotel had burned. Boasting 35 rooms, this hotel was run by the Patton family in the early part of this century. The postmark on this card reads 1911.

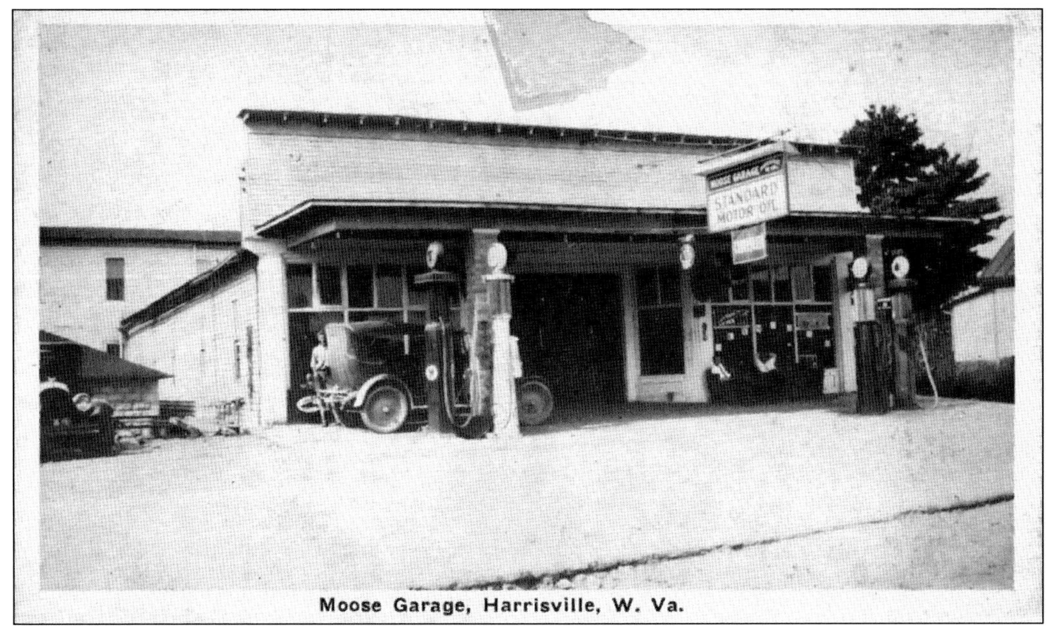

The Moose Garage in Harrisville was named for the many moose heads that decorated the interior. The garage, owned by R.E.L. Frymire, was located in the place that later became Keith Brothers and is now Shrader's Exxon. This structure was destroyed in 1967 when the new building was constructed on the site at 701 E. Main Street. This *c.* 1930 card was published by the Auburn Greeting Card Company in Auburn, Indiana.

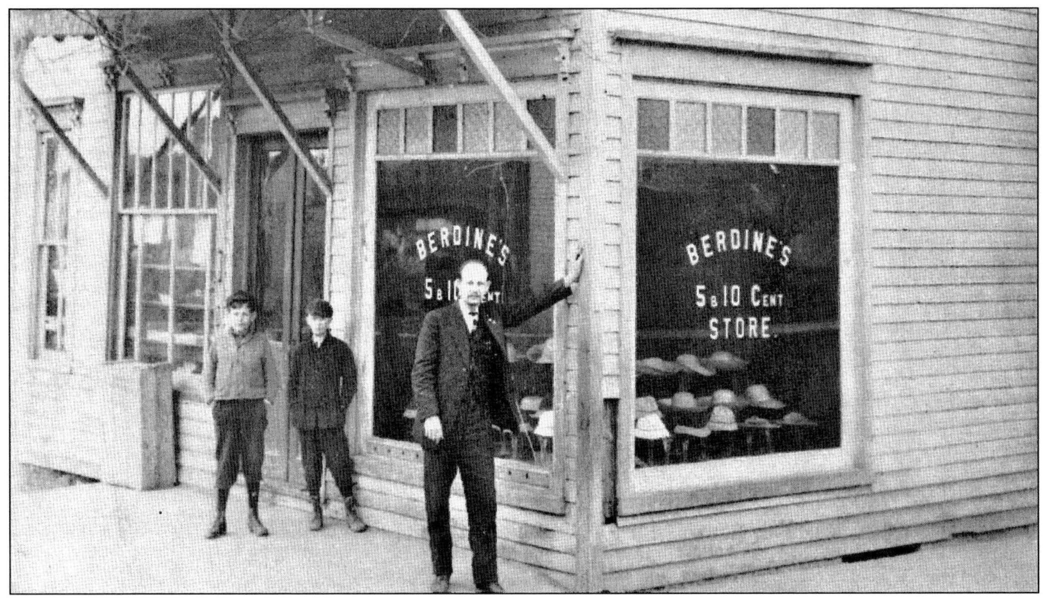

This is a reproduction postcard produced by Berdine's Variety Store. Berdine's still operates today at 106 N. Court Street and claims to be the oldest continually operating five-and-dime store in America. This photo was taken when the store was in its original location in the Layfield building on the corner of West Main and Court Streets. The sign in the window says "ladies hats 10 cents." The photograph for this card was taken in 1908.

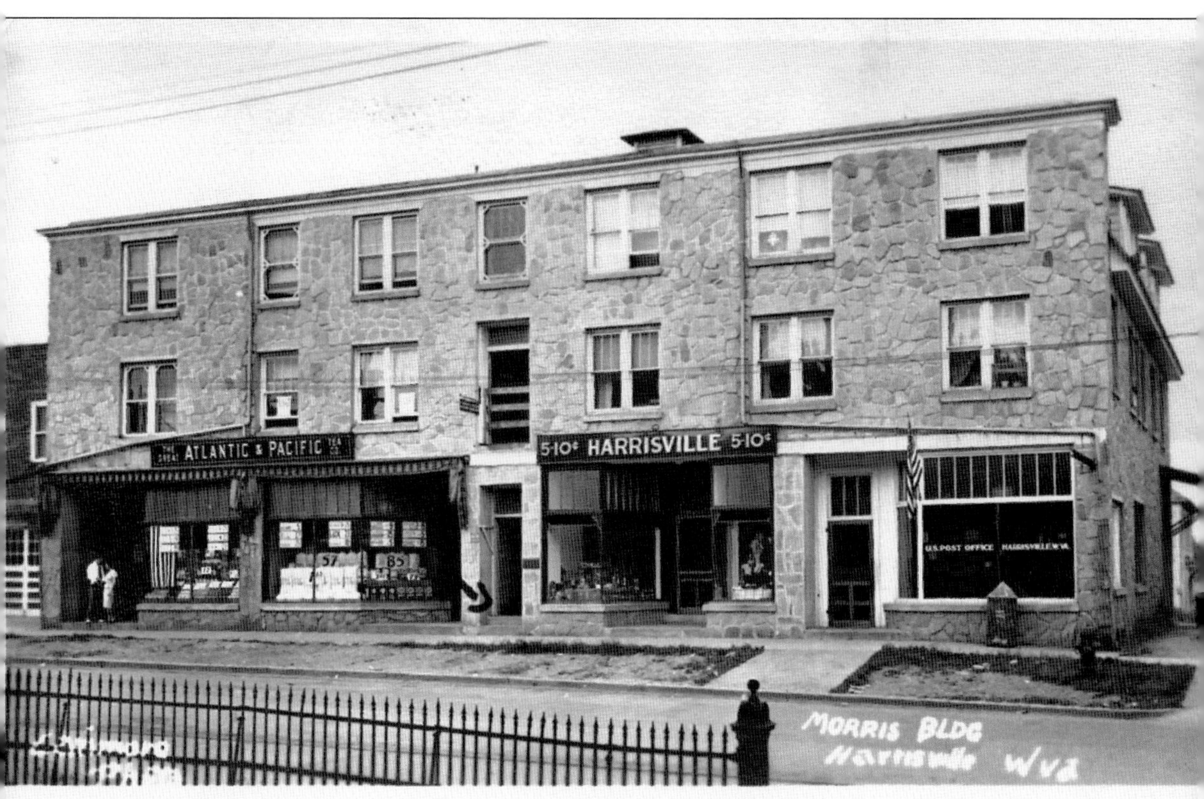

This *c.* 1955 card shows the Morris Building, which is located in Harrisville at 311-319 East Main Street. Pictured at the time of this photo are McCoy's five-and-dime store, the Atlantic and Pacific Store (A&P), and the U.S. Post Office. The message on the back of this particular card indicates that there was a doctor's office upstairs. The edifice, built in 1930, now houses the Ritchie County Magistrate Court, the Hometown Pharmacy, and the Heritage Inn.

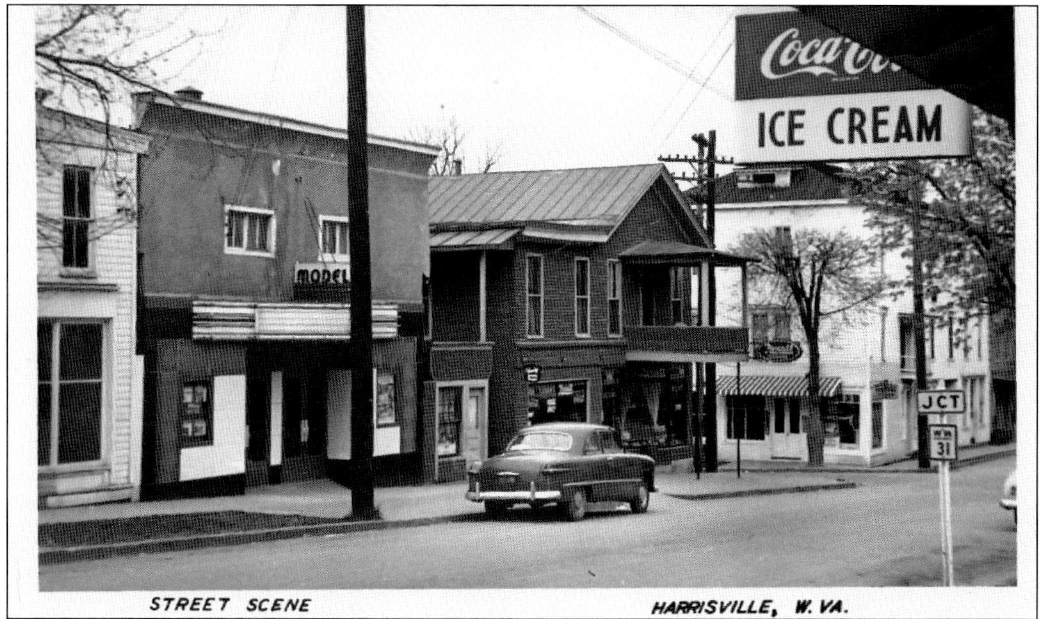

This view of Main Street from a postcard dated 1953 shows the Model Theatre and Flesher's Drug Store. The theatre operated here until 1973, and the building was razed in 1984. The Cokeley building just beyond the drug store was torn down in 2002. Its last occupant was Layfield's Hardware.

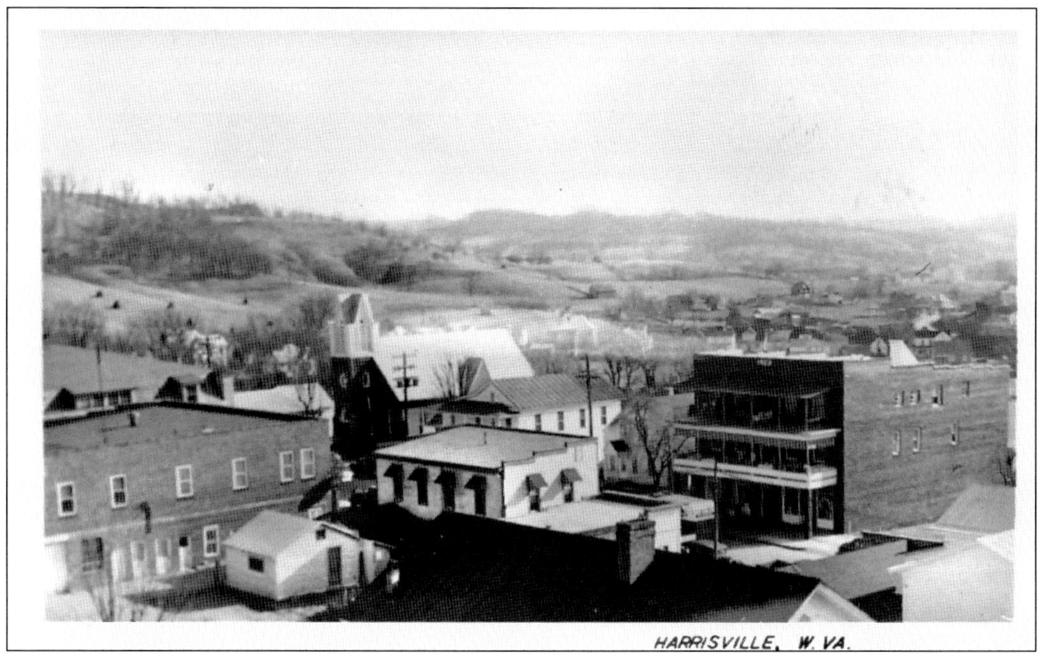

This view of Main Street shows St. Luke's Methodist Church. The photo was probably taken from the roof of the courthouse. Note the porches on the Broadwater building to the right. The Broadwater building, constructed in 1923, is still standing, but the porches are now gone. This card, dated 1953, is from the same series of cards as the one shown at the top of the page.

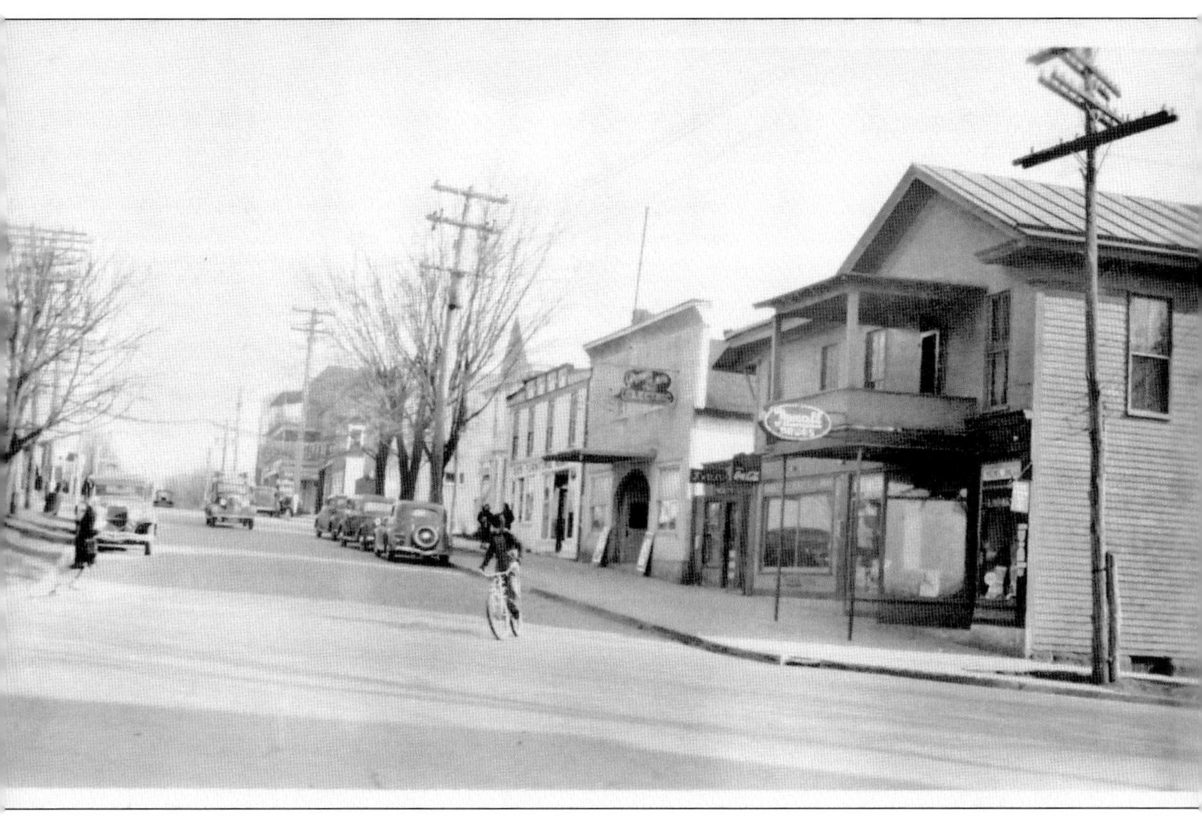

Shown here is another view of Main Street, *c.* 1940. Flesher's Drug Store is the first building on the right with the Electric Theatre just beyond. The last building in view on the right is the three-story Broadwater building with the second- and third-floor porches still intact.

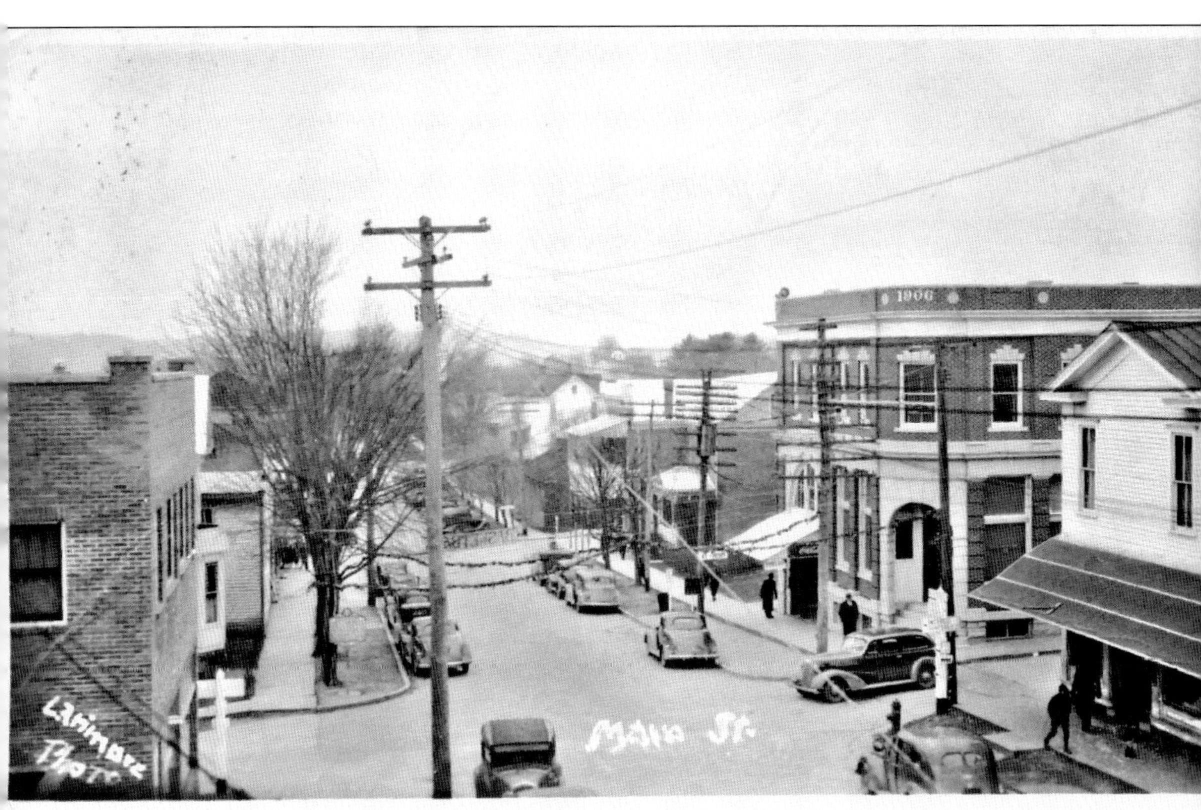

Main Street is shown looking west at the intersection of Main and Spring Streets in this *c.* 1940 card.

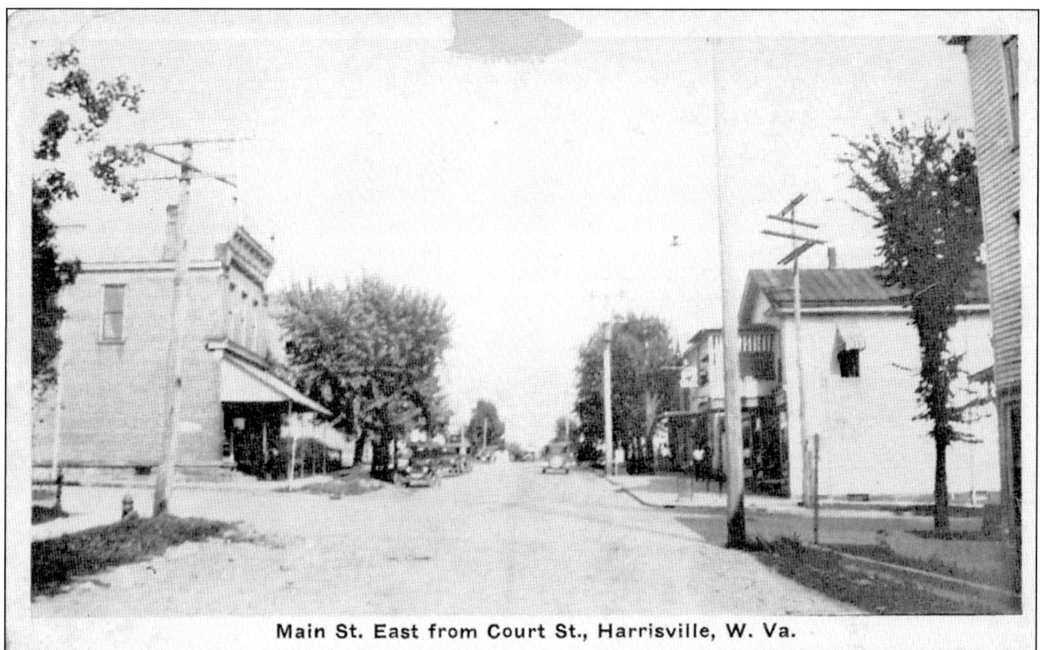

This view, postmarked in 1932, shows Main Street East from Court Street. Flesher's Drug Store is on the right and the Electric Theatre is just beyond it. This card was published by Auburn Greeting Card Company in Auburn, Indiana.

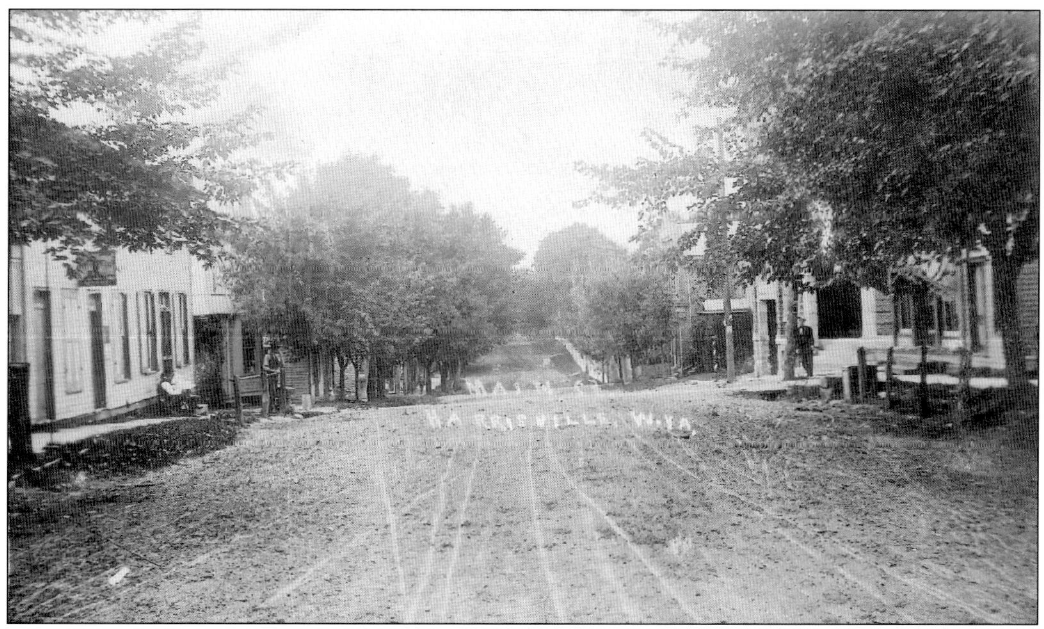

E. Main Street is shown looking west just before the intersection of Main and Spring Street in this *c.* 1910 postcard. The man to the right is standing in front of the First National Bank building. Note the dirt/mud streets.

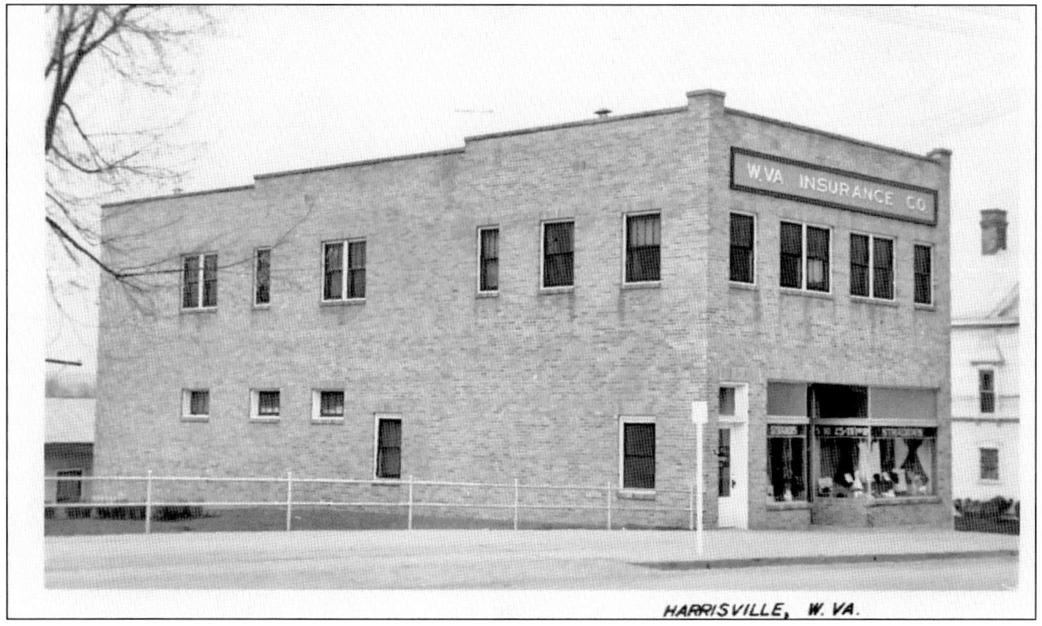

This card depicts the West Virginia Insurance Building, which is on the corner of Main Street and Spring Street. This structure, built in 1937, now houses *The Ritchie Gazette* office and the law office of Rodney C. Windom. At the time this card was made in 1953, the insurance company was upstairs and Strader's store was on the ground level.

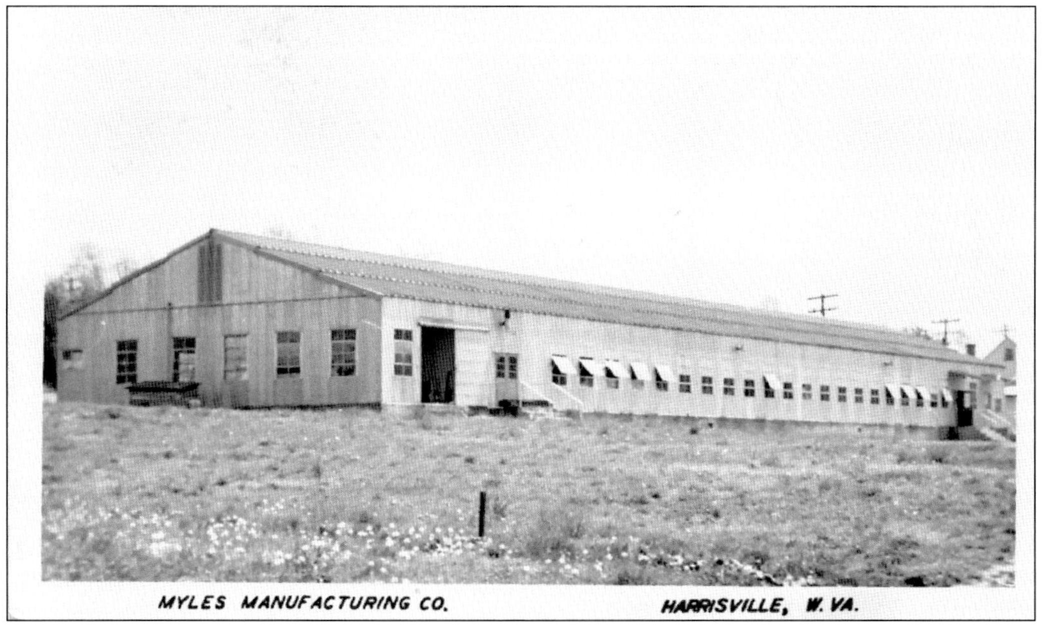

This 1953 card shows that Myles Manufacturing was located on Cross Street behind the Harrison Street Methodist Church. This building housed varying garment manufacturing industries that provided hundreds of jobs for the work force of Ritchie County over the span of several decades. Myles Manufacturing was one of the many garment industries in the county that were instrumental in the county's economy. The building still exists, but stands empty as of 2004.

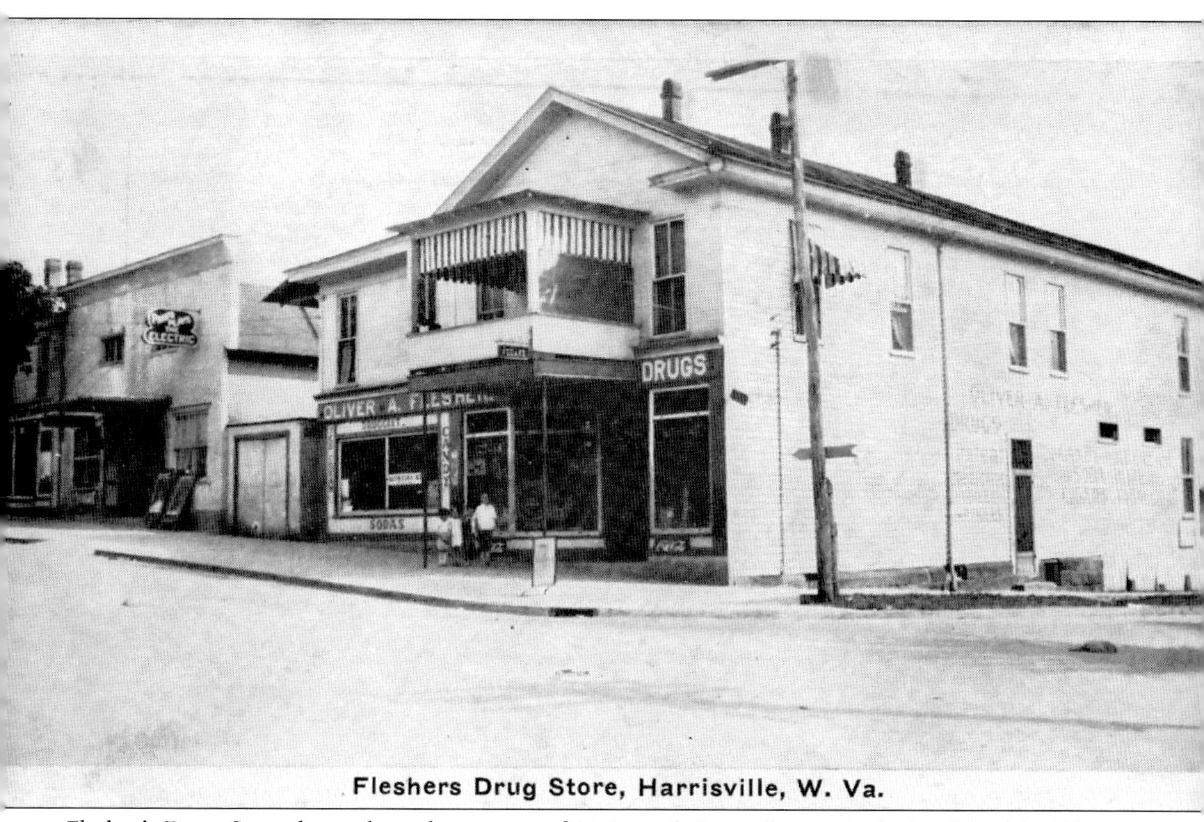

Flesher's Drug Store, located on the corner of Main and Court Streets, is depicted in this 1933 postcard. Oliver A. Flesher was the druggist at the time. This structure, built in 1890, is one of the oldest in Harrisville. It later became the B&B Pharmacy.

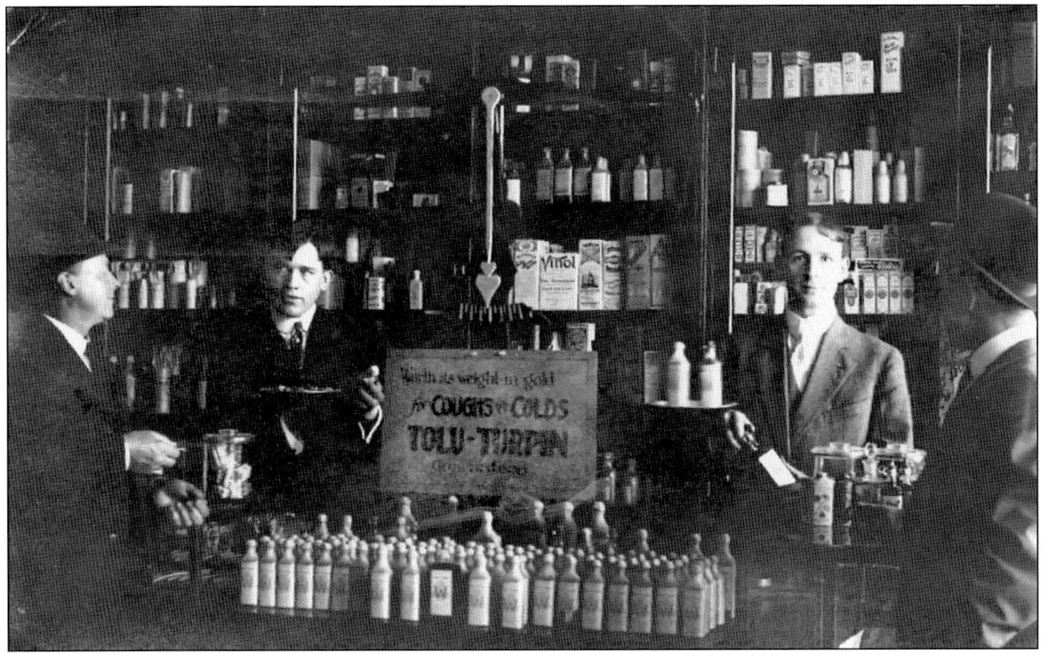

The interior of Flesher's Drug Store in Harrisville is shown in this card, *c.* 1915.

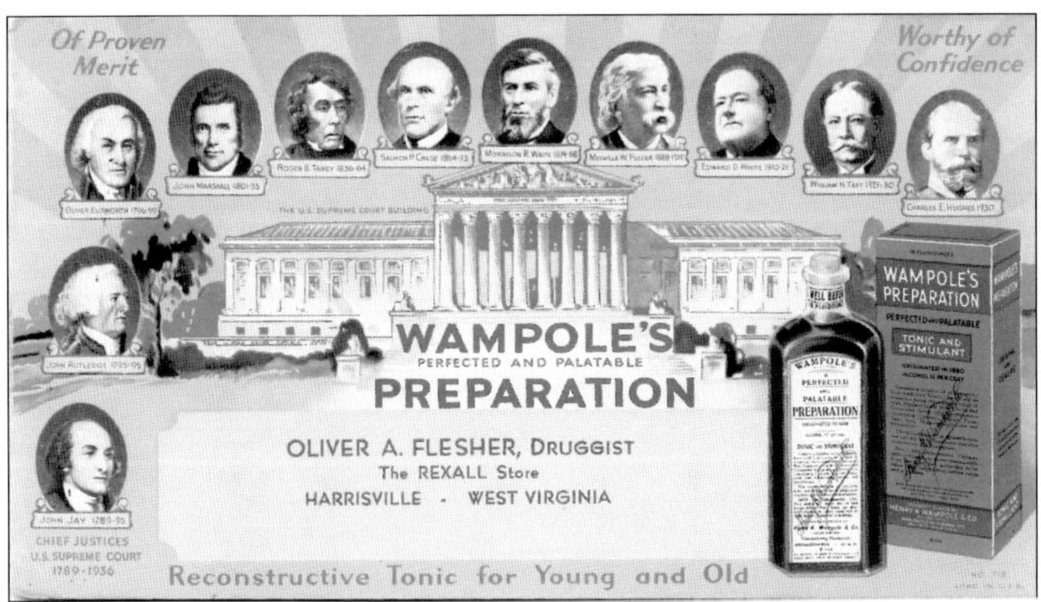

Depicted here is a *c.* 1936 advertising blotter from Oliver A. Flesher, the druggist at Flesher's Drug Store. These were often used as postcards, though they were made for advertising.

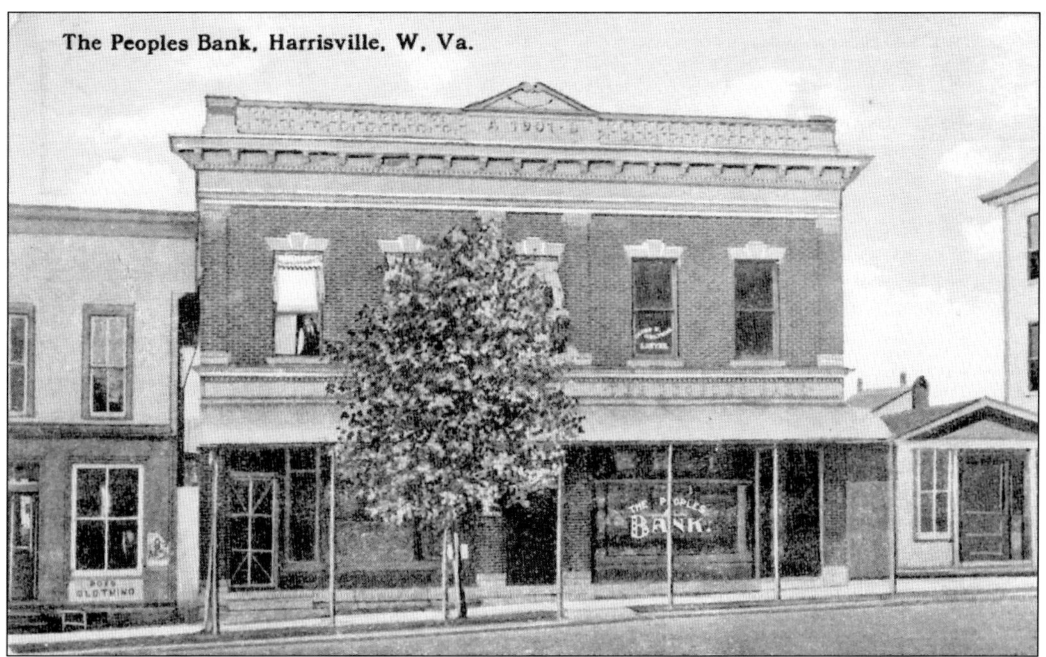

The Peoples Bank was located at this building, which was erected in 1901 at 121 N. Court Street. The message on this card, postmarked in 1921, indicates that a lawyer's office was located on the second floor. The edge of the three-story White Hall Hotel can be made out to the far right. The building is now the home of Huntington National Bank.

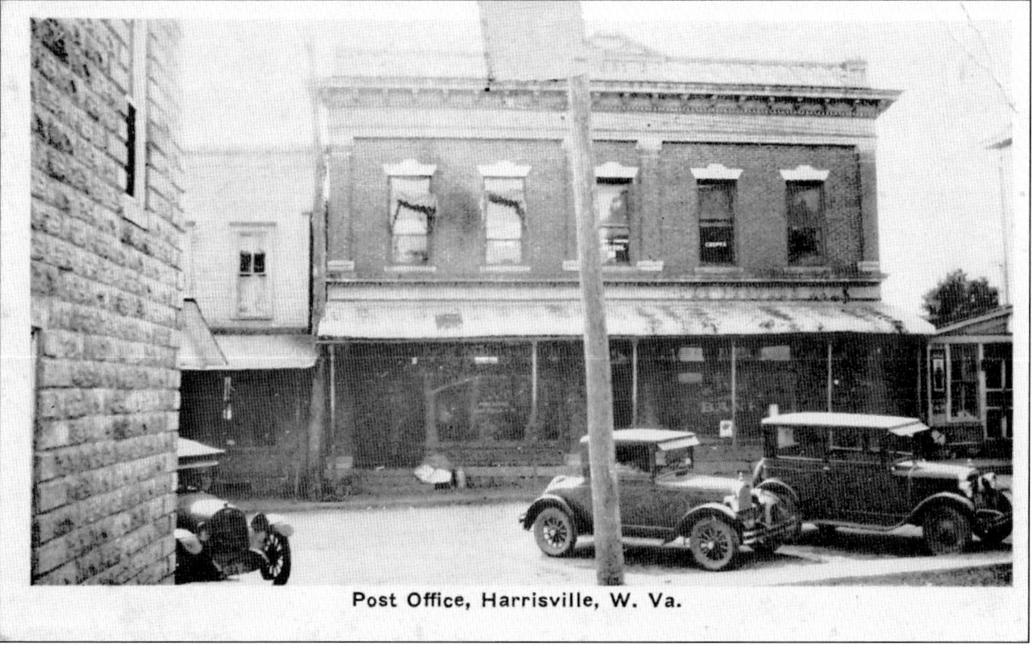

This *c.* 1930 card shows the original Peoples Bank building. At this time, the building housed the U.S. Post Office, which was located was to the left of the bank office. Wards Sandwich Shop, shown in the next card, stands just to the right.

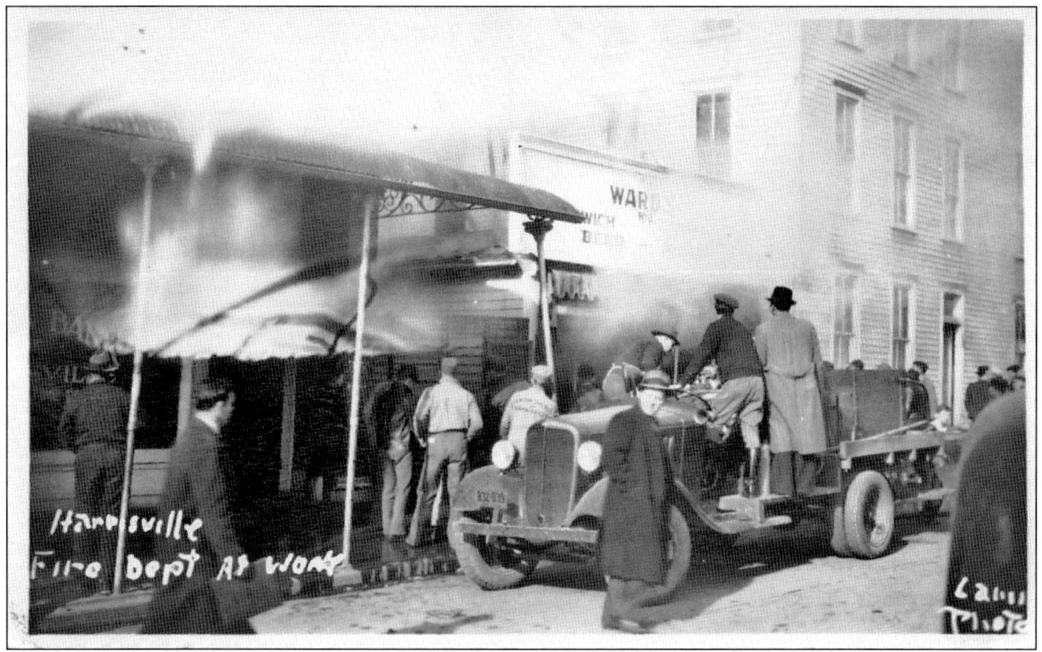

The Harrisville Fire Department is shown here fighting a fire at Ward's Sandwich Shop in this *c.* 1935 postcard. This building sat between the Peoples Bank building and the White Hall Hotel on N. Court Street.

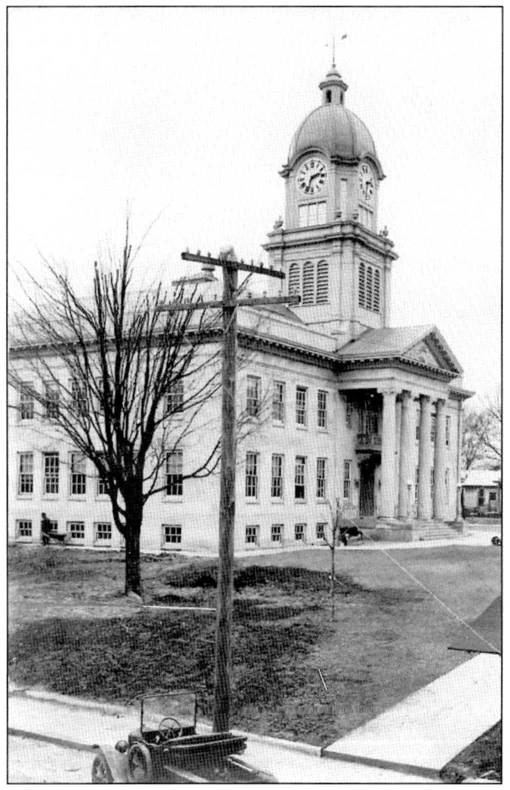

This and the two cards on the next page show the present courthouse, which was built in 1923. The clock was added later with money raised by the Harrisville Woman's Club. This remains one of the most attractive courthouses in the state of West Virginia and is the focal point of town. The card on this page is *c.* 1920.

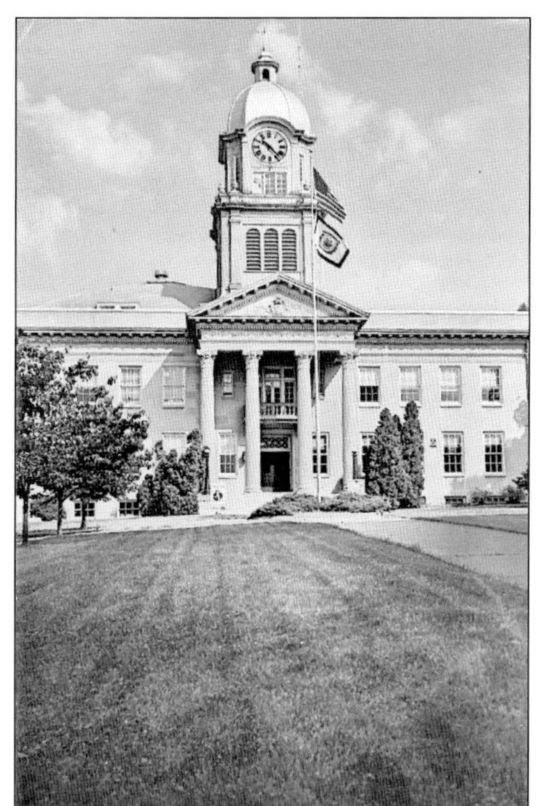

The picture at the right was published *c.* 1975 by Colorpicture Publishers of Boston, and the postcard below was published in 1990 by R. Daniel Simmons.

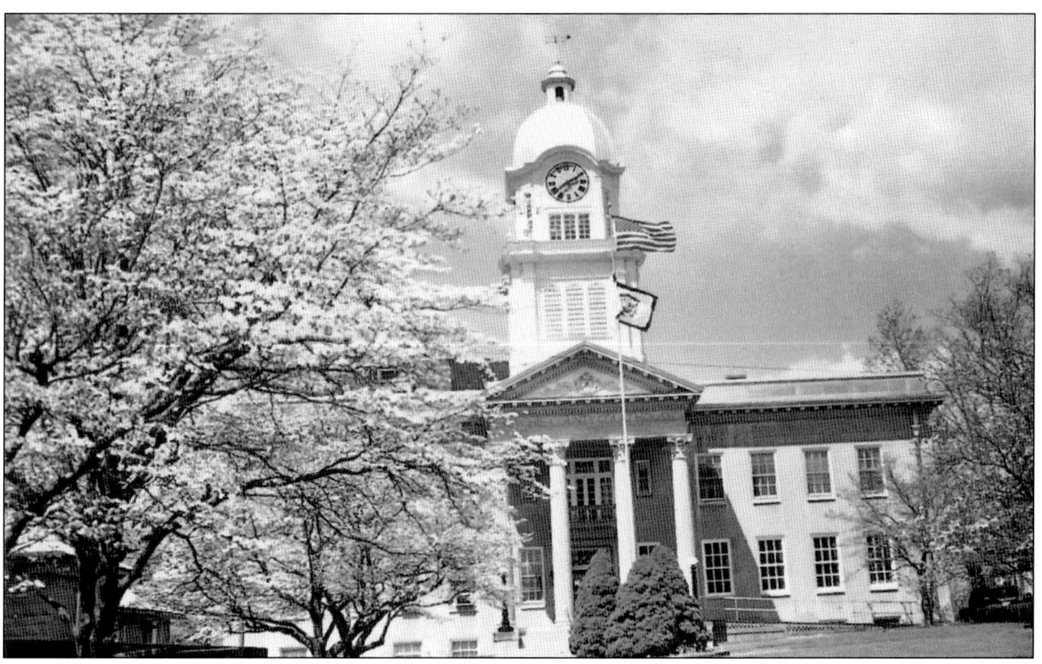

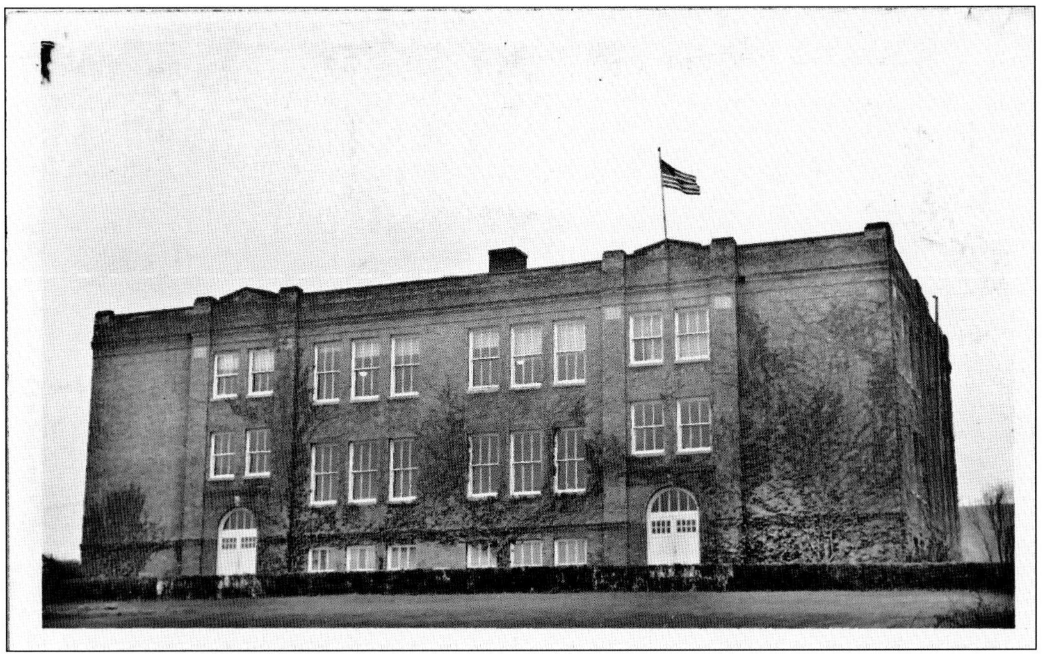

This image, dated 1953, is a real photo postcard of Harrisville High School. This structure was built in 1924 and served as the high school until 1985. At that time, it became Ritchie County High School until the new school was built in Ellenboro in 1993. The main structure of the building is now empty.

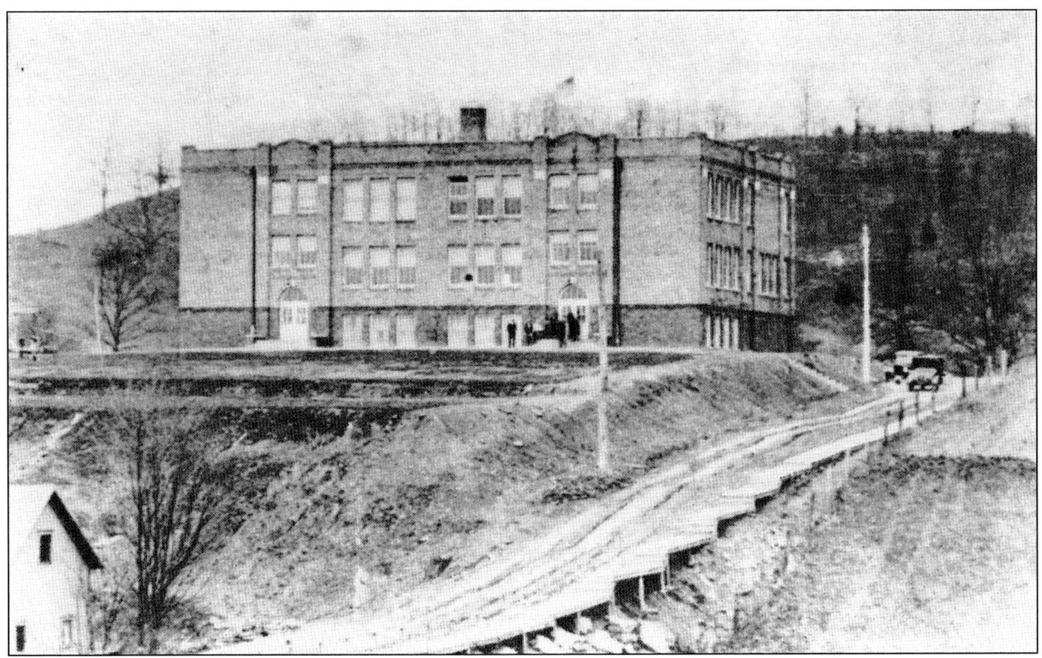

Depicted here is another view of Harrisville High School, probably shortly after its construction. Note the wooden boardwalks and steps. This *c.* 1924 card is a reprint by Berdine's Variety store in Harrisville.

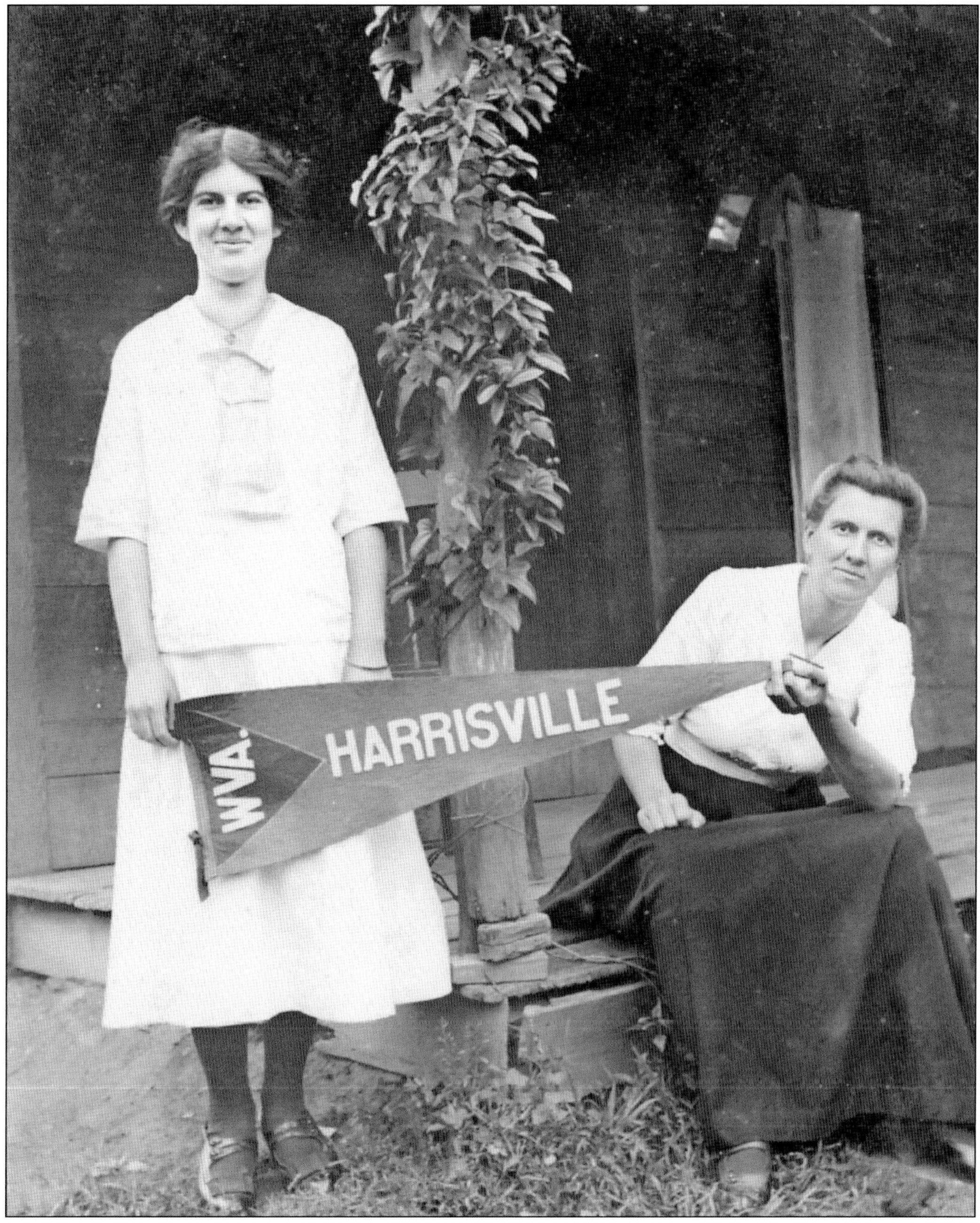

This undated postcard shows some early fans of Harrisville.

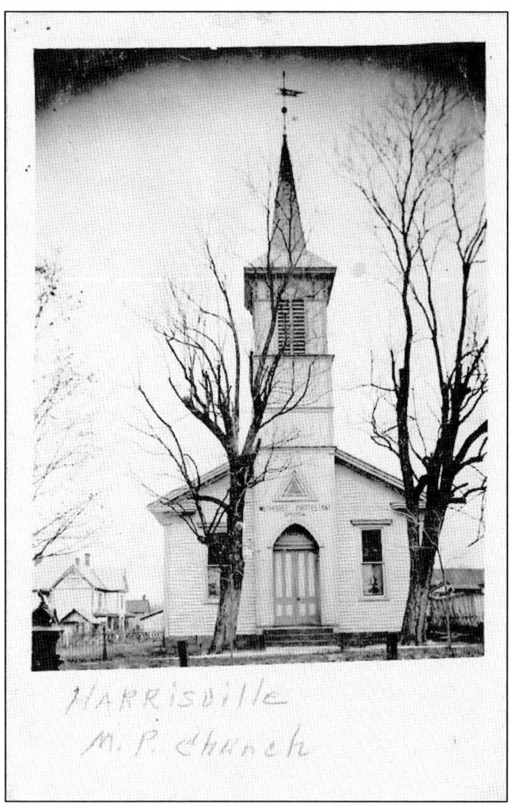

The Methodist Protestant church, which was located across from the grade school building on W. Main Street, is on a site now occupied by the Department of Human Services. The church, shown in this *c.* 1910 image, was razed in 1988.

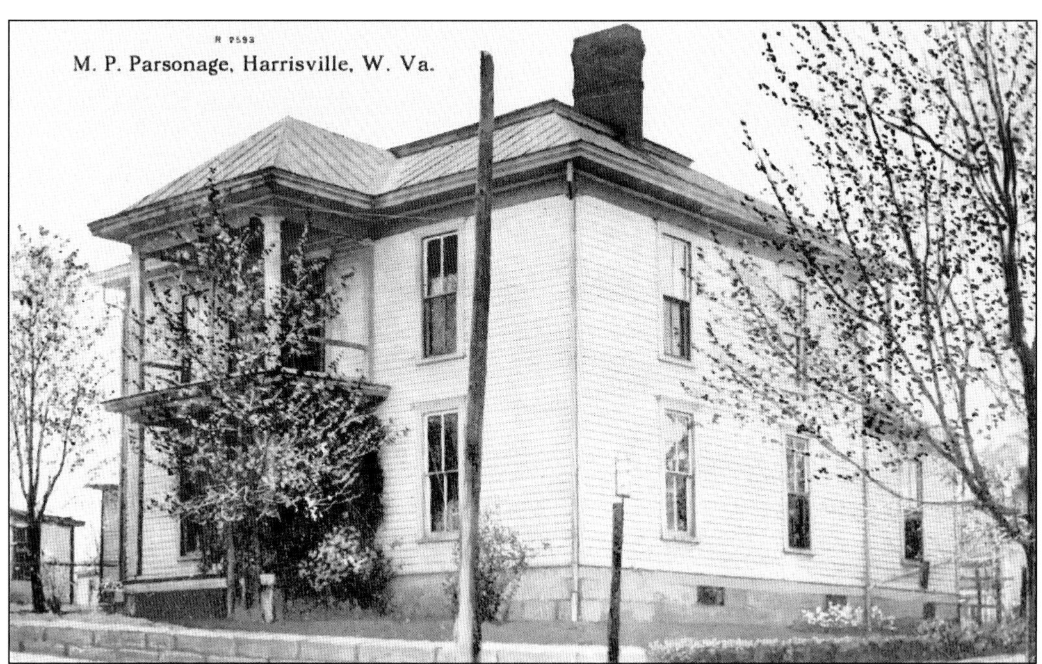

This image, postmarked in 1915, depicts the parsonage for the Methodist Protestant church. Located at 217 W. North Street, the house is now being used as a residence.

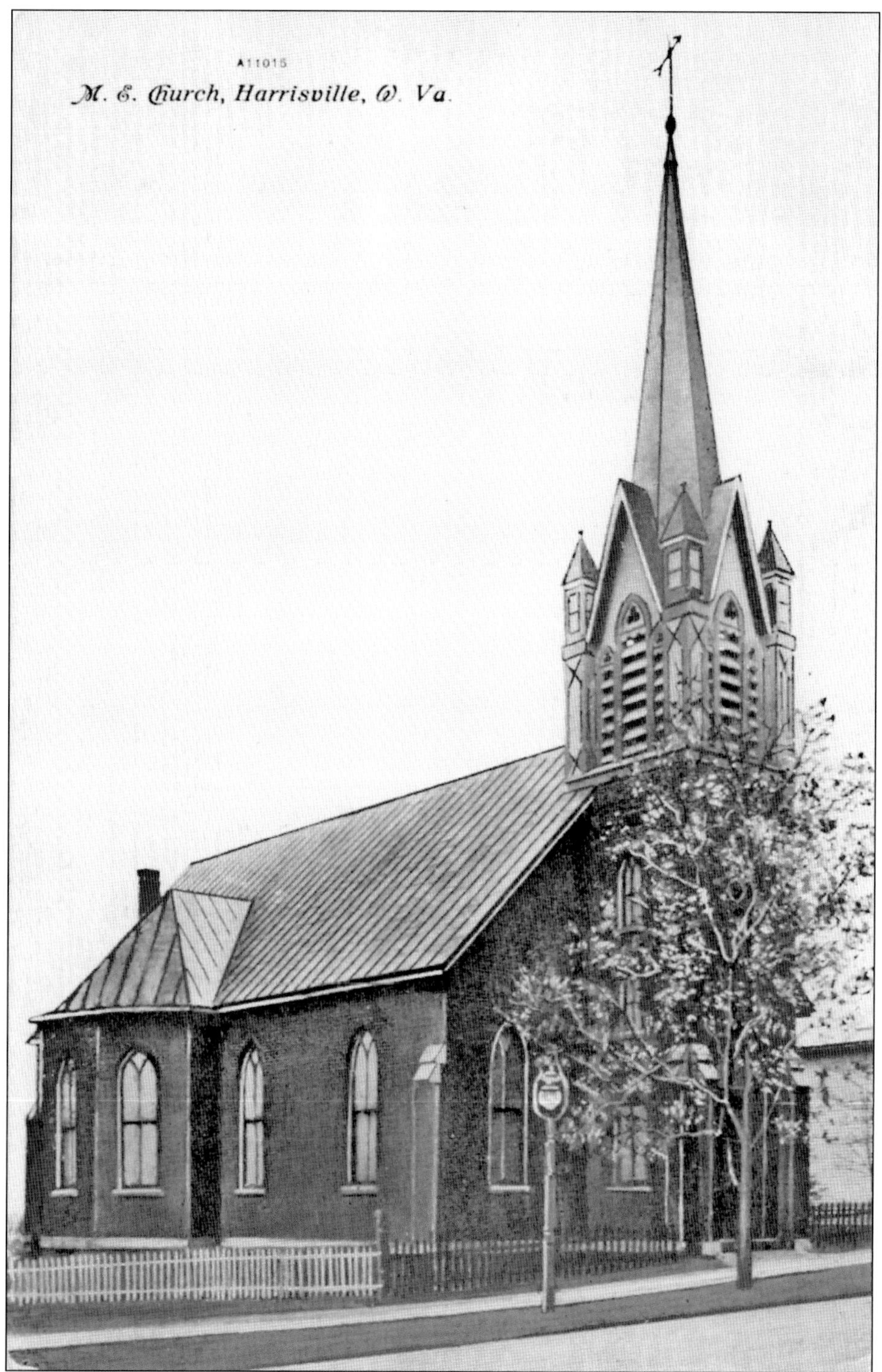

The Methodist Episcopal church, shown in this 1911 card, was built shortly after a fire destroyed the church's previous building in 1888. It is now the site of St. Luke's Methodist on Main Street and has been added to and remodeled over the years.

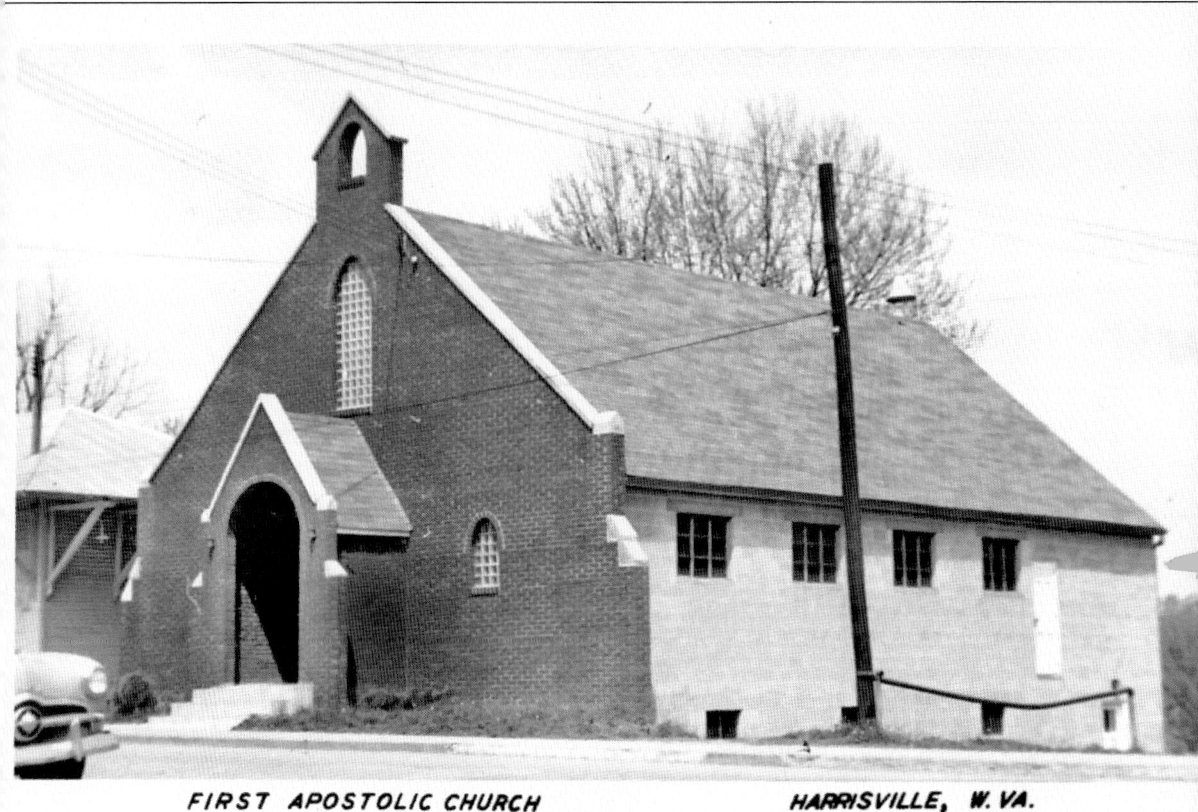

The First Apostolic Church at 601 E. Main Street, shown in this *c.* 1953 postcard, was built in 1949. This view of the church does not show the parsonage, as it was added on several years after the church was built. The church still holds services at this location today.

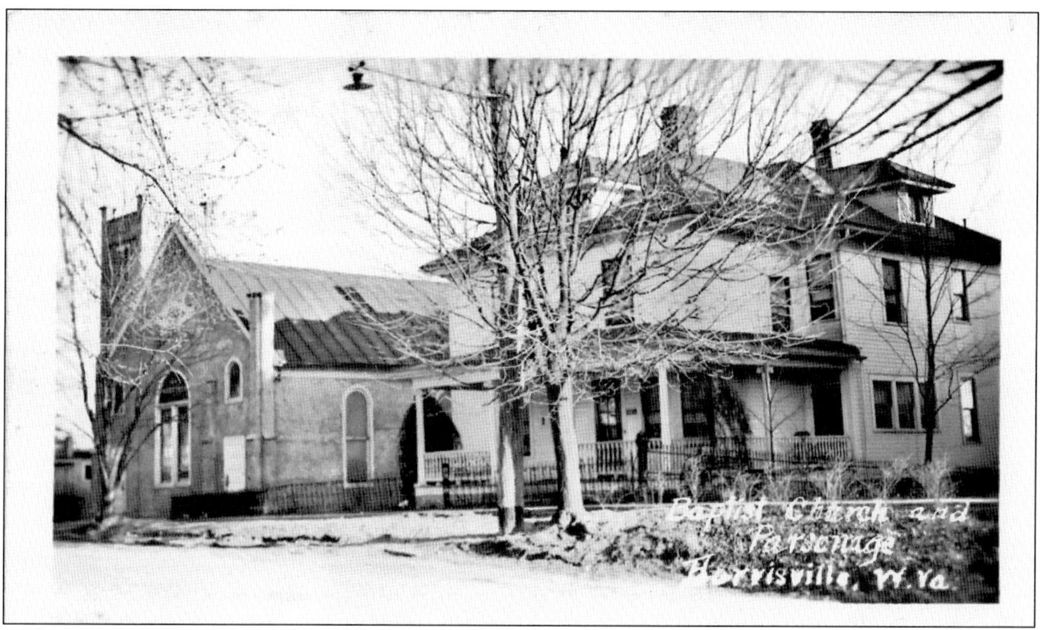

The Baptist church and its parsonage were located on West Main Street, as seen in this *c.* 1953 postcard. The church is now gone, but the parsonage still stands next door to the left of the Gen. Thomas M. Harris School Museum at 127 W. Main Street.

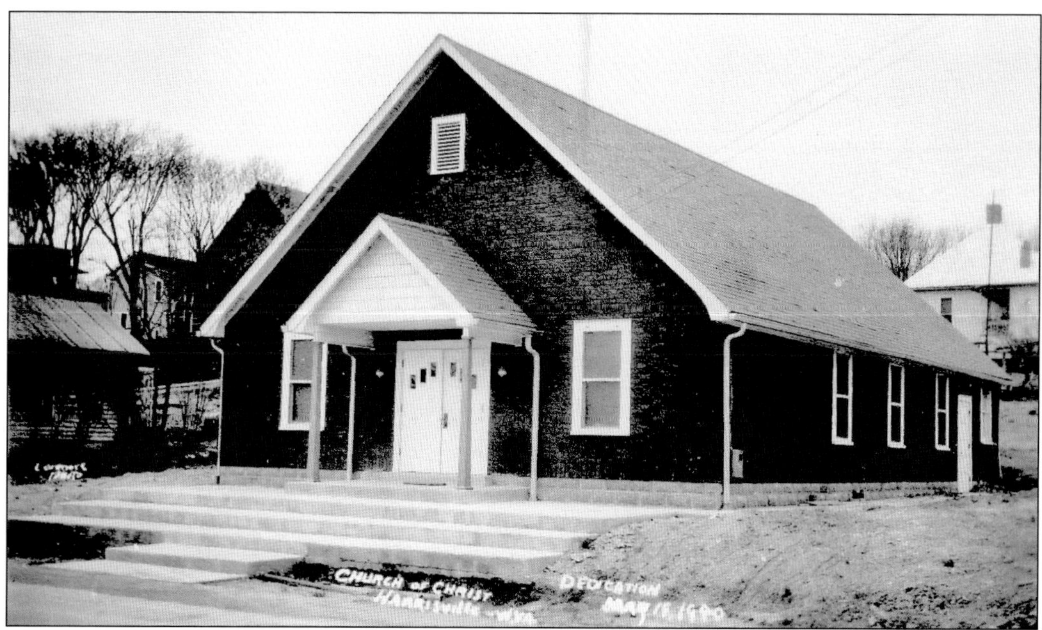

This card from 1940 shows the Church of Christ on Stout Street. This church was built in 1940 and continues to hold services at this location.

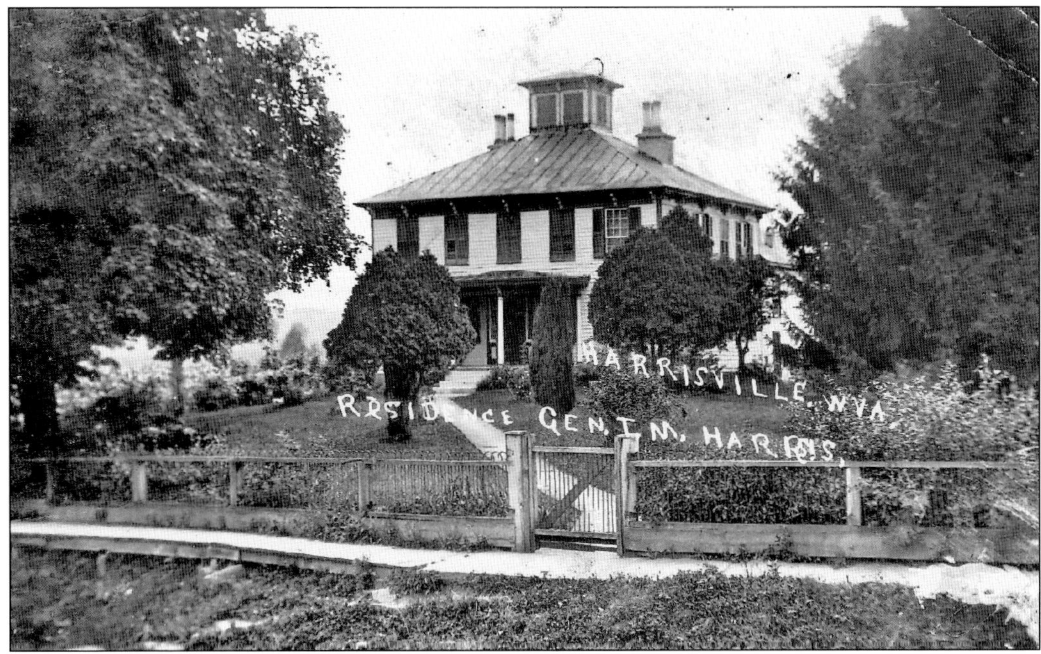

This card, postmarked in 1908, depicts the home of Gen. Thomas M. Harris, for whose uncle Harrisville was named. His home stood at the site of the current Baptist church, which is located at the corner of S. Court Street and South Street.

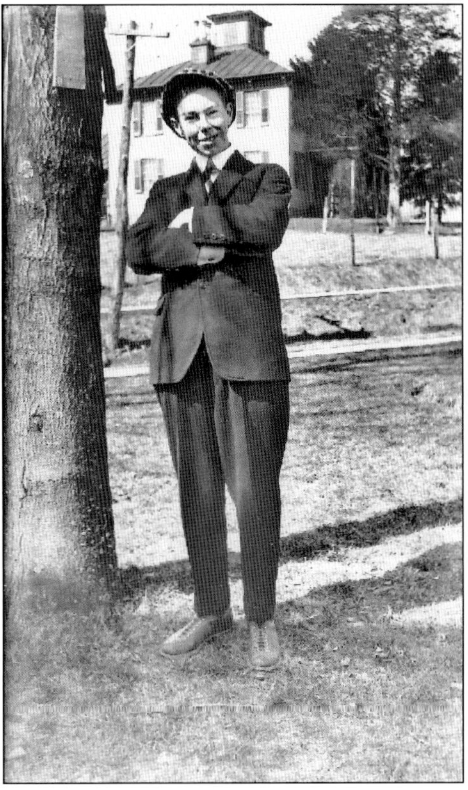

An unidentified gentleman stands in front of the Harris house in this postcard, *c.* 1910.

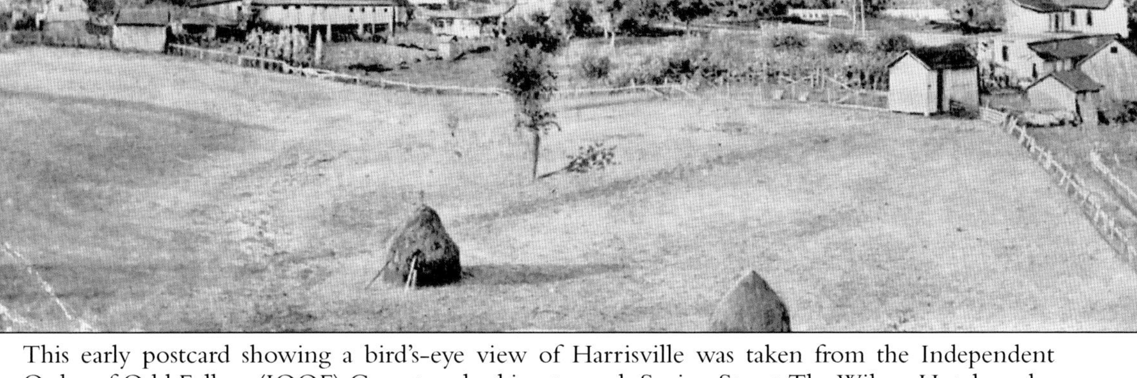

This early postcard showing a bird's-eye view of Harrisville was taken from the Independent Order of Odd Fellow (IOOF) Cemetery looking towards Spring Street. The Wilson Hotel can be seen in the center at the corner of Spring and Pierpoint Streets in this card, which was postmarked in 1912.

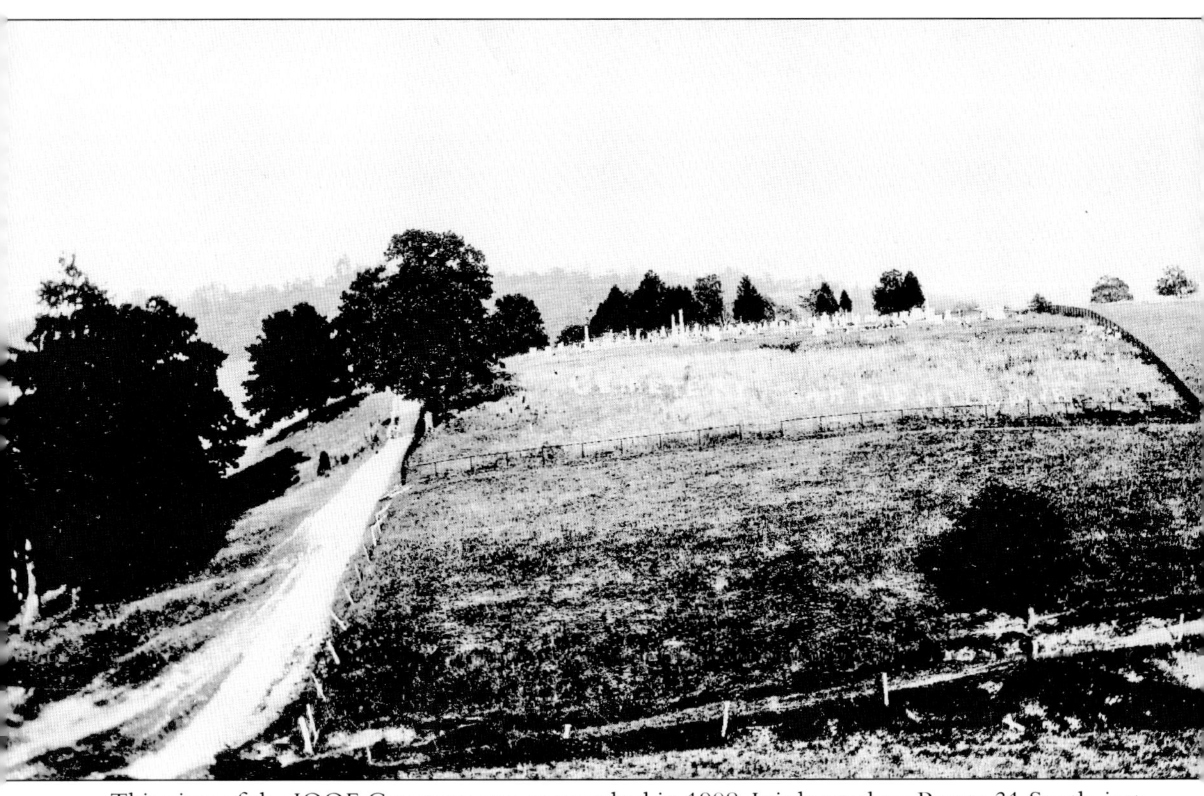

This view of the IOOF Cemetery was postmarked in 1908. It is located on Route 31 South, just at the edge of Harrisville.

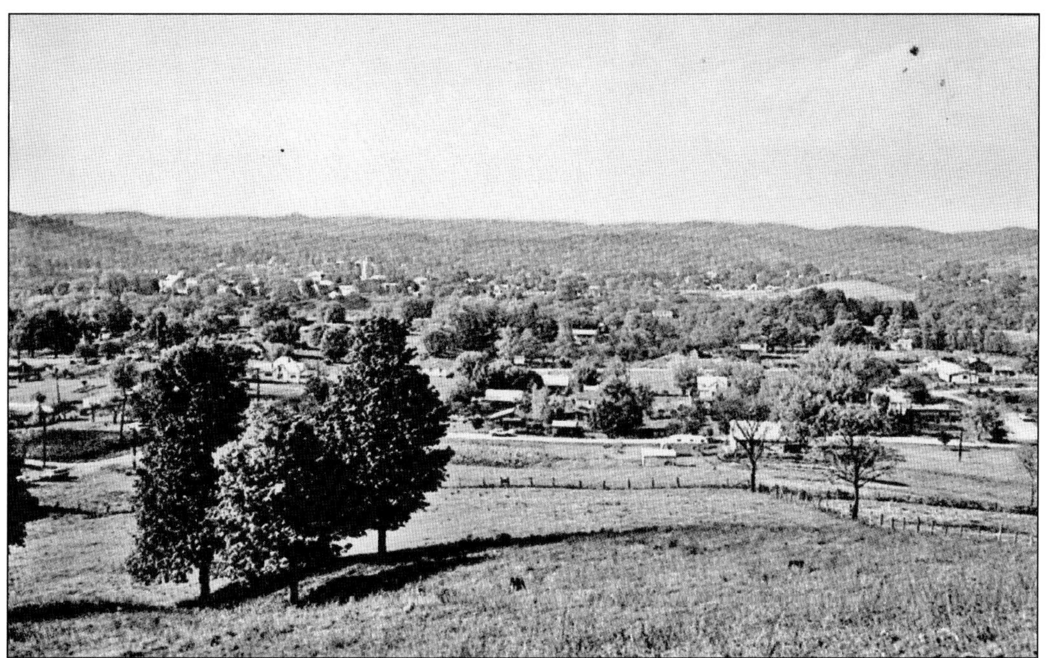

This *c.* 1960 postcard depicts a bird's-eye view of Harrisville.

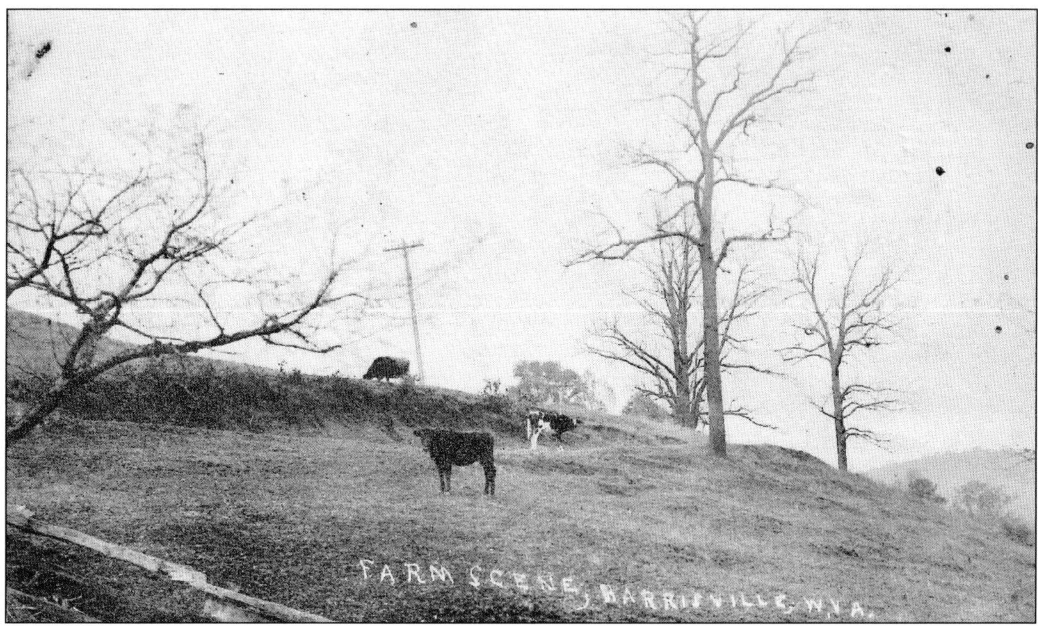

This *c.* 1908 image portrays a farm scene in Harrisville. This view is one of the images shown on the first card in this chapter.

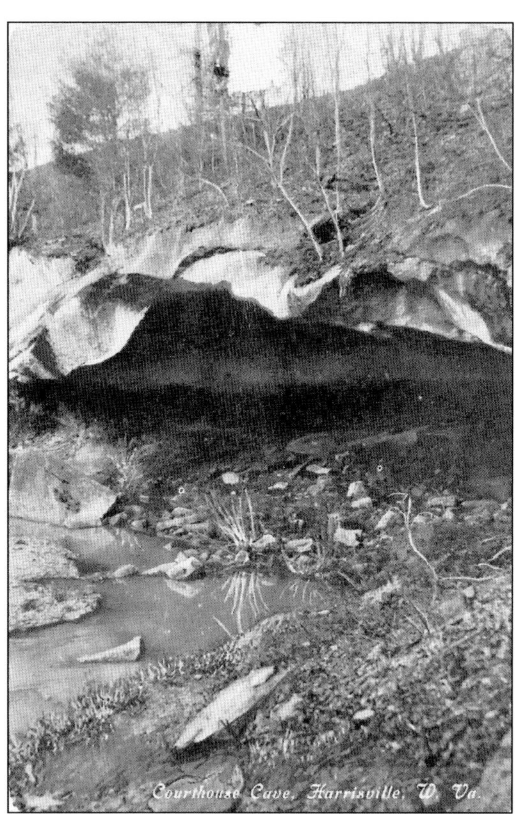

Court House Cave is shown in this *c.* 1925 postcard. The cave is located along the old Harrisville Southern railroad roadbed, just outside Harrisville.

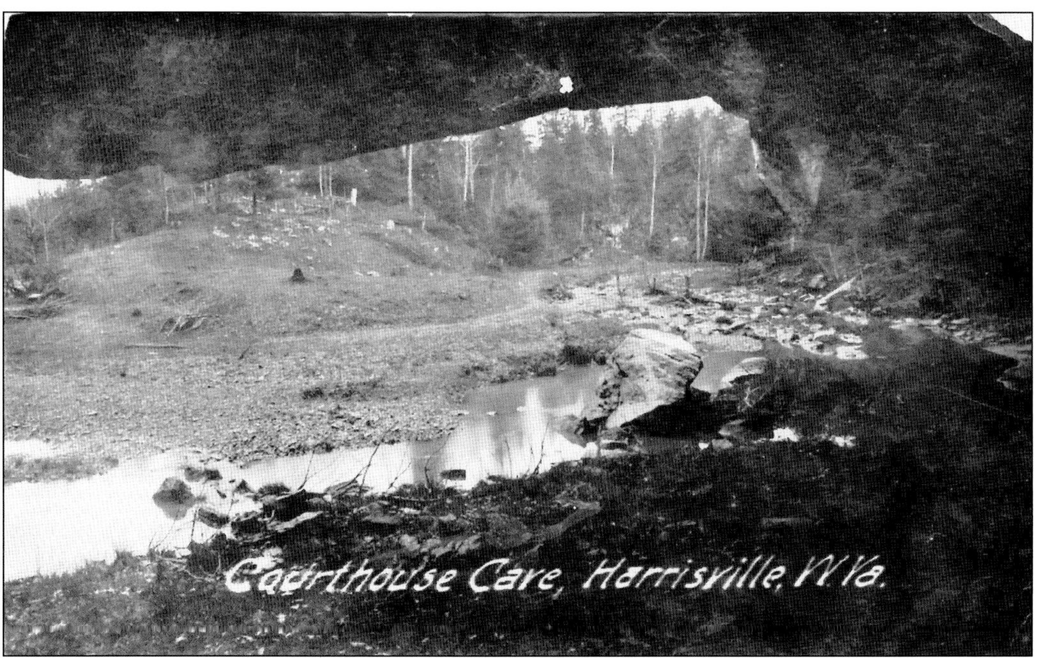

This *c.* 1920 card depicts another view of Court House Cave, from the inside looking out.

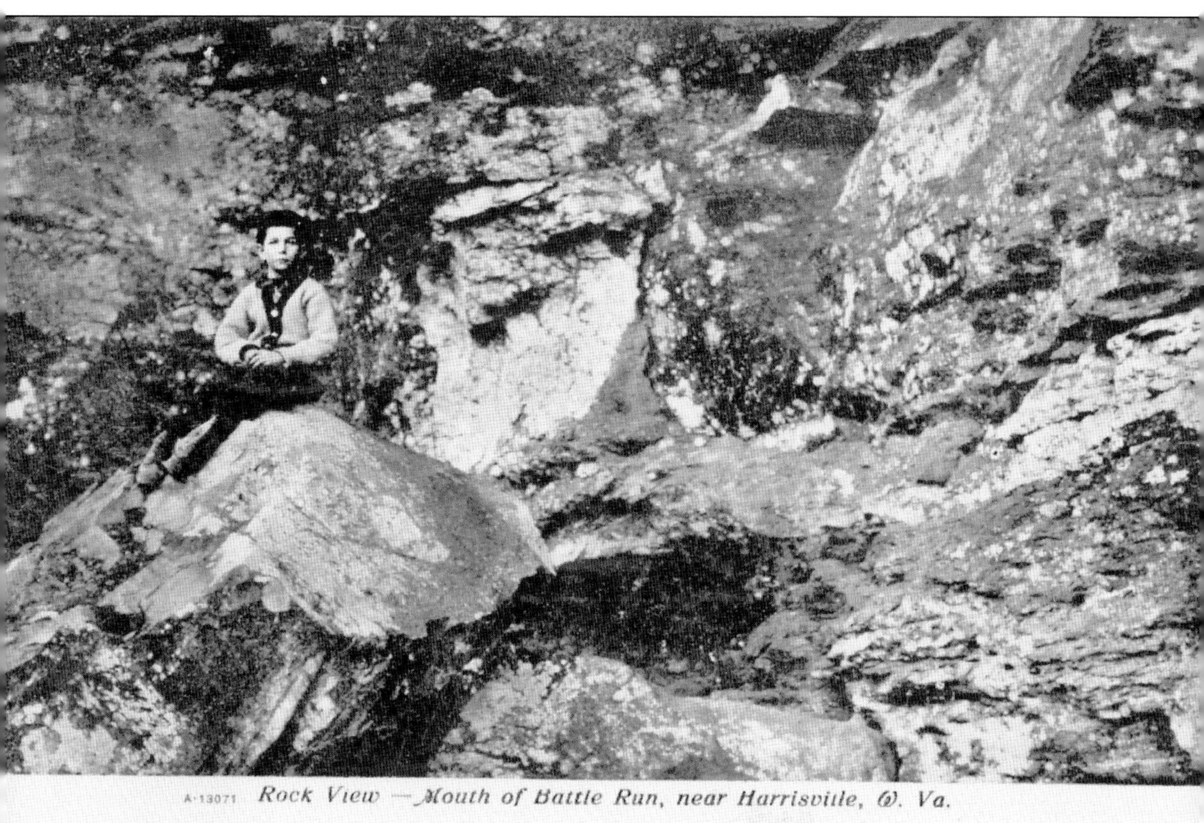

Rock View can be found on the mouth of Battle Run near Harrisville, located where Route 31 crosses Buck Run. This card was postmarked in 1911.

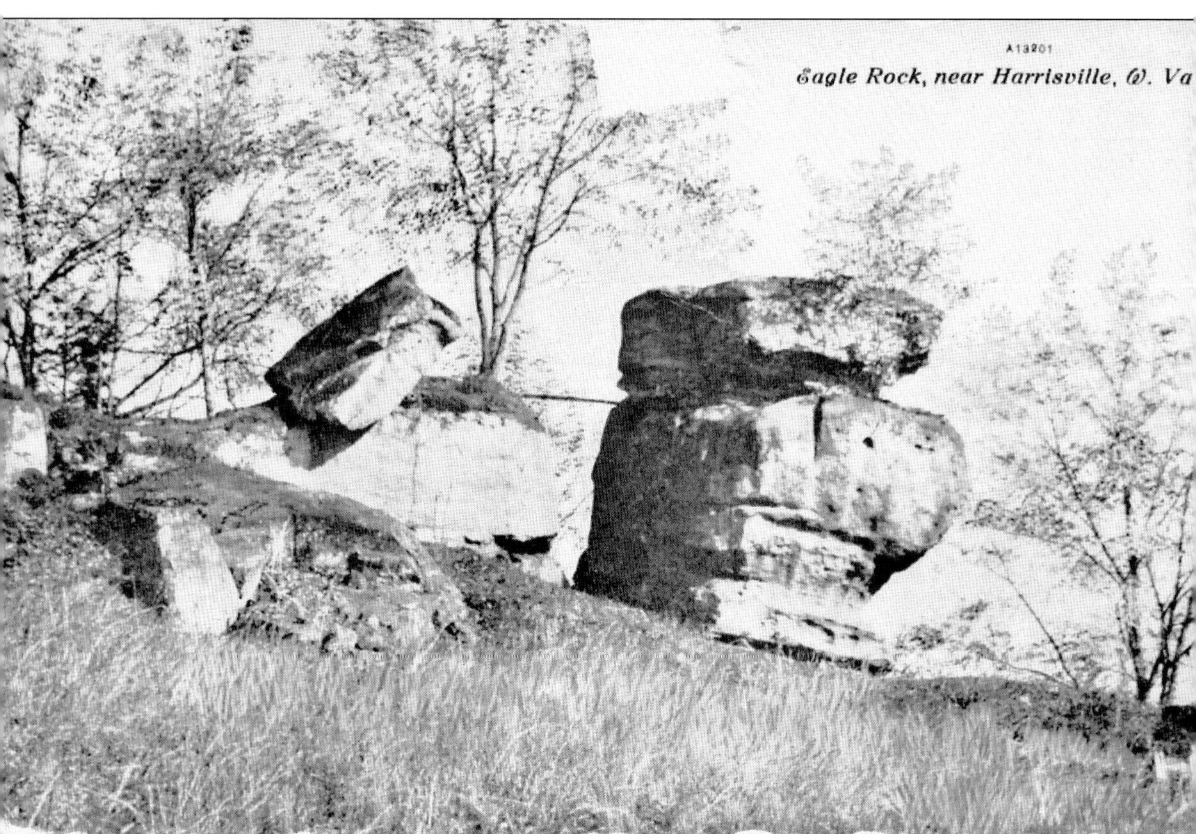

Eagle Rock, located near Harrisville, got its name because it was in the shape of an eagle. The rock, shown in this *c.* 1905 card, was destroyed by the building of the Harrisville Southern Railroad. It overlooked Buck Run and the cut through the hill that is known as Kroger's Pass.

Two

PENNSBORO

Pennsboro was established in or around 1858. Historically, Pennsboro was a thriving town of industry due to its location on the Parkersburg-Staunton Turnpike and along the B&O main line. Pennsboro served as the center of most of the early business enterprise in the first part of the 20th century. As evidenced by this first card, Pennsboro meant business. This chapter will first explore the early business cards for Pennsboro and then see the many cards of other buildings and places of interest.

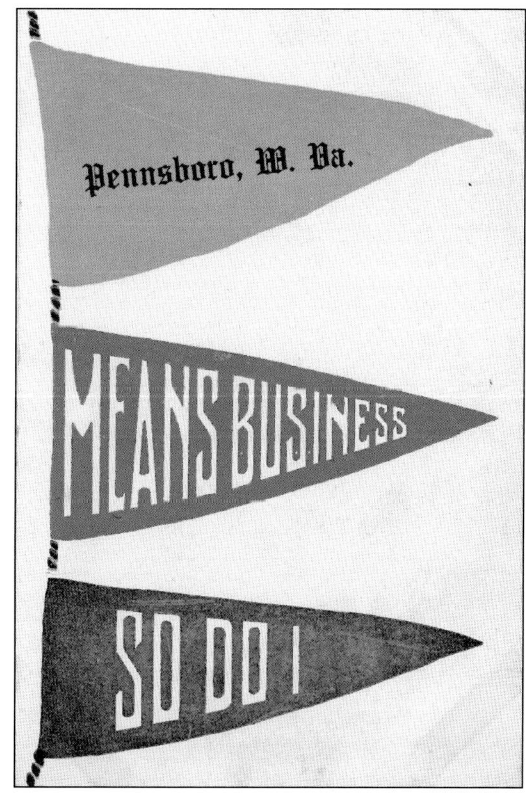

This *c.* 1915 card was an early advertising card for business in Pennsboro.

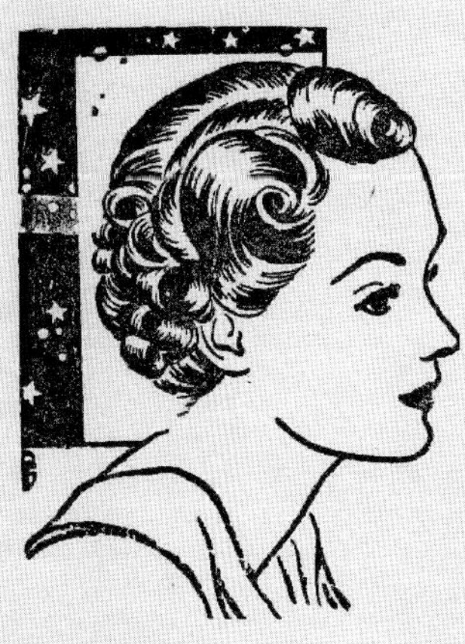

I take this means to invite my Old Friends and New Ones to

BEA'S BEAUTY SHOP

Located in Pennsboro, over McKinley and McCullough Furniture Store.

OPENING DATE, JULY 9, 1947

Bell Telephone-- 106R   Pritchard Phone

This advertising postcard announces the opening of Bea's Beauty Shop.

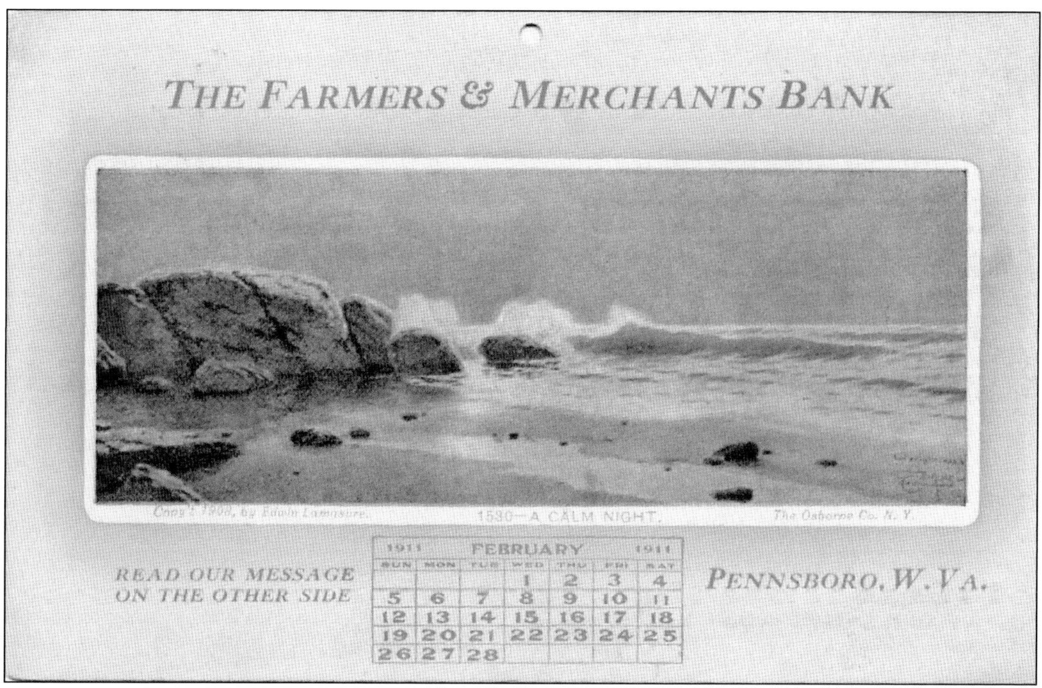

Depicted here is an early advertising calendar postcard from the Farmers and Merchants Bank, which was organized in 1897. The president of the bank was Creed Collins. The back of this 1911 card has advertising information about the bank and lists H.J. Scott as the cashier.

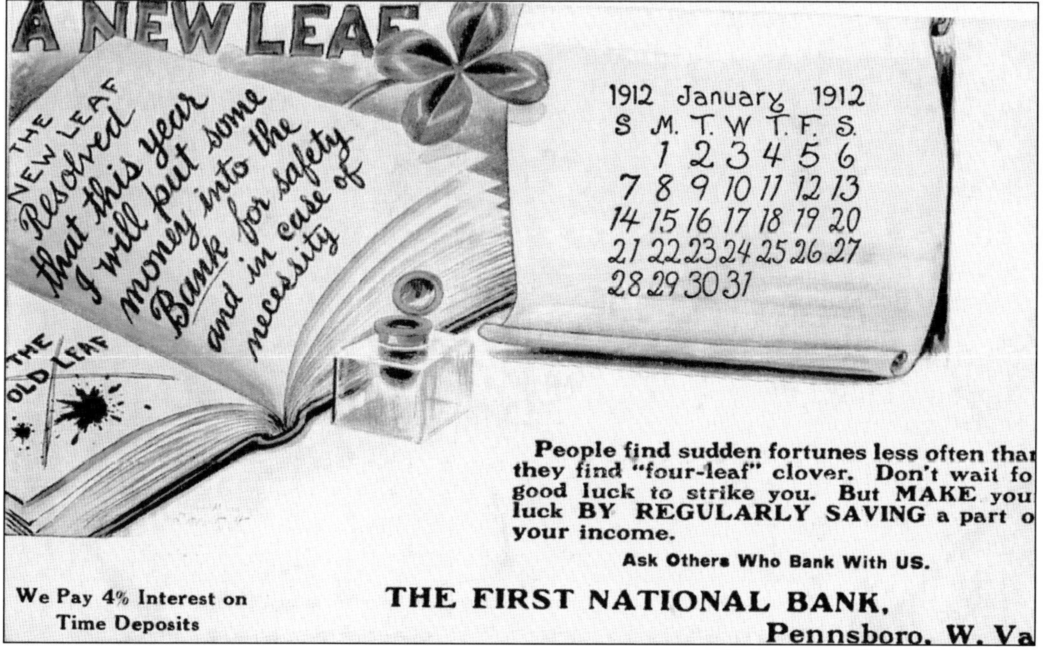

Another early advertising calendar postcard, this one from the First National Bank, is shown here. Creed Collins was also president of this bank, which was organized in 1904. The calendar and the card were dated in 1912.

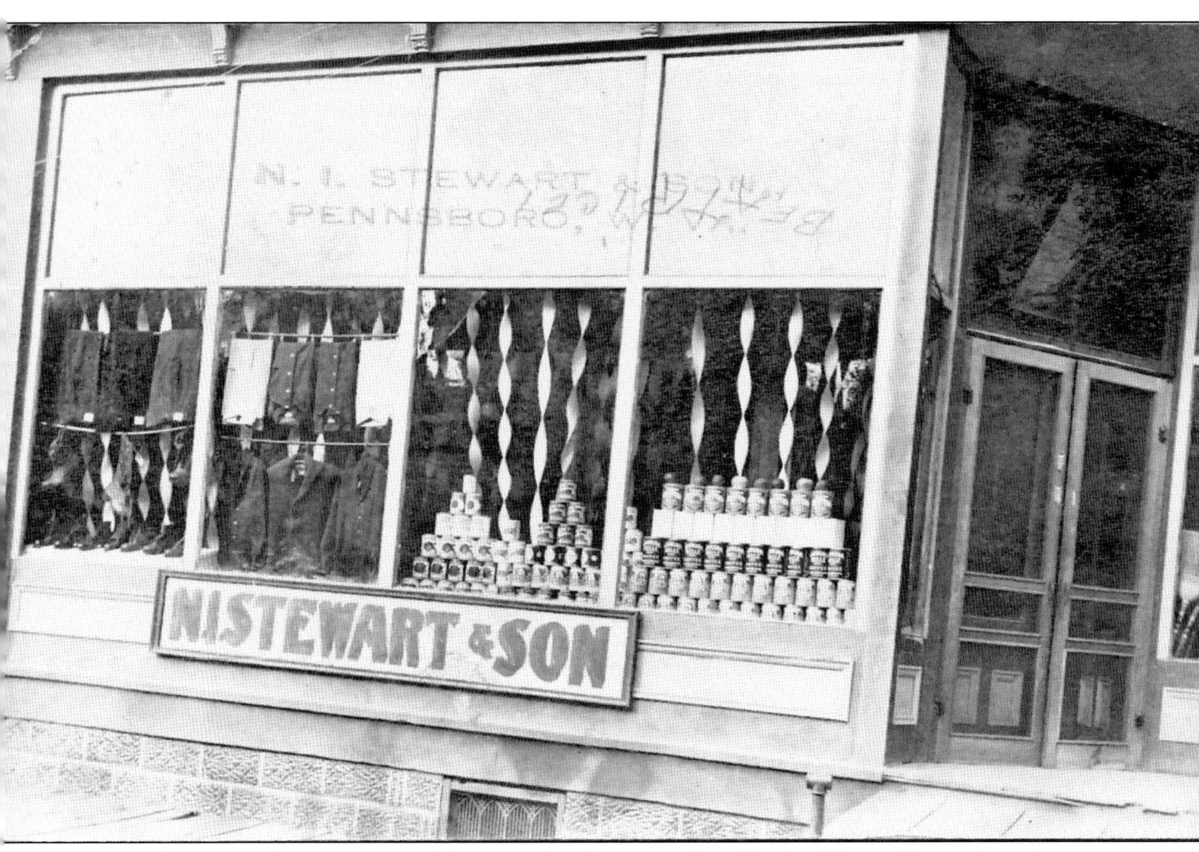

N.I. Stewart & Son was one of the early local mercantiles. The building still stands at the corner of Masonic Drive and Main Street and was the recent site of a ceramics shop. The entrance has changed little since this card was produced. This card was postmarked in 1914.

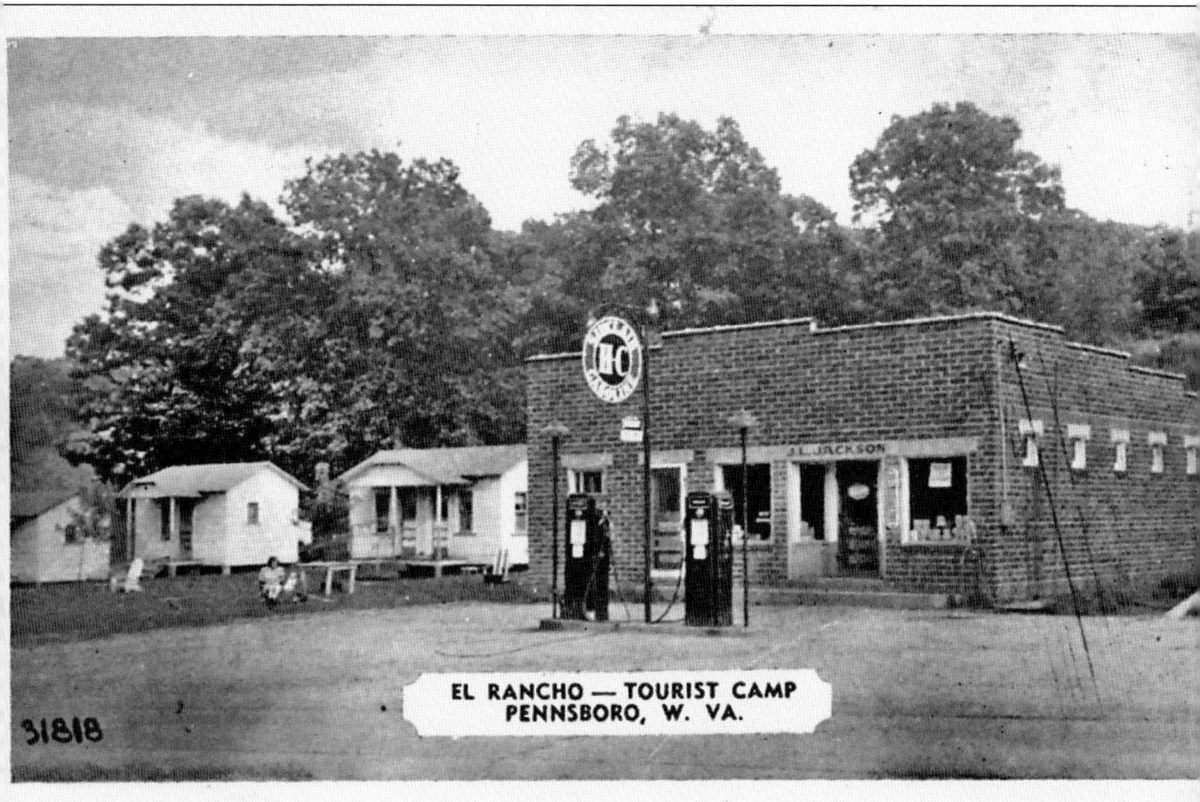

This postcard depicts El Rancho Tourist Camp in Pennsboro. The building stood on the far east end of Pennsboro on the right side of old U.S. Route 50 heading out of town toward Tollgate. It also served as Jackson's Store, a small grocery that was built by J.L. Jackson. The building was recently razed, and all the cabins are now gone as well. The text on the back of the card reads, "El Rancho. Modern Clean Quiet. For the 'rest' of your life."

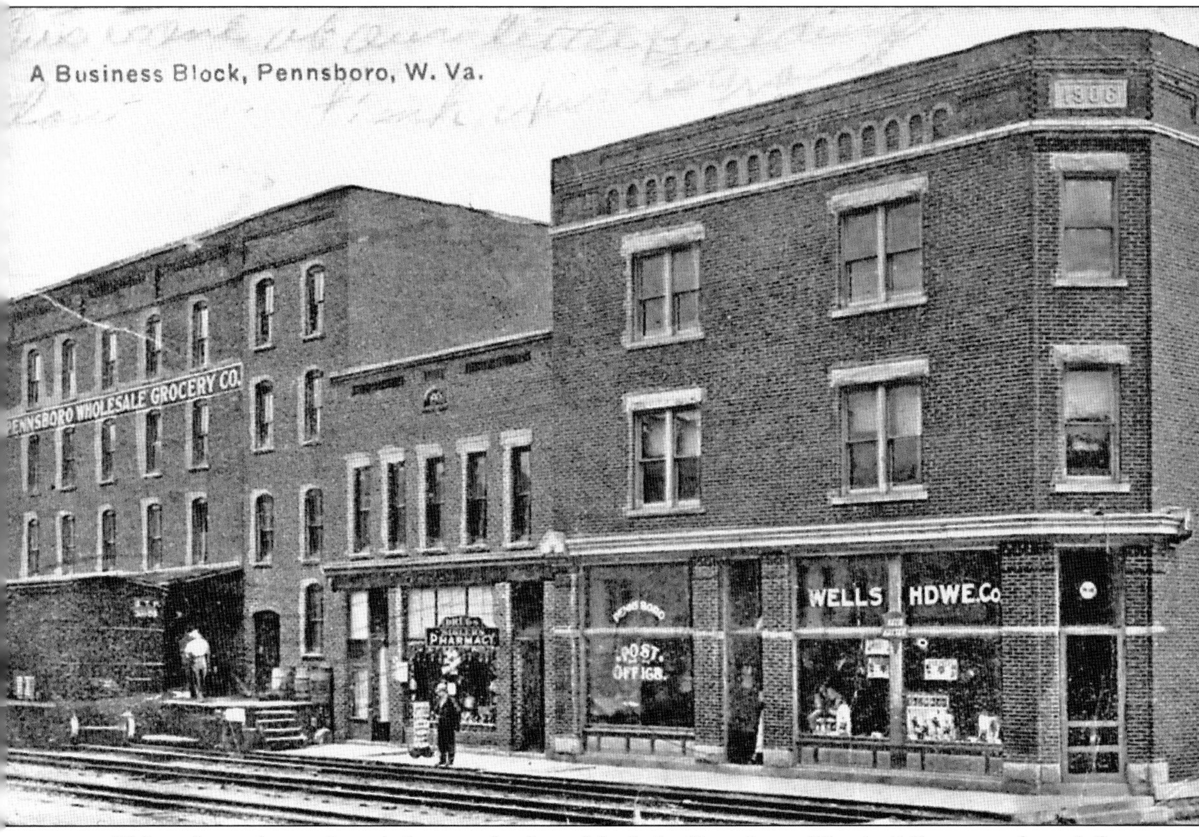

This color-enhanced card shows a business block in Pennsboro. The buildings are, from left to right, the Pennsboro Wholesale Grocery Company (built in 1906), Sigler's Pharmacy (built in 1908), the U.S. Post Office, and Wells Hardware (built in 1906). These businesses thrived because of their close proximity to the depot, which was immediately across the street in a diagonal direction. The Wells Hardware building burned down in the mid-1990s and the remaining buildings are now part of Harvest Time Ministries. However, the top two floors have been removed from the grocery company structure. This card was postmarked in 1911.

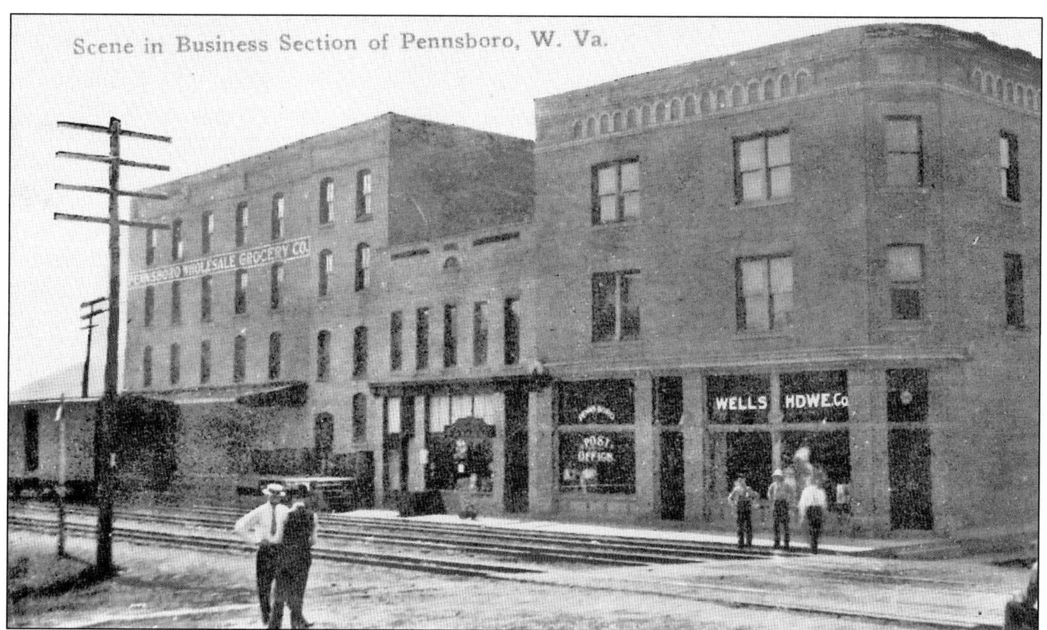

This *c.* 1910 card also depicts the business section of Pennsboro. It is a much more accurate view because it is a real photograph. Note the three railroad tracks at the intersection.

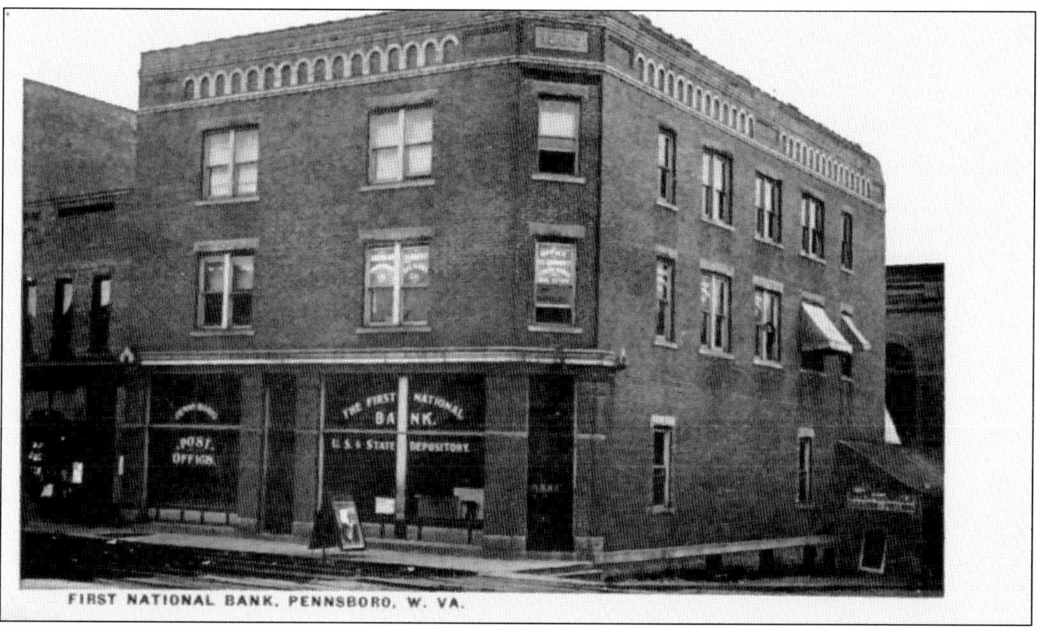

The First National Bank was formerly the Wells Hardware. This card is postmarked in 1912, shortly after Wells Hardware relocated across the street into the Wells Building and the bank began to occupy the building. The bank purchased this building from E.E. Wells and Bert Bradford on May 3, 1911. The windows on the second floor say, "Office of __ Lambert, Real Estate, Stocks, Bonds." At one time, the top floor housed the IOOF order. This building later became home to Michel's Pharmacy.

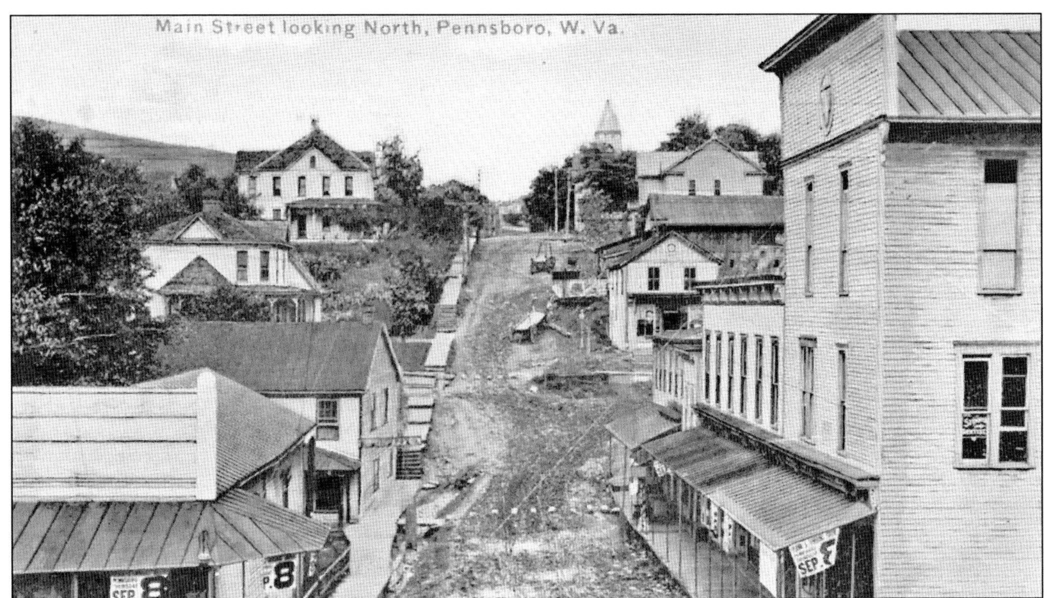

This image, postmarked 1910, is a color-enhanced view of looking north up Main Street. On the left are, from bottom to top, Lantz' Store and Ice Cream Shop, the Brown Hotel, the Dollie Thomas home (which was owned by Love A. Prunty at the time of this photo and later became the Sarah Nutter home), and the Brown/Pfeltz (later Statler) home at the top of the hill. These homes, both built in 1910, still stand today. On the right are, from bottom to top, the Pratt Store, the marble works, and the home of Dr. Jones. The steeple of the Methodist Episcopal church can be seen at the top of the hill. A sign on the window of the second floor of the Pratt Store reads "Stoops-Dentist." The signs advertise an event in town on Thursday, September 8.

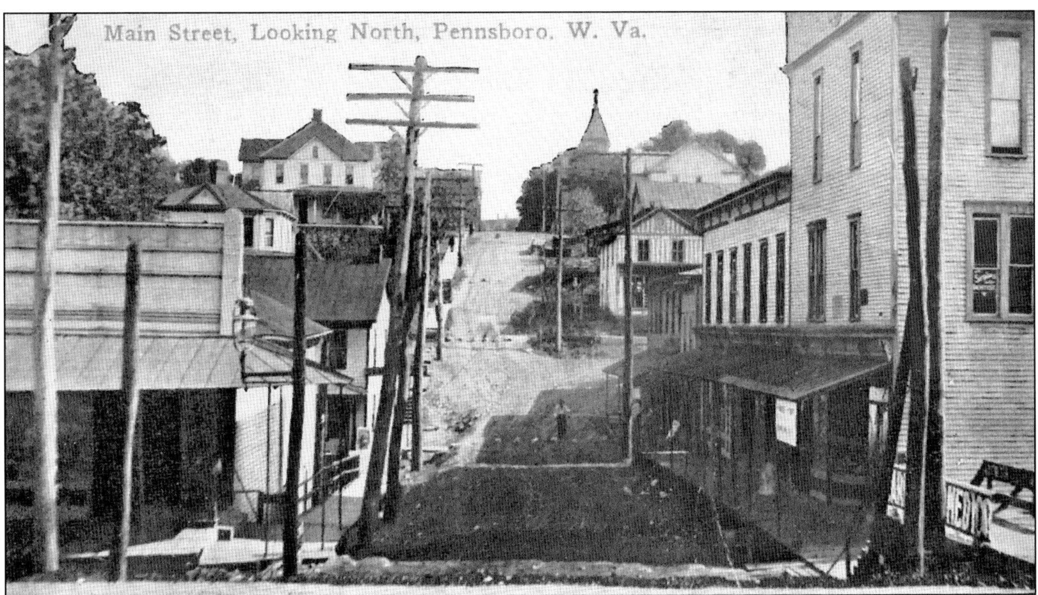

This card shows the same view as the previous card, though it is obviously a different time period. One can tell that this card, postmarked in 1914, is later because of the addition of the utility poles. All of the buildings on the right burned in 1917 in what must have been a tremendous fire.

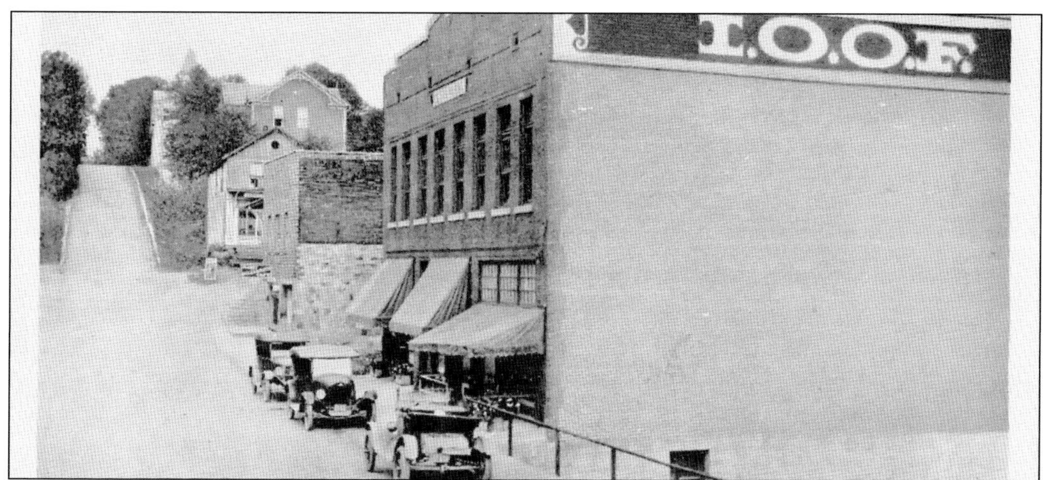

The first building to the right is the IOOF Building, which at one time housed Weekley's five and dime store, McCulty and McKinley Furniture and funeral home, and the McCullough funeral home. It now houses the Pennsboro branch of the Ritchie County Public Library. The awning in this photo reads "Cunningham" and is possibly the same insurance company that is pictured in the following card at a different location. The next building is the current law office of the author and also the Flower Station. In this photo, this building has a sign that reads "Billiards/Café," indicating it is from the time in which Flannigan's Pool Hall and Café was located here. The IOOF building was constructed in 1924, and the Flannigan building was constructed in 1917. This card was published by Sigler's Pharmacy in Pennsboro, *c.* 1925.

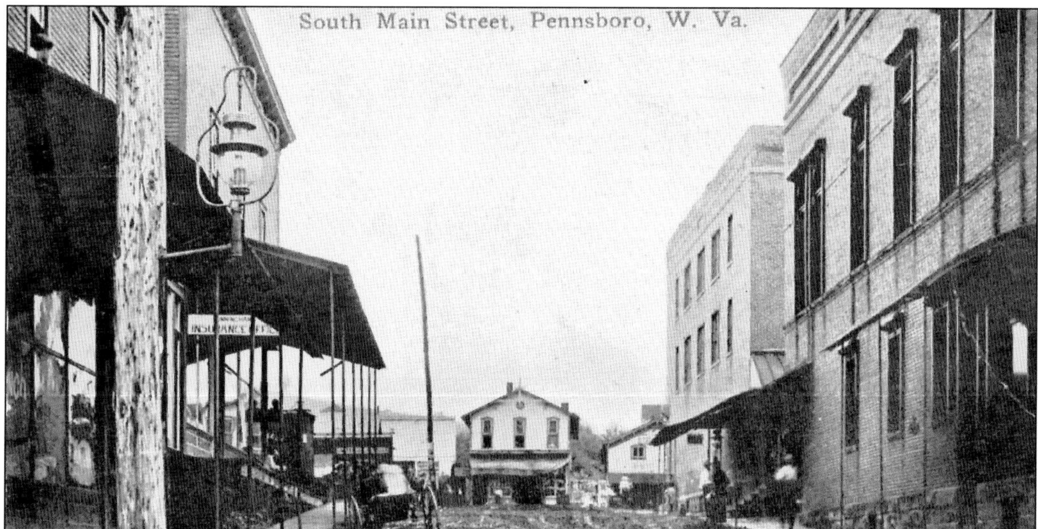

This card, postmarked 1912, shows South Main Street looking toward what is now Davis Marbles (at one time T. Lamberts store), Mrs. Doyles' Restaurant, and Corra's Confectionery and Beer Hall. The Citizens National Bank is to the right of that building, and the office of Dr. A.P. Jones is located upstairs in that building. On the left is Cunningham Insurance office. The adjoining business was once a hardware store. The buildings to the right contained, from closest to furthest, the Farmers and Merchants Bank and the Cyclone Cash Store, the Gaiety Theatre (later known as the Penn Theatre and the Heaton Theatre), Stoop's Dentist Office, and the First National Bank. These buildings on the right are all now part of Harvest Time Ministries.

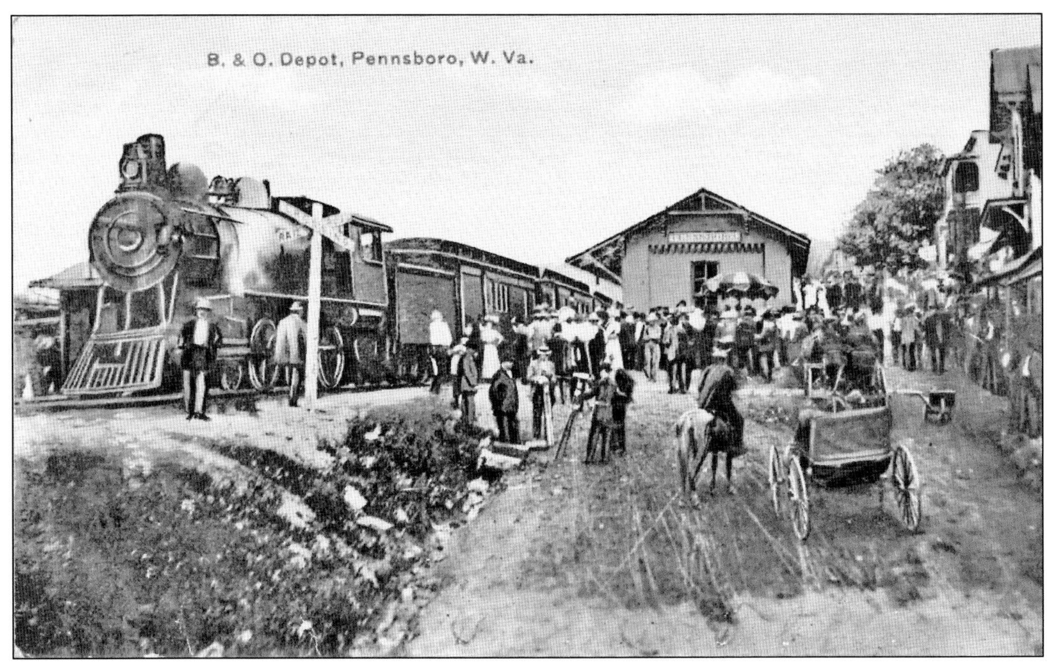

This color-enhanced card of the B&O depot was postmarked in 1910.

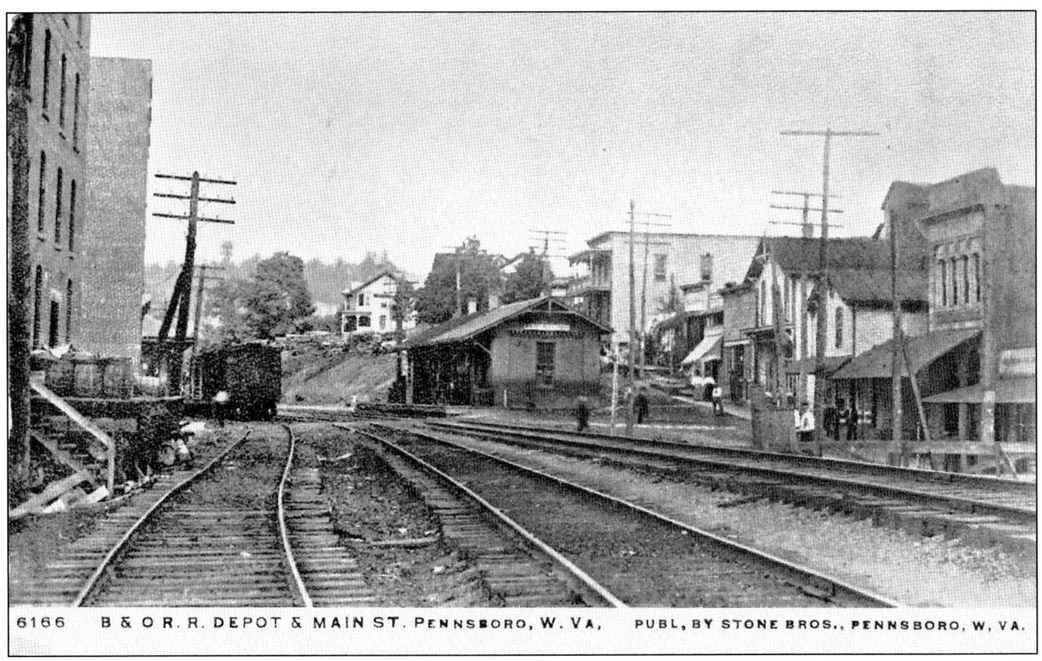

The color-enhanced card on this page, postmarked in 1906, shows the B&O depot and much of the downtown section of Pennsboro prior to the building of the current Wells Building to the right of the depot. Dr. J.B. Wilson's home and office, seen above to the left of the depot, is now the Rose Hill Bed and Breakfast.

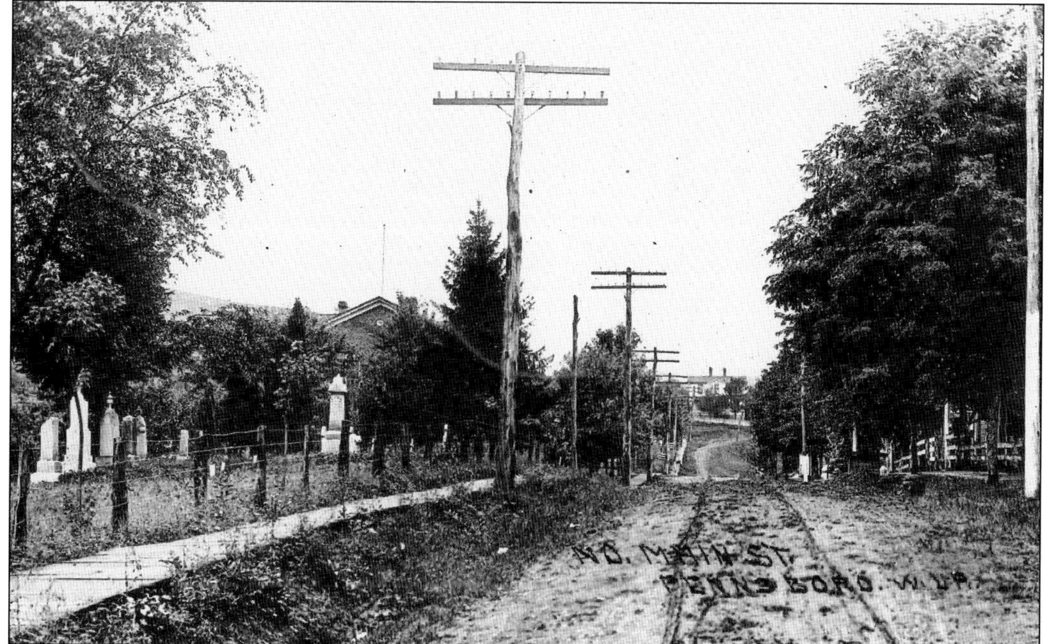

This *c.* 1908 view of North Main Street was made from its intersection with West Penn Avenue and the St. Josephs Catholic Church cemetery to the left. The top of the school can be seen in the distance.

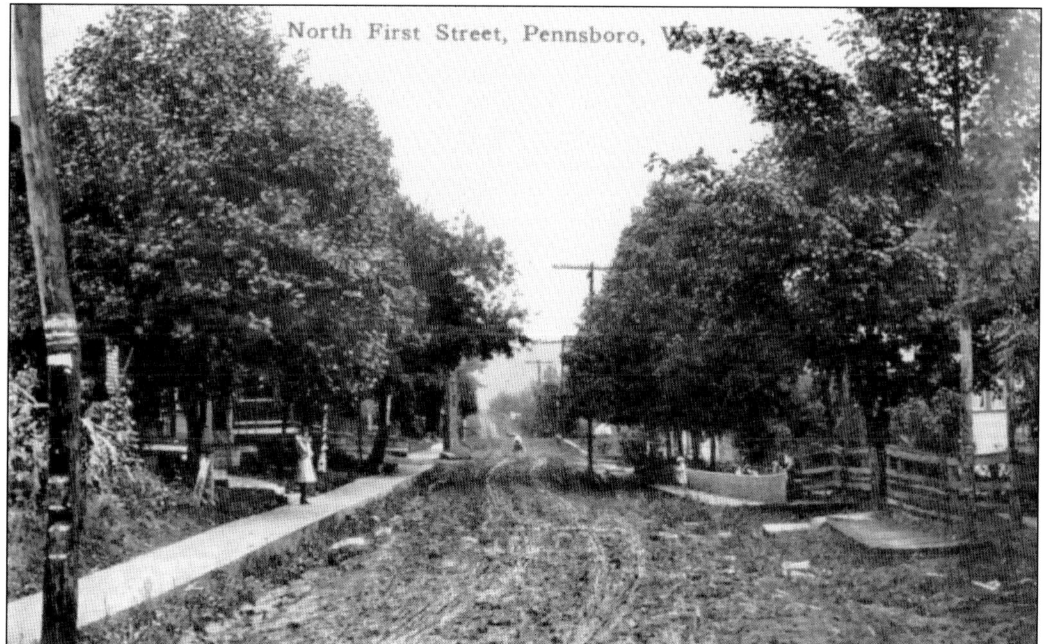

A view of North First Street just past the turn on West Wells Avenue is shown in this card, which was postmarked in 1912.

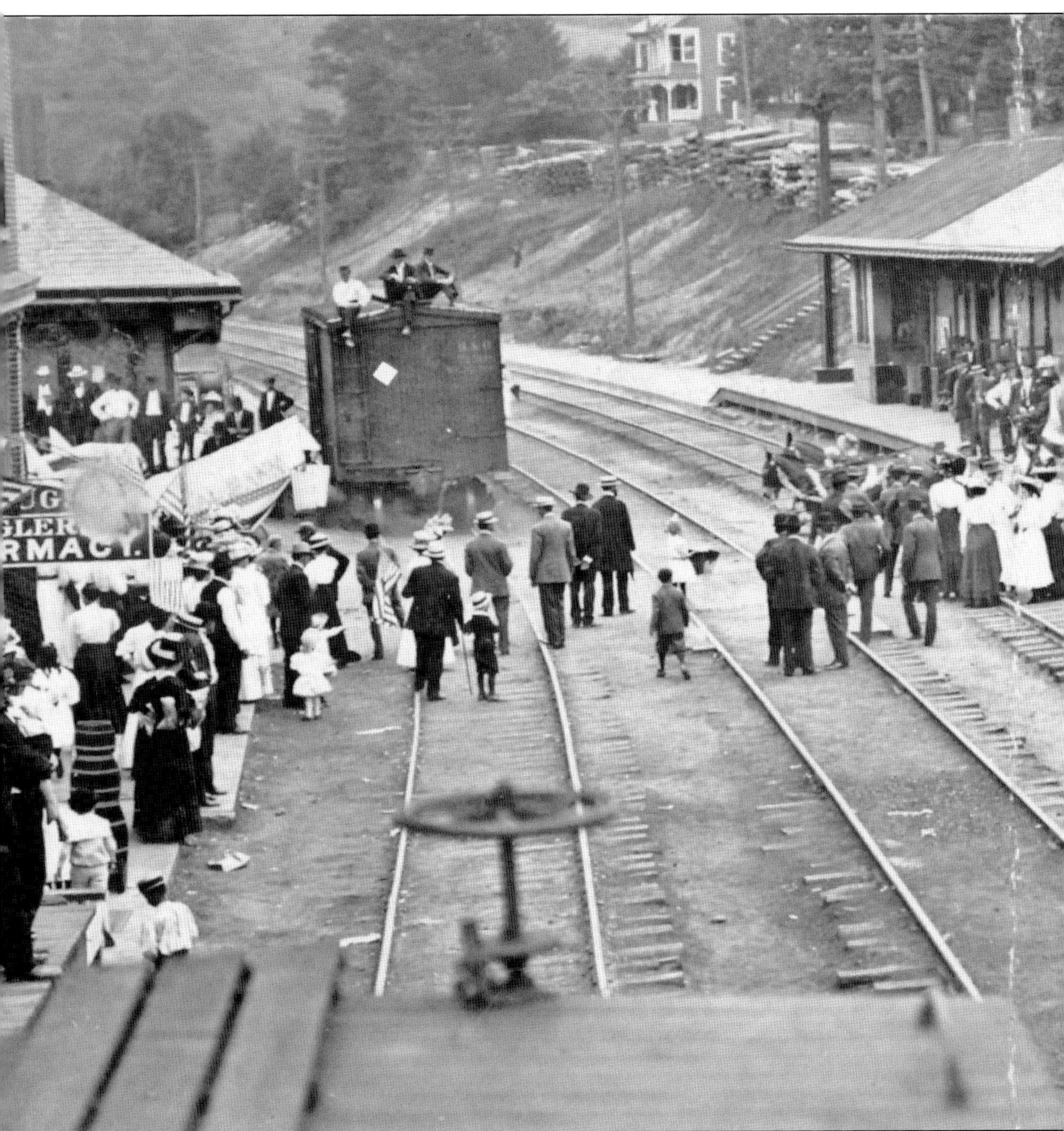

This oversized *c.* 1915 postcard provides a great view of the downtown section of Pennsboro. At first glance, one would think that these people are waiting on the next scheduled train. Closer inspection reveals a parade going through town with at least three floats visible. Floats can be seen

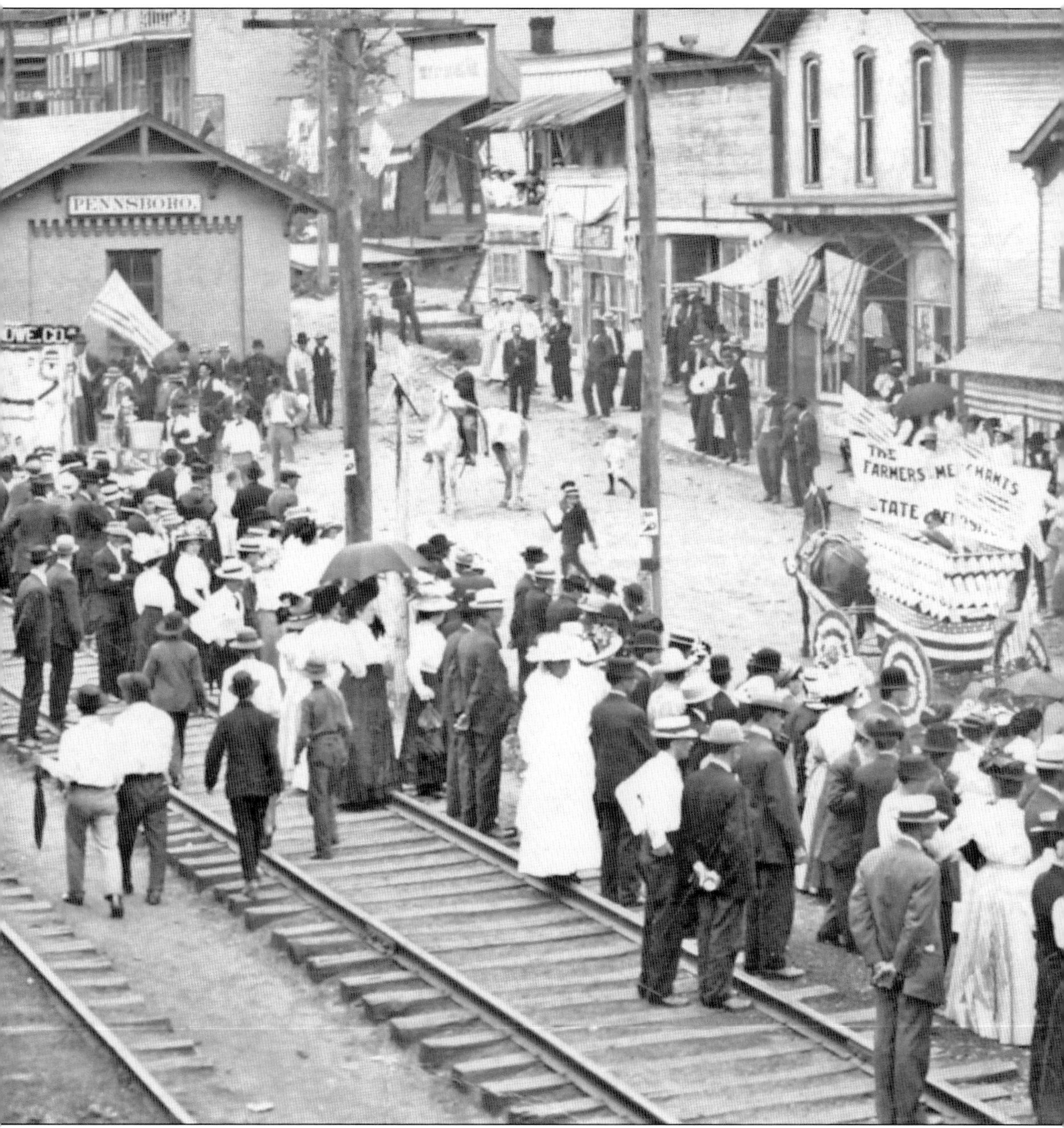

for Farmers and Merchants Bank and Wells Hardware Company. The sign for Sigler's Pharmacy can also be seen on the left. The depot shown still stands in Pennsboro, though most of the buildings seen here are now gone. One can see a feed store just above the depot.

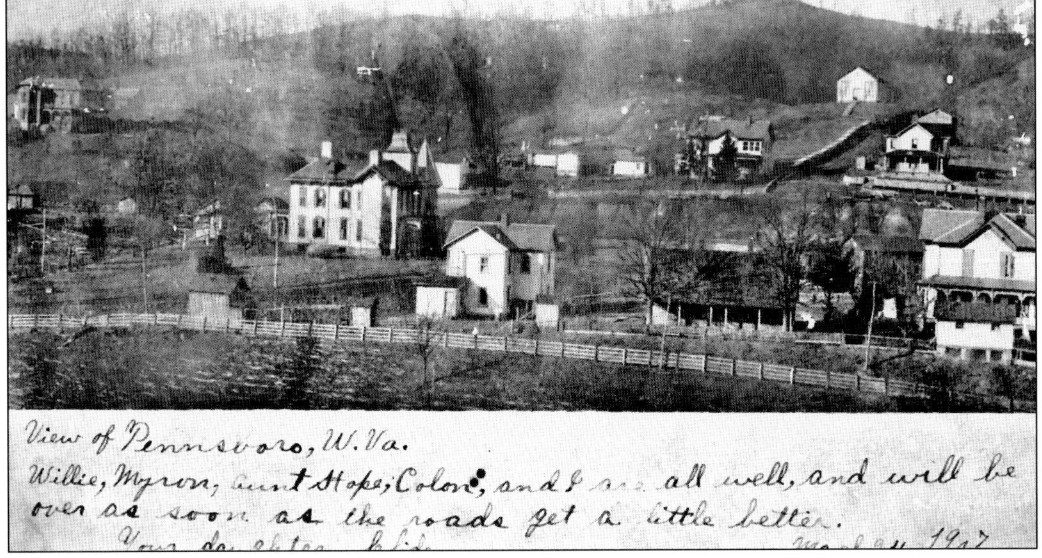

A view of Pennsboro is shown in this 1907 card. The home to the far left is the Creed Collins mansion, which was built in 1884, demolished in the 1960s, and is now the site of Creed Collins Elementary School. The large home in the center-left is the Kimball/Davis home, which was built in 1865 and later served as a hotel and then the Pennsboro Eagles Club from 1941 until being razed in 1988. The West Union Bank now sits on this site. The only home in this photo that is still in existence is the one in the upper-center-right, which was built in 1860 and was at one time the residence and office of Dr. J.B. Wilson. It is now the Rose Hill Bed and Breakfast.

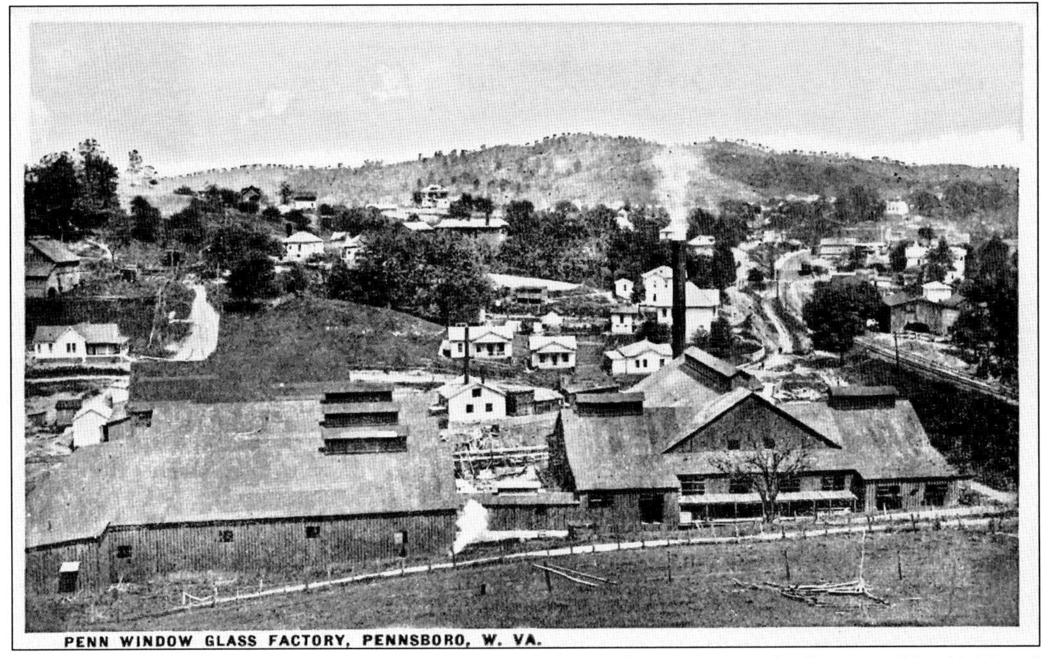

Shown here is a *c.* 1920 color card of the Penn Window Glass Factory, which opened in 1914 and closed in 1928. This site is now occupied by Champion Agate, and none of the buildings seen in this postcard still exist.

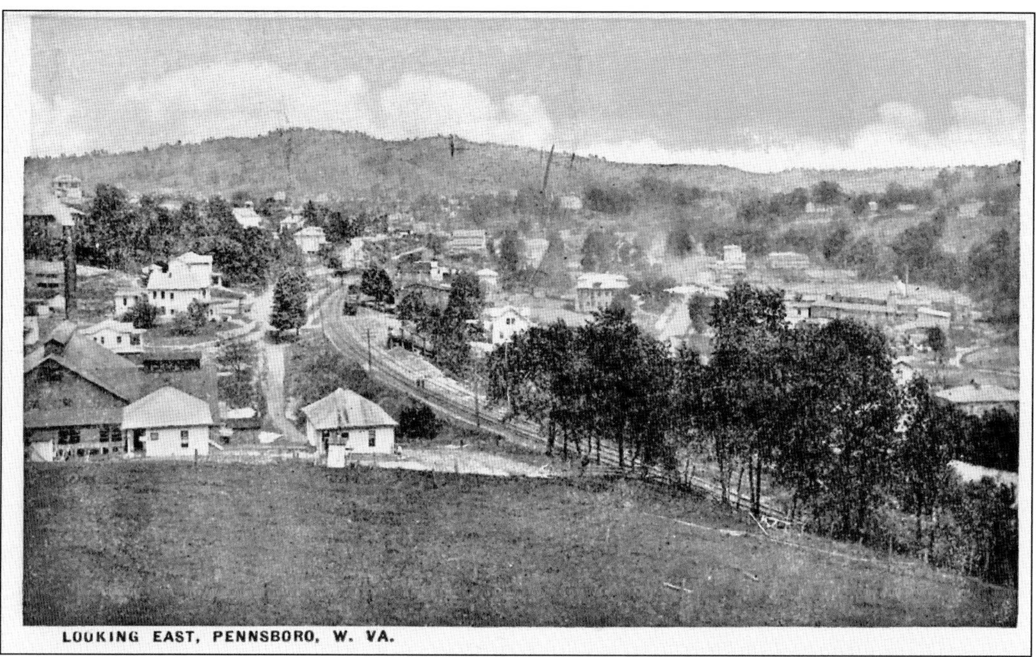

LOOKING EAST, PENNSBORO, W. VA.

This color card was made at the same time as the card on the left bottom. It also provides the same view as the card on the left bottom, although it was taken closer to the B&O line.

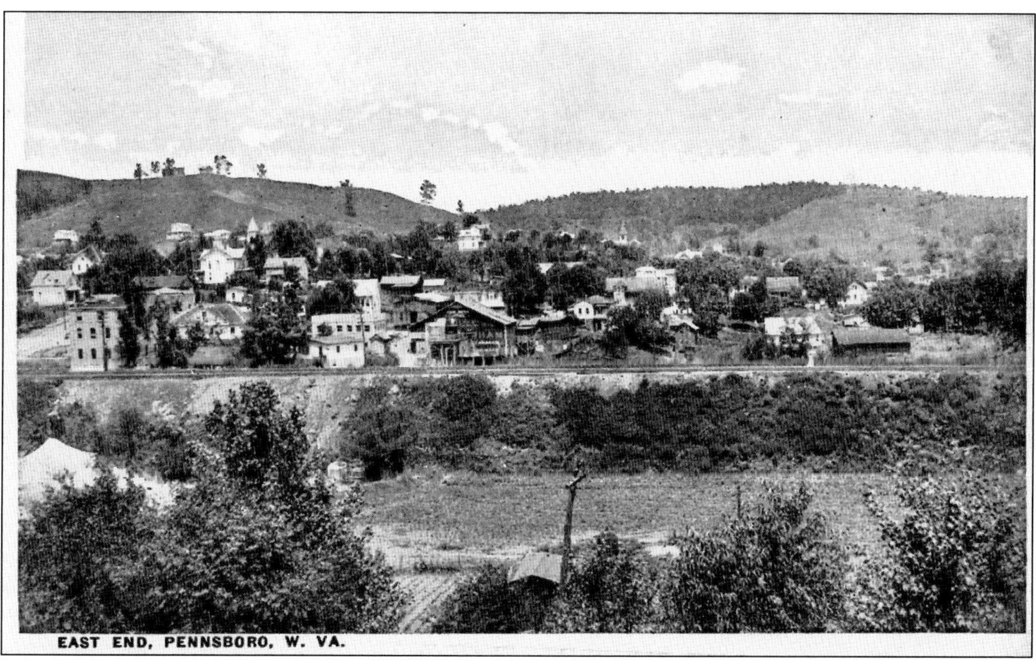

EAST END, PENNSBORO, W. VA.

This color card shows the east end of Pennsboro looking over the B&O mainline in 1919. Main Street can be seen to the very far left. Also, the livery stable can be seen in the center in the large black structure, which would have been at the current site of the Pennsboro Church of Christ.

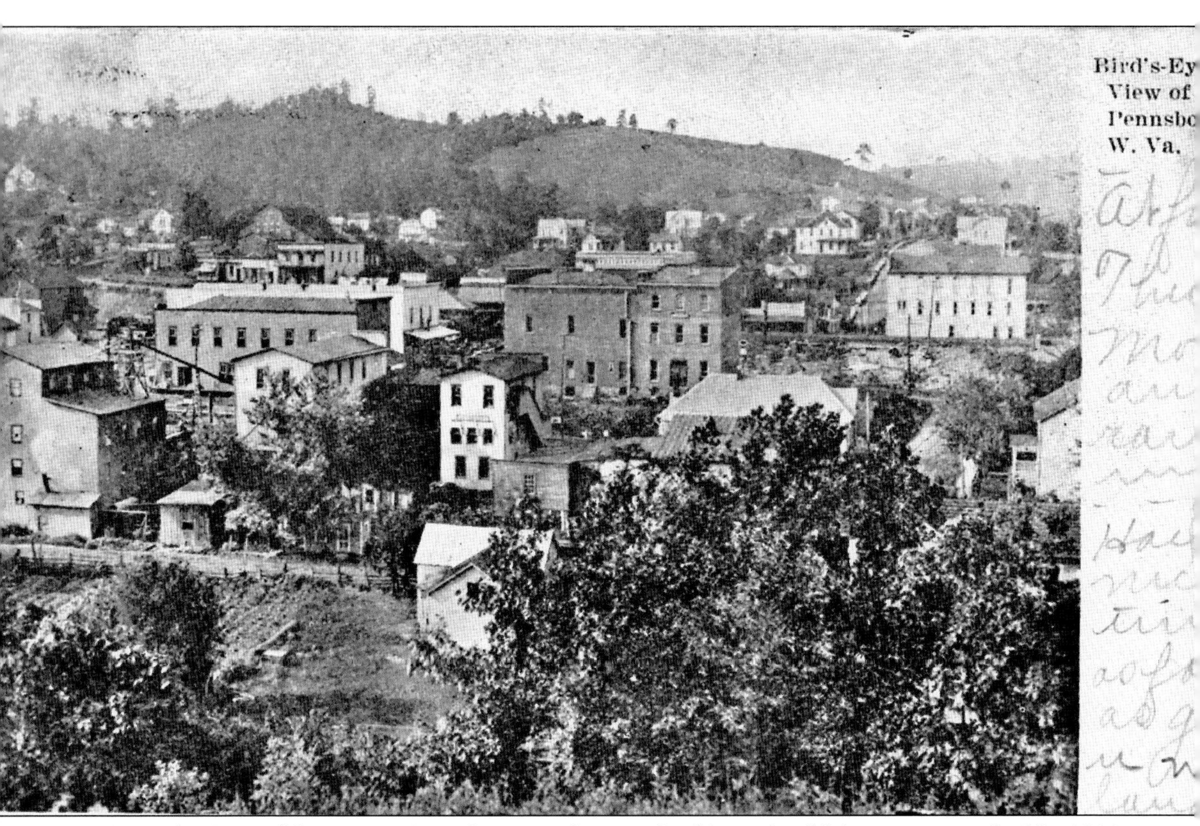

An early view of downtown Pennsboro can be seen in this card, which was postmarked in 1906.

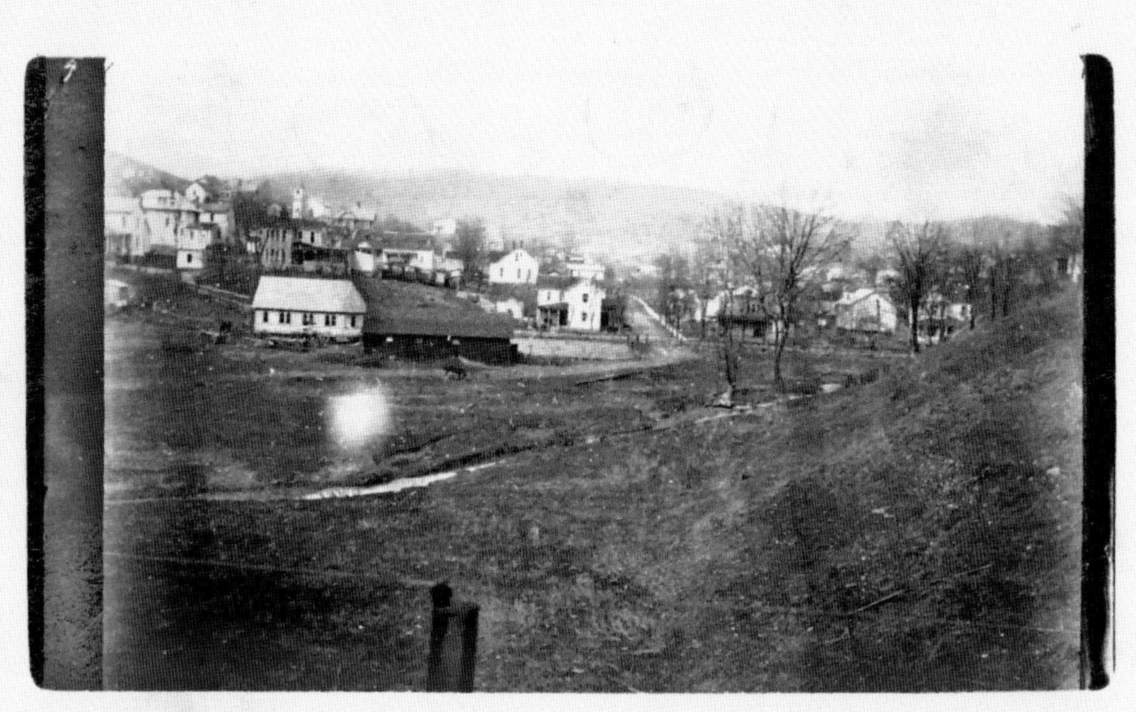

This *c.* 1910 card provides a view of the Fream Street section of Pennsboro. The street leading away from the viewer in the center of the card is Fream Street. The buildings in the foreground are where the Pennsboro Church of Christ now sits.

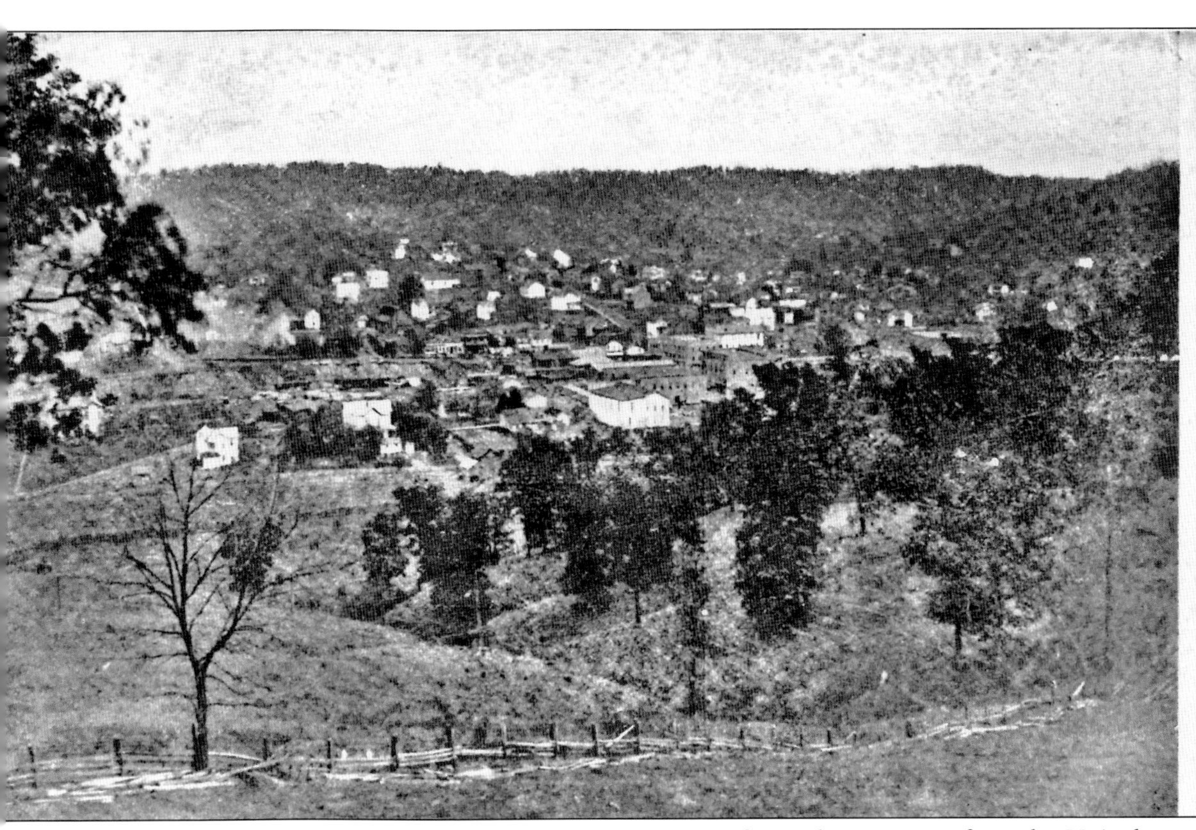

This card, postmarked in 1907, depicts a bird's-eye view of Pennsboro as seen from the United Brethern Church.

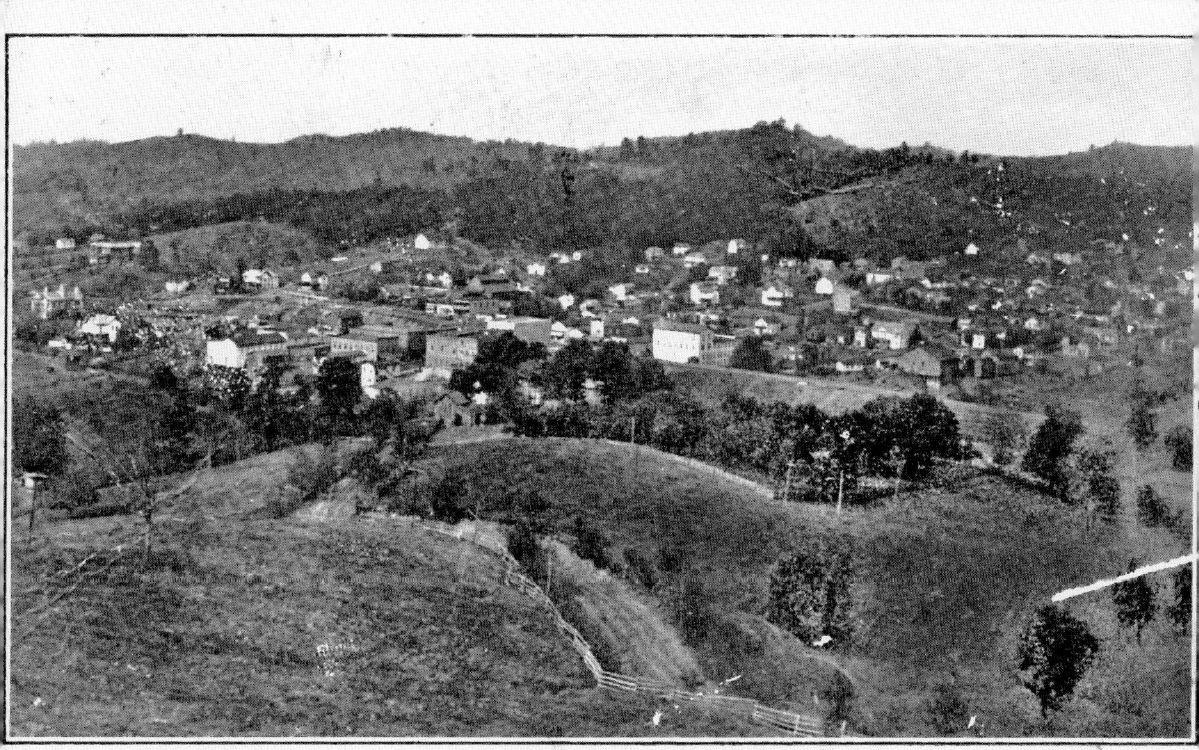

South Pennsboro is shown looking northwest in this 1907 postcard.

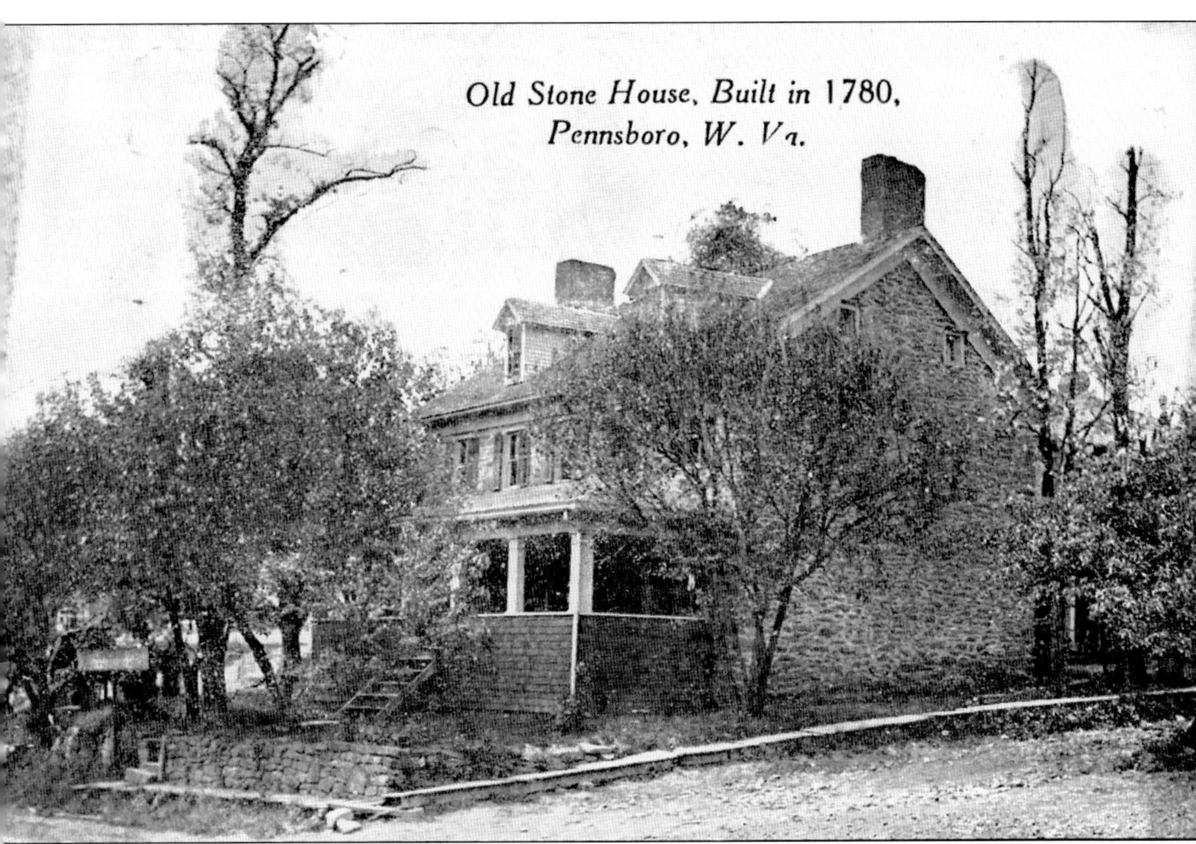

The Old Stone House shown in this image is the most historically significant structure in Ritchie County. The first permanent home built in Ritchie County, it was begun in 1810 and served as the only stagecoach stop between Clarksburg and Marietta, Ohio. The house was then known as Martin's Inn. It now serves as a museum and the home to the Ritchie County Historical Society. This undated card was published by Gibson, Chaney and Company in West Alexander, Pennsylvania, and incorrectly states the date built as 1780.

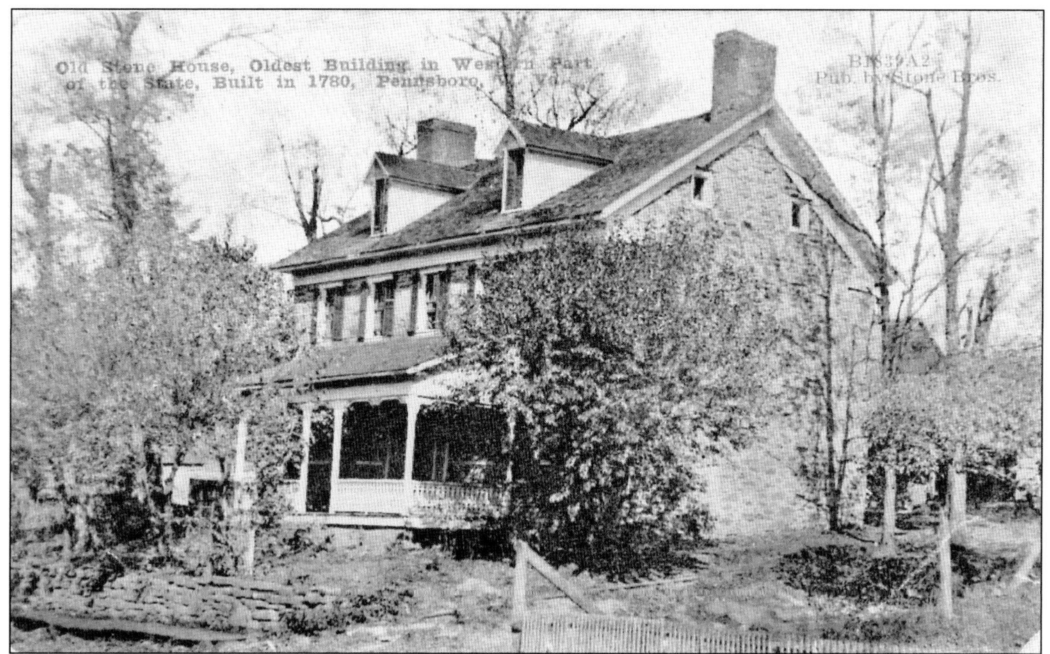

Depicted here is a color enhanced card of the Old Stone House. This card was published by H.G. Zimmerman and Company of Chicago and postmarked in 1909. This card also shows an incorrect building date.

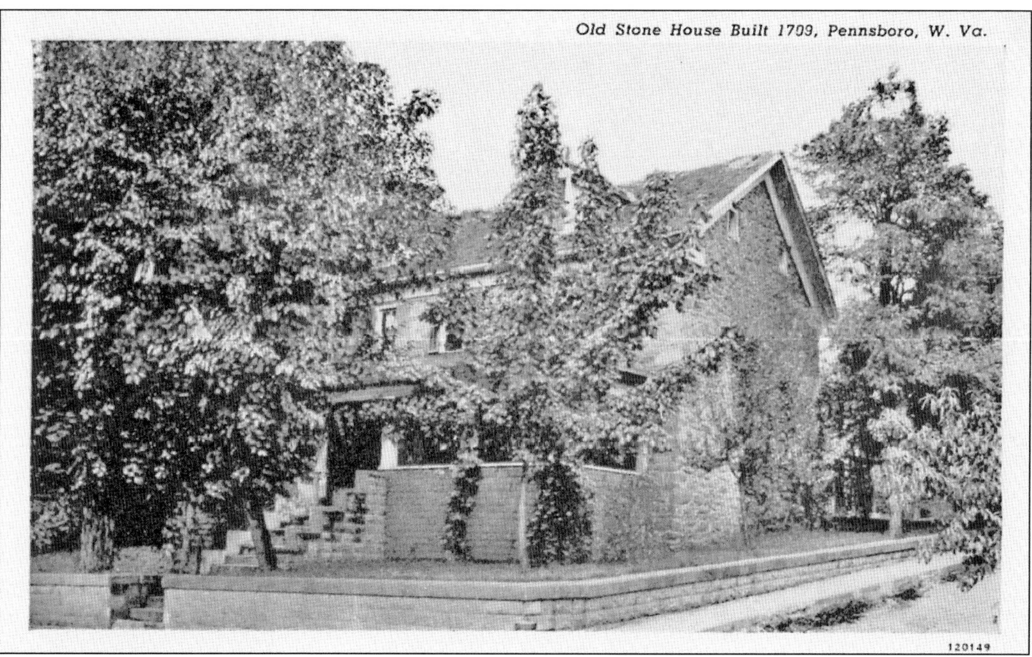

This card showing another view of the Old Stone House incorrectly states that the house was built in 1709. The card was published by Sigler's Pharmacy in Pennsboro.

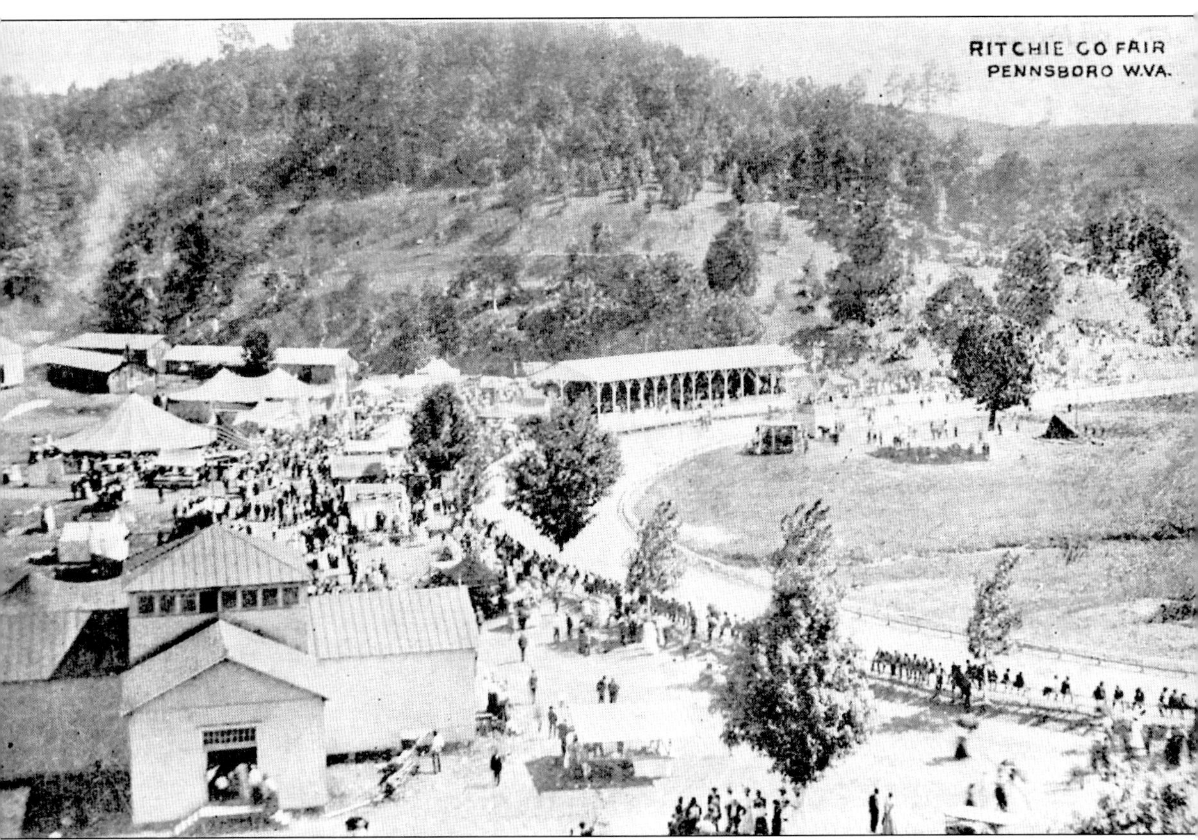

The Ritchie County Fair was certainly one of the grandest fairs in the state when it was in its prime. This early postcard from 1909 shows the vast crowds that would gather each year for the fair. Horse races were quite prevalent there. Although all of the buildings shown in the cards are now gone, the track, Pennsboro Speedway, has recently been used for auto races. It has been home to some very large, world-renowned dirt track races.

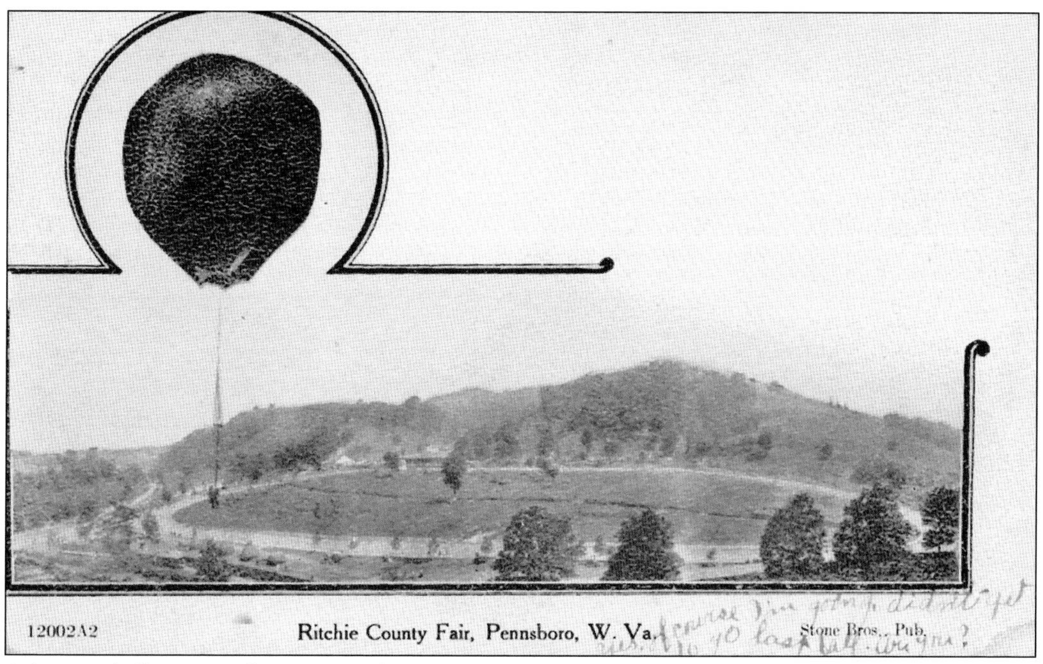

A hot air balloon can be seen in the distance at the fair in this card, which was postmarked in 1908. Stories say that a man was once killed at the fair in a hot air balloon.

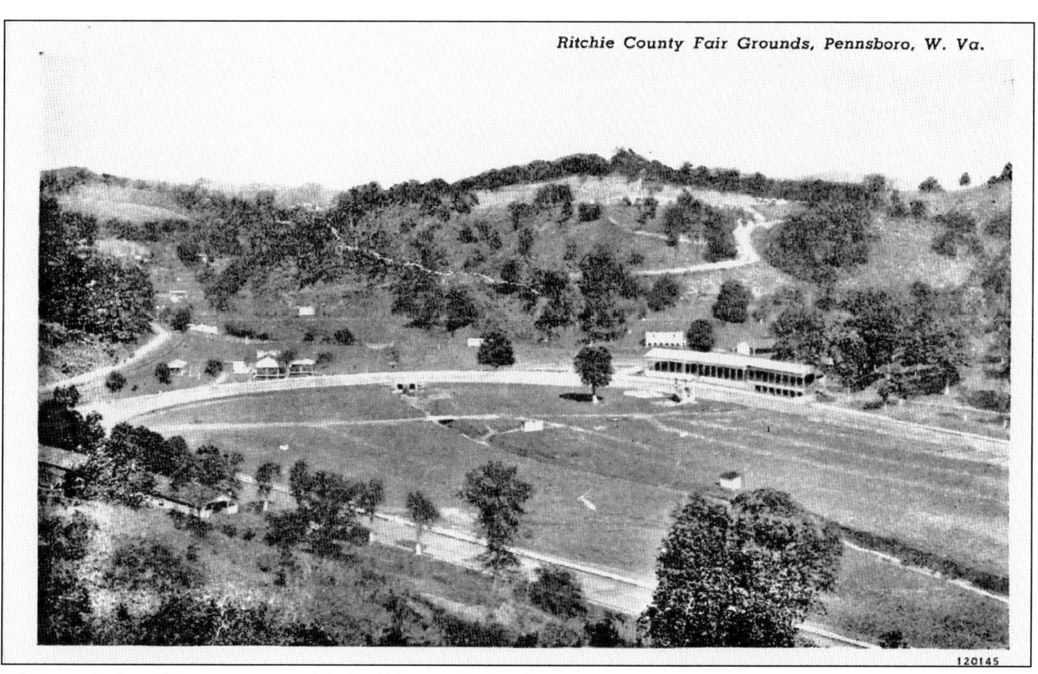

This card, dated 1950, was published by Sigler's Pharmacy of Pennsboro.

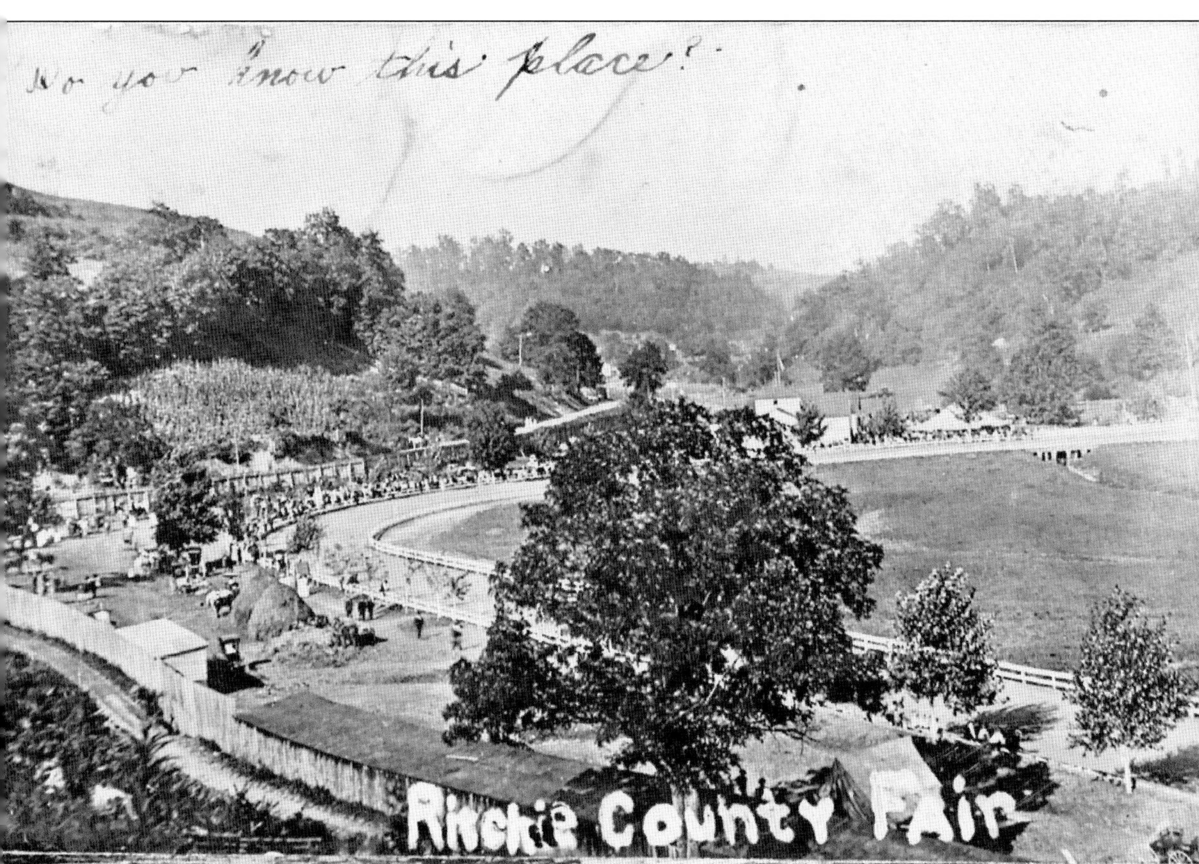

The message from the writer of this particular card (J.W.) indicates that he went to the fairgrounds for the Fourth of July celebration in 1910 and had quite a time. He stated that it was almost equal to the fair.

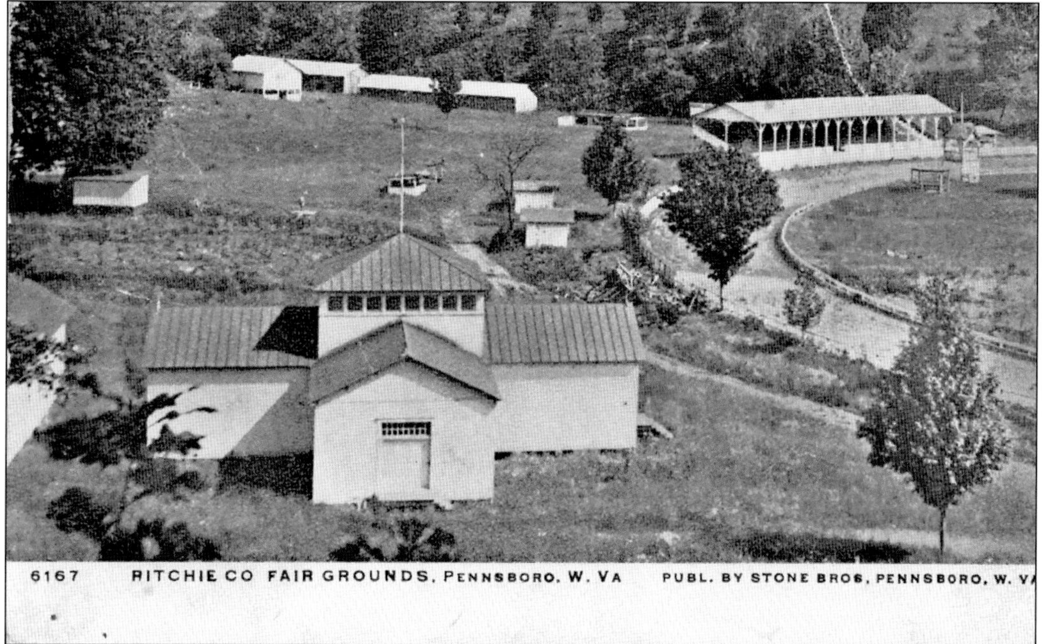

The Ritchie County Fairgrounds are shown in this 1907 postcard. The agriculture building is the one visible to the far left, the Floral Building is the center structure, and the horse barns can be seen in the distance above. The grandstand was the last of these structures standing, but it burned down in the 1970s. This card was published by Stone Brothers in Pennsboro and was postmarked 1907.

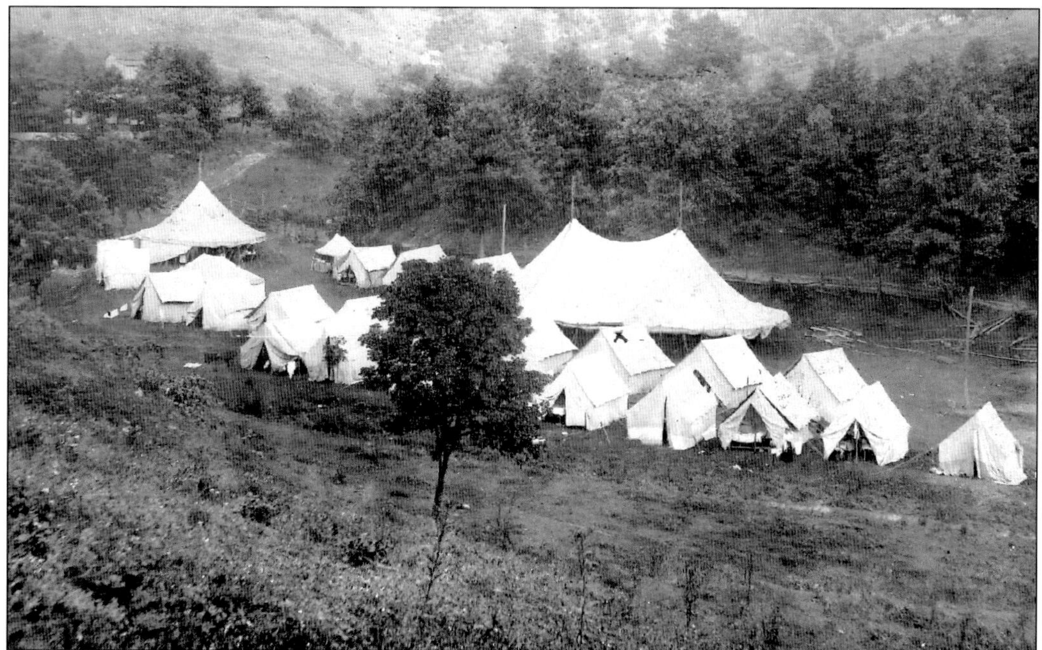

This image depicts the Seventh Day Adventists Camp at the Ritchie County Fairgrounds. This card was postmarked in 1907.

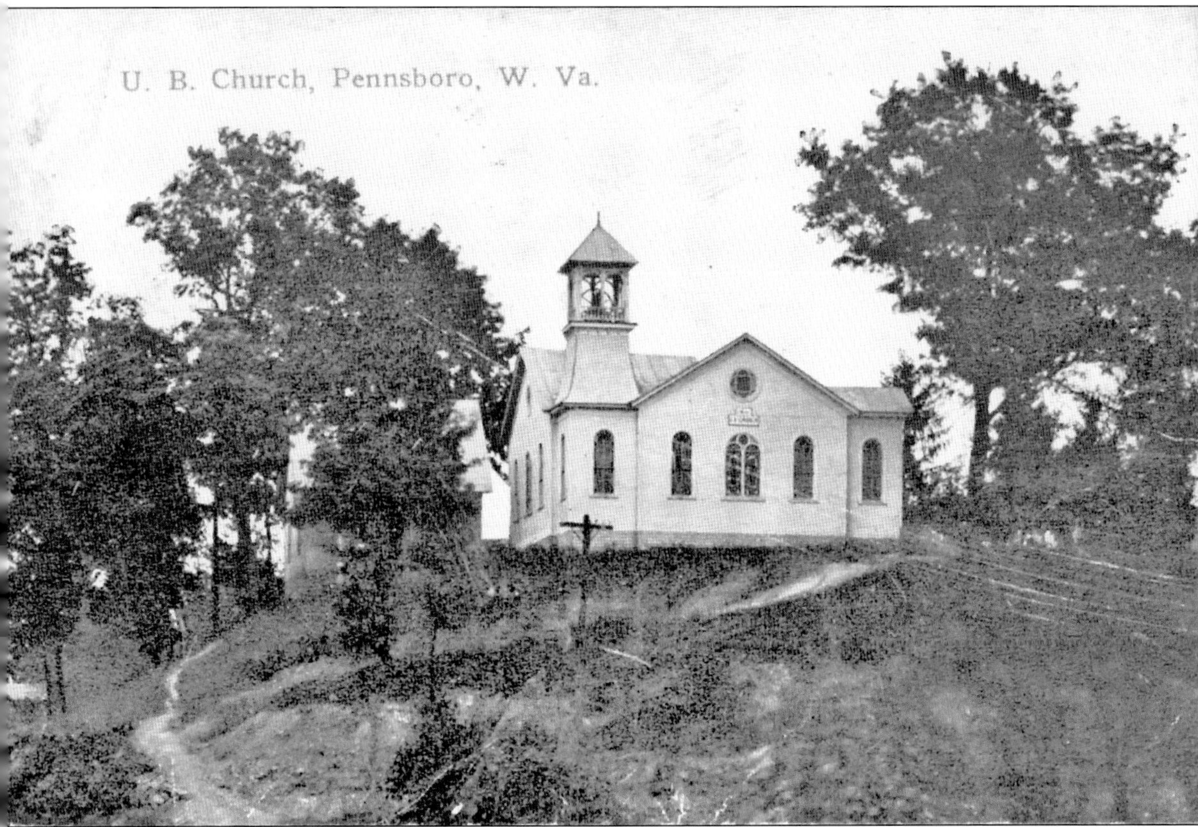

The church shown in this undated postcard, the United Brethren Church, was built in 1869 after the original building, which was built in 1864, burned down. Though the church still stands, it ceased to be used in 2003 for safety reasons. The structure was weakened when a basement was added in 1922. At the time it ceased to be used, it was known as the First United Methodist Church. The author's great-great-grandfather, Archibald Blackburn Wilson, was the first person to be interred at the cemetery here in 1865, and was instrumental in the establishment of this church.

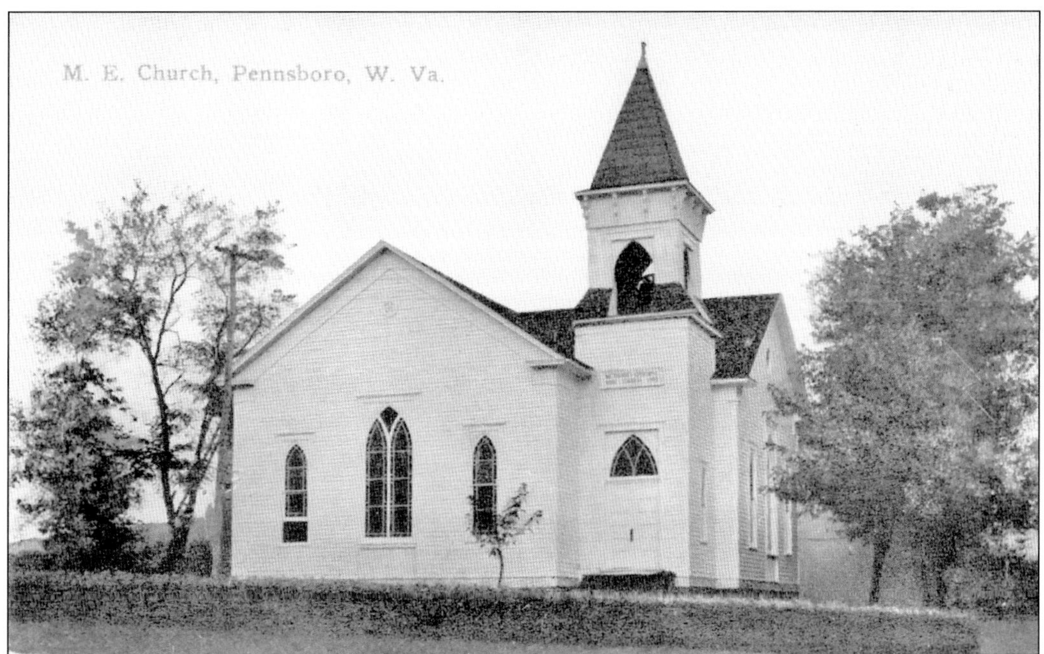

The Methodist Episcopal church was located at the corner of Main Street and Penn Avenue. The lot was purchased for this church in 1880 for $75. The church burned down in 1957 and is now the site of the Pennsboro United Methodist Church, formerly known as the Trinity United Methodist. This card, postmarked in 1917, was published by R.E. Pratt & Company of Pennsboro.

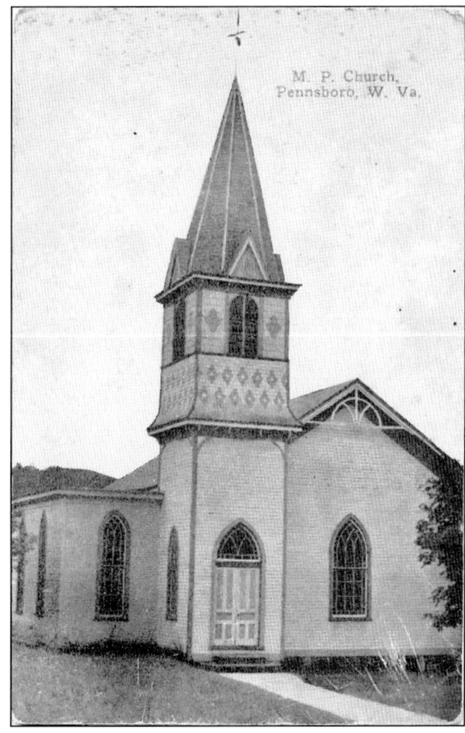

The Methodist Protestant church was built in 1901 and was also known as Payne Memorial in honor of Rev. Josiah Payne. This church was destroyed by fire in 1952. This card, postmarked in 1910, was published by R.E. Pratt & Company of Pennsboro.

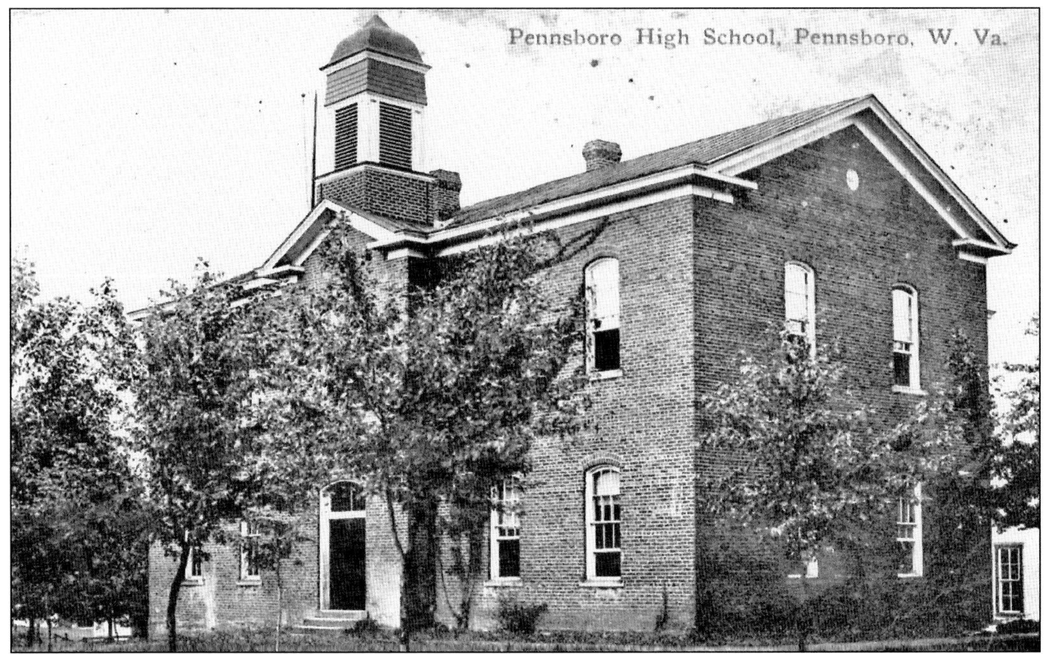

Shown in this *c.* 1910 image is the original grade school, which was built in 1890. It later became Pennsboro High School, originally a two-year high school.

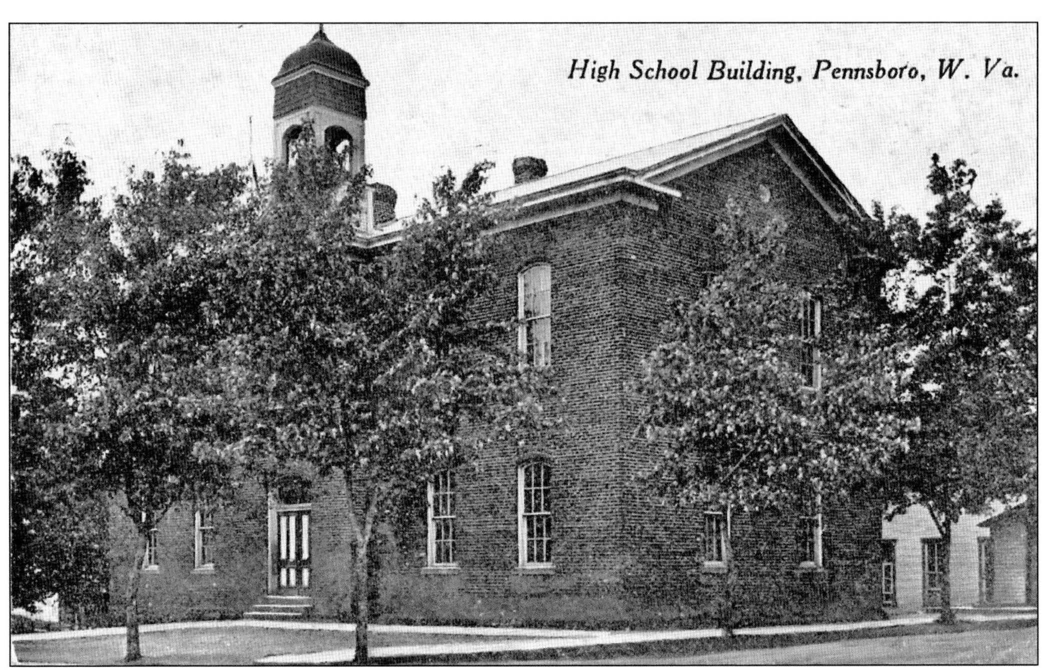

Here is another view of the original Pennsboro High School, a public school. In comparison to the previous cards, it appears some remodeling was done to the tower of this structure. This card, postmarked in 1916, was published by Gibson, Chaney and Company of West Alexander, Pennsylvania.

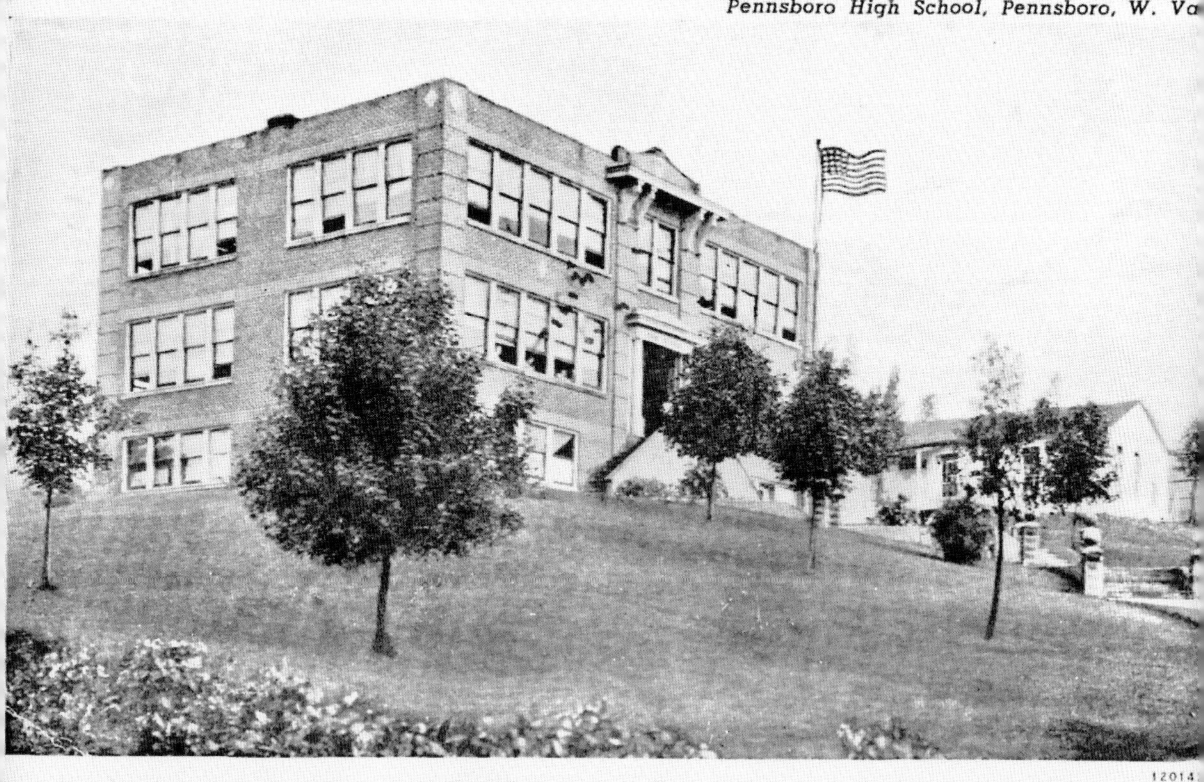

This high school was built in 1916. The first principal was Goff D. Ramsey. The high school closed in 1985, when it was consolidated with Harrisville High School to form Ritchie County High School. This card was postmarked in 1950.

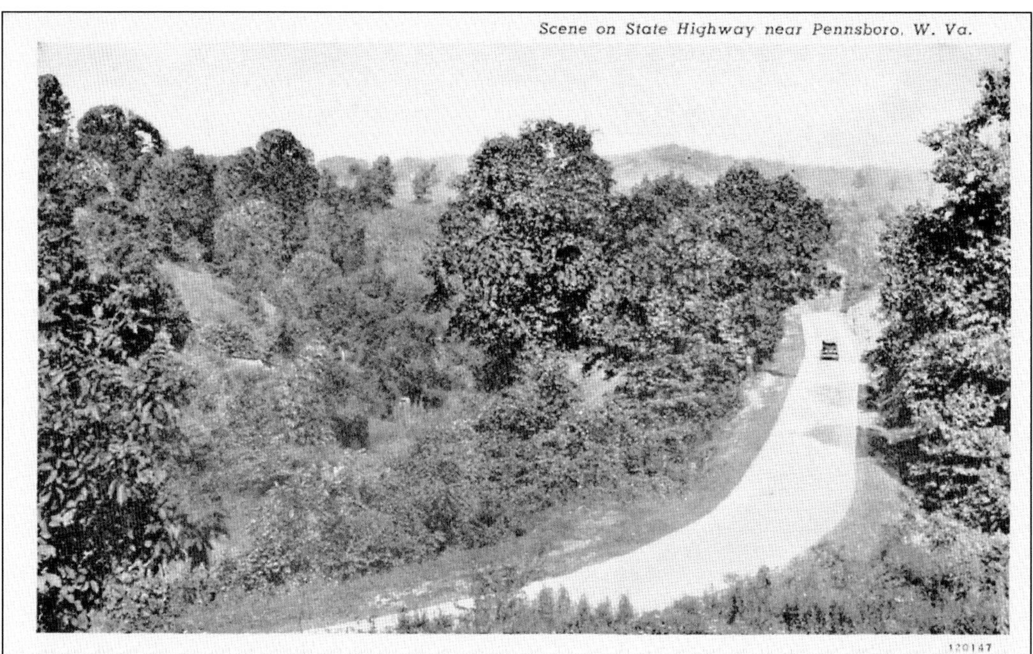

This scene on a state highway near Pennsboro is believed to be between Pennsboro and Tollgate on old U.S. Route 50. This undated card was postmarked in 1931 and published by Sigler's Pharmacy in Pennsboro.

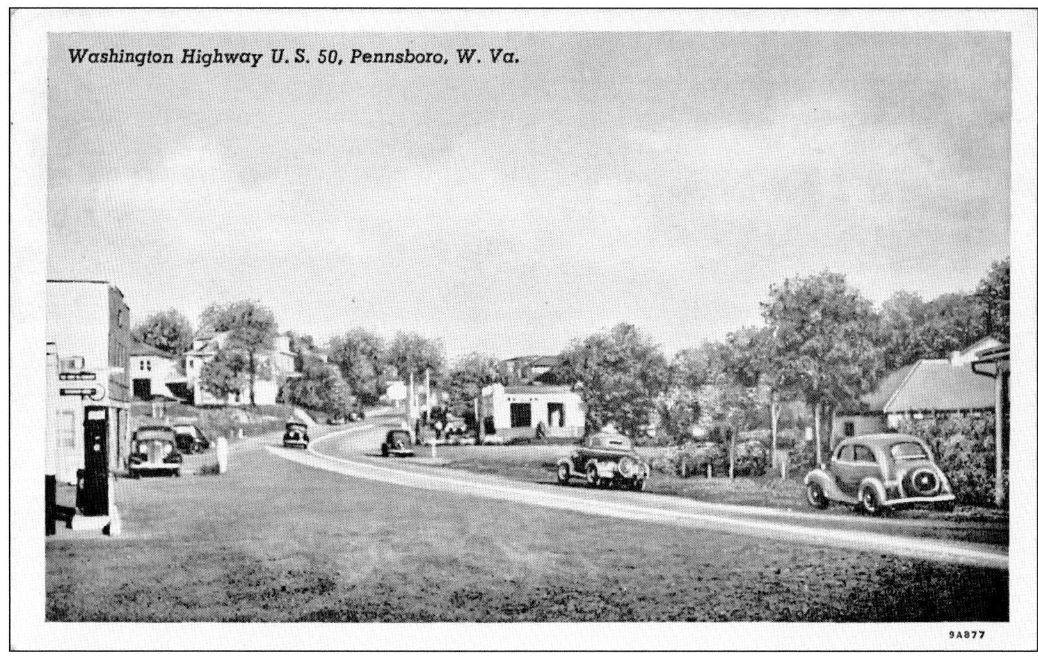

U.S. Route 50, the Washington Highway, went right through Pennsboro, as shown in this *c.* 1940 card. It is now called Myles Avenue. The pump for Hopkin's Gas Station can be seen to the left, and Koogan's gas station can be seen on the right. The Old Stone House can be seen in the distance.

Three

Cairo

Cairo is one of the oldest towns in this part of the state. It became a railroad station in 1856 but was not officially incorporated until 1895. Cairo was one of the B&O mainline boomtowns. Wooden boardwalks paralleled dirt streets and the town boasted thriving businesses, including an opera house. The discovery of great veins of oil and gas here in the late 1800s, along with the many other natural resources, made Cairo quite a town in the early part of the 20th century. From the early photos of this town, one can see an incredible amount of oil derricks all throughout the town. When the oil and gas began to decline, so did the town. However, its recent resurrection as a tourism focal point for Ritchie County has brought new life to this once thriving area. The existence of many of the town's early, original structures makes Cairo very historically significant.

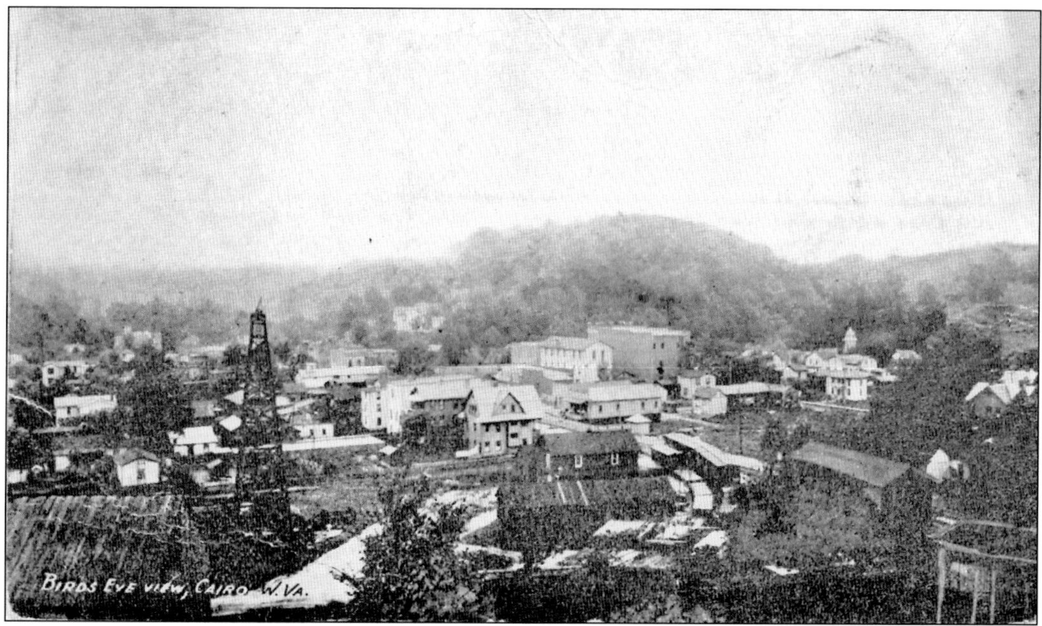

This early postcard depicts a bird's-eye view of Cairo. The Cairo & Kanawha (C&K) Railroad can be seen in the lower portion of the card. Cairo High School would later be built atop the hill in the center. A great deal of the business part of this town still exists. This card, postmarked in 1908, was published by I.&M. Ottenheimer in Baltimore, Maryland.

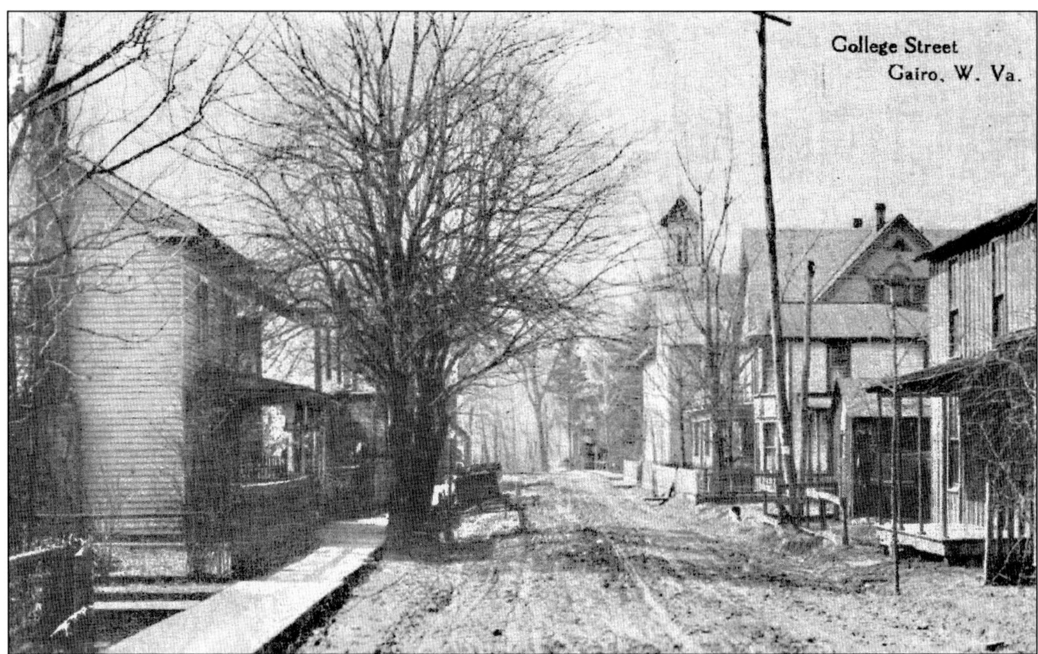

This *c.* 1910 postcard shows College Street in Cairo. At the far end of the street on the right, one can see the public school that was built in 1873 and served until 1915. It was a high school from 1905 to 1913, when a new school was built.

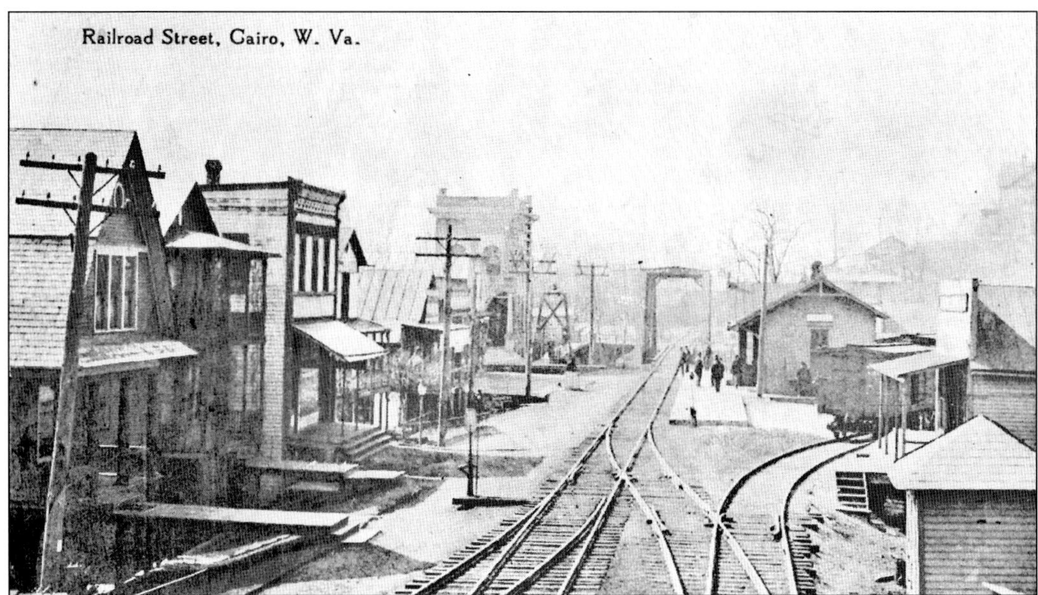

Here is a view of Railroad Street. The depot is shown on the right of the tracks in the distance. The building just before it is the Cairo Supply building, now the Country Trails Bike Shop. The Cairo Bank is shown on the left of the tracks in the far distance. The Cairo Bank, the stout building to the left with the awning, and the Cairo Supply buildings are the only ones still in existence. Note the wooden boardwalks on the left extending out to the rail line. This *c.* 1910 card was published by Vinton Printing Company of Vinton, Ohio.

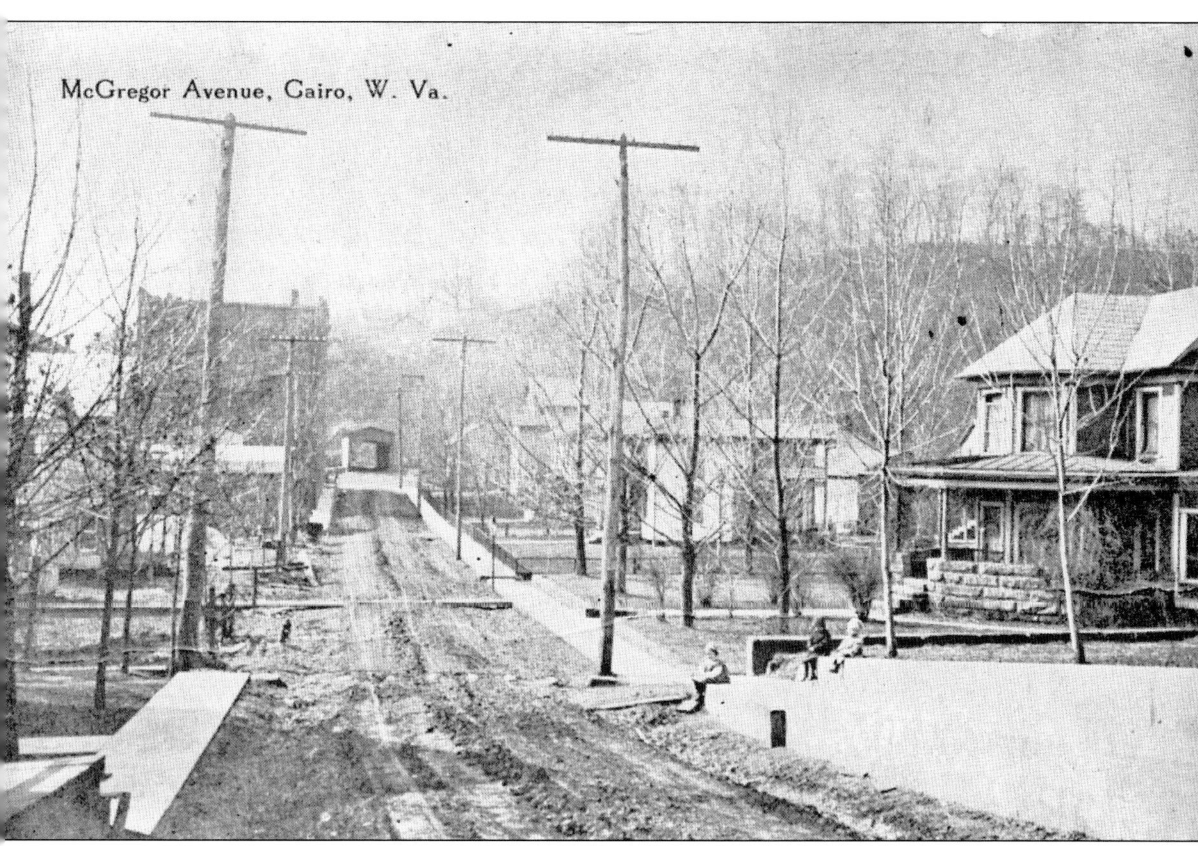

Depicted in this *c.* 1914 image is McGregor Avenue, shown looking toward the covered bridge across the Hughes River. The building to the right is now McCullough-Rogers Funeral Home (formerly Raiguel's), which was originally the Leeton Home. The building to the left is the rear of R.C. Marshall Hardware. This card was published by Vinton Printing Company of Vinton, Ohio, as part of a Cairo series. Other cards from this series are pictured in this chapter, as evidenced by the same print style on the front of the card.

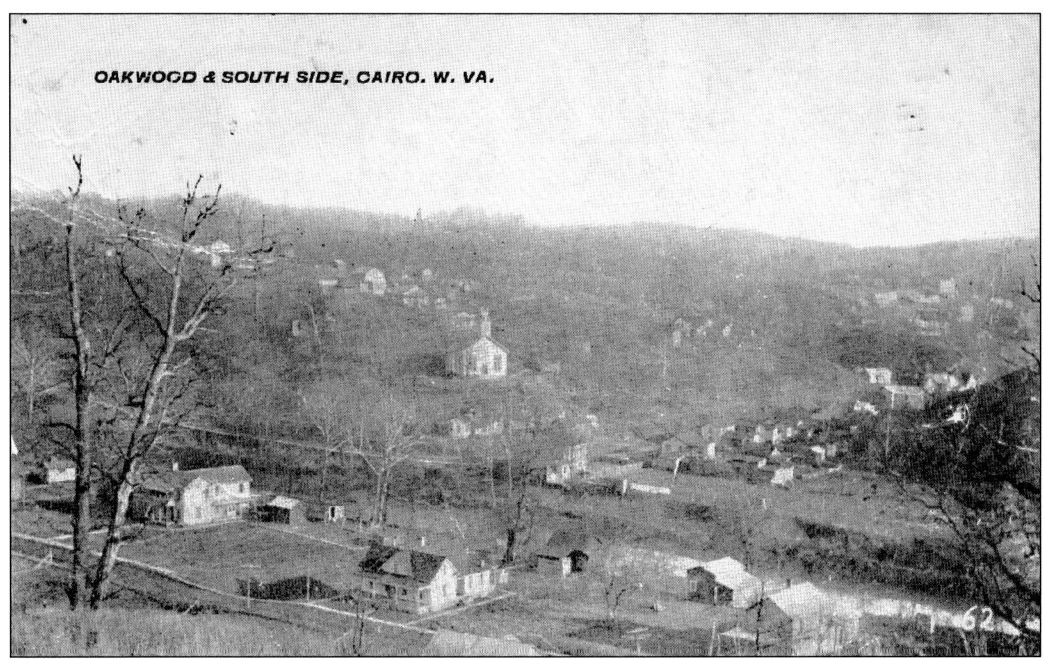

Shown in this image is a view of Oakwood and South side taken from the B&O line across the Hughes River. The Presbyterian church is in the center of the car on what is now known as Smith Hill. This card was postmarked in 1916.

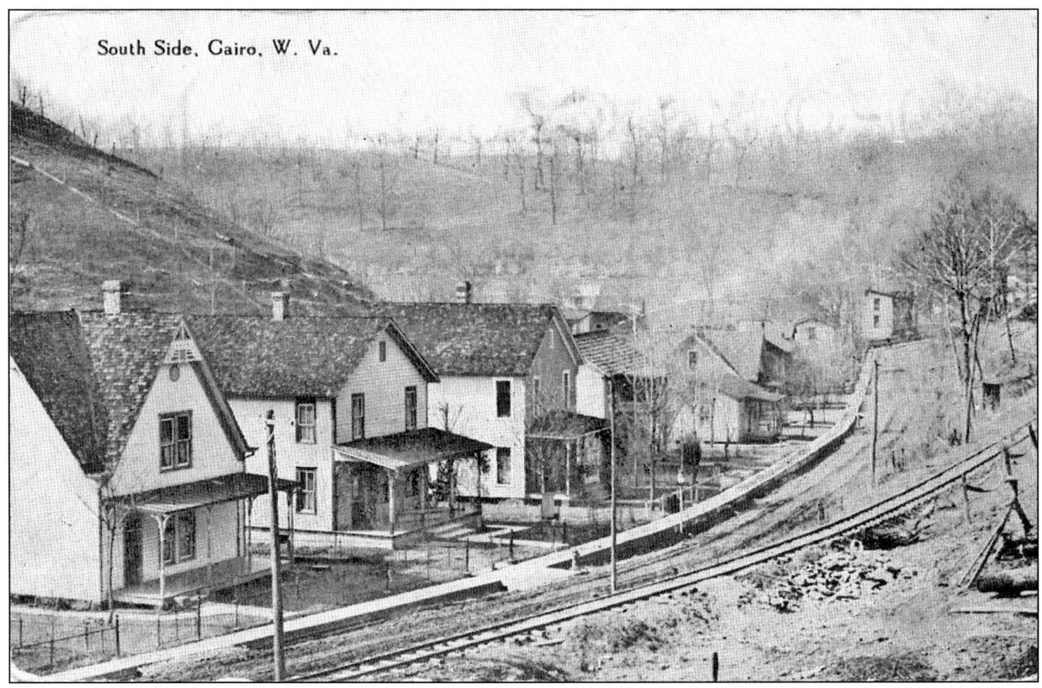

This view of the south side of Cairo along the C&K Railroad looks towards the river. This view is now Route 31 looking toward Marshall Turn. This *c.* 1910 card was published by Vinton Printing Company of Vinton, Ohio.

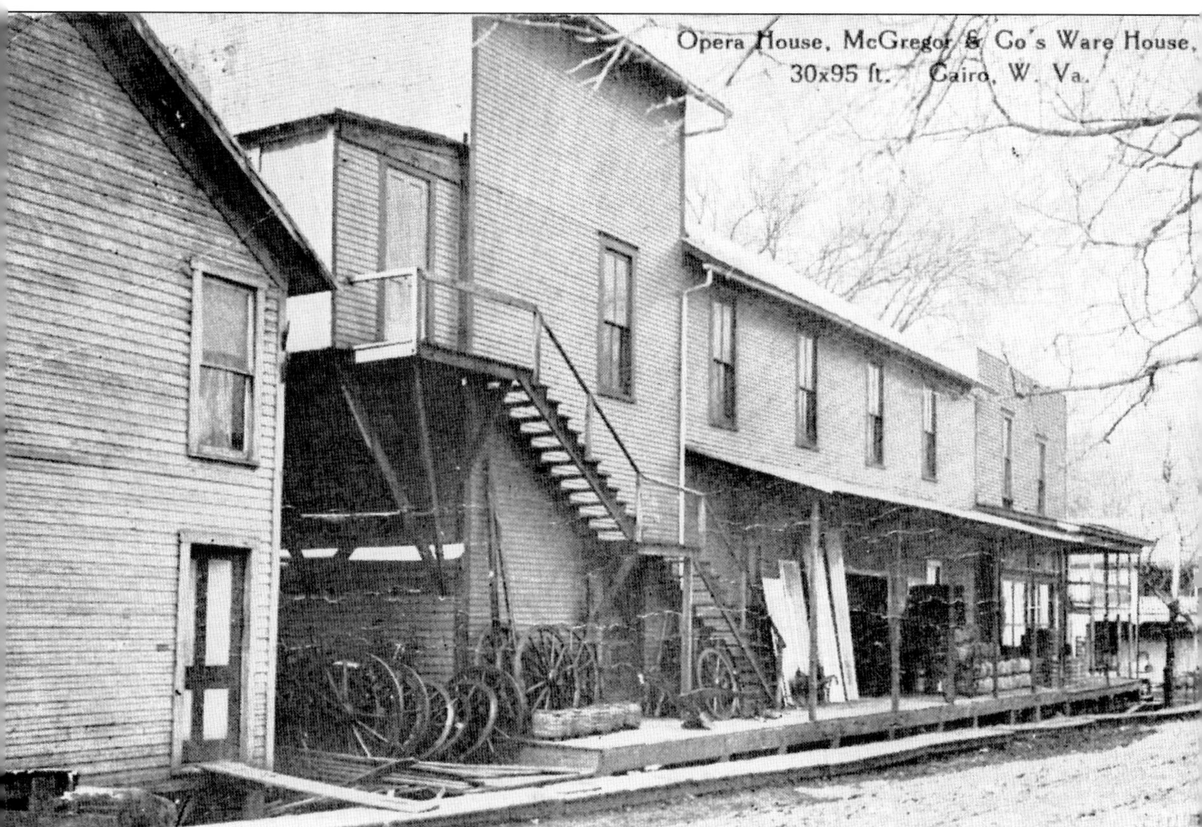

The structure in this *c.* 1910 postcard contained McGregor and Company's Warehouse; the Opera House was located upstairs. The structure sat near the corner of Main and McGregor diagonal to R.C. Marshall Hardware, beside the covered bridge. It is also visible in the distance in the next card. This structure later housed Max Mason's garage and later a retreading facility run by Ruperts. This card was postmarked in 1913 and published by Vinton Printing Company of Vinton, Ohio.

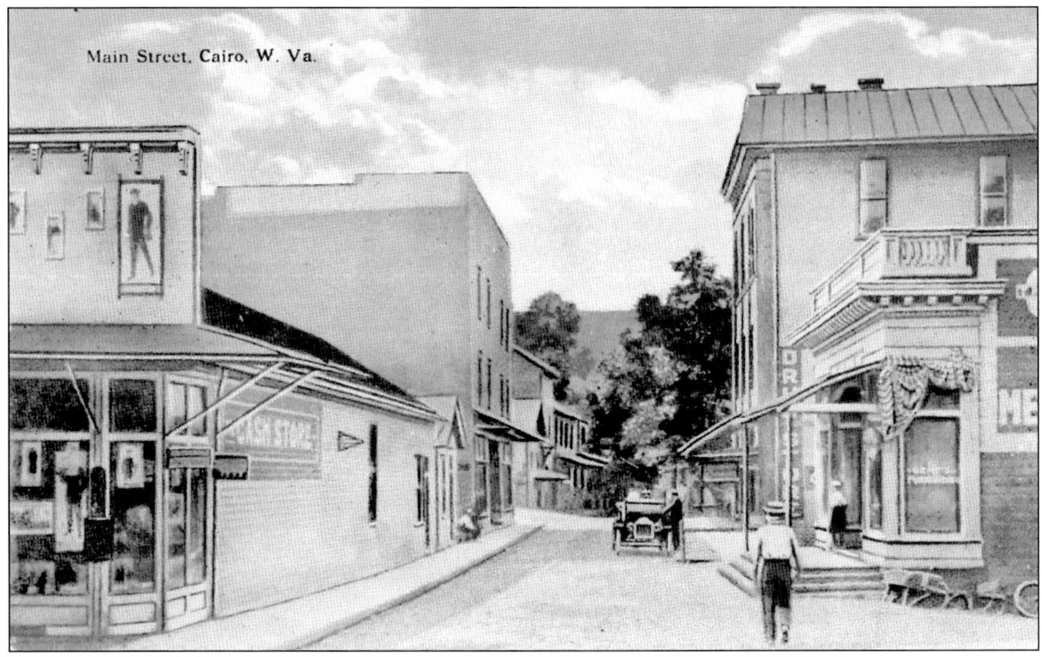

This *c.* 1920 color card shows downtown Main Street looking from the B&O mainline up Main Street.

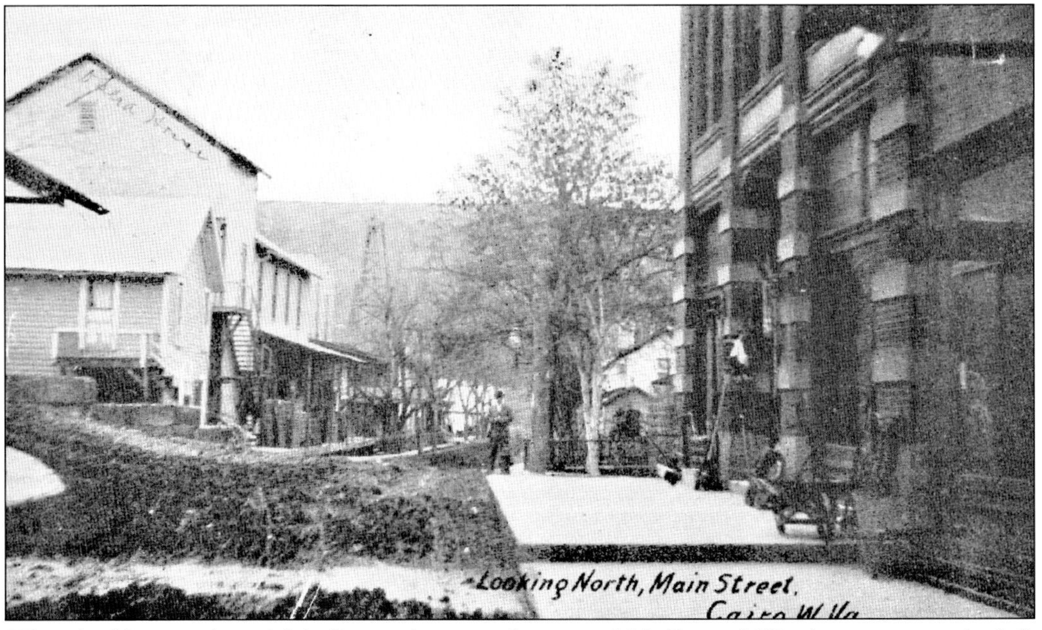

When looking north on Main Street, the opera house and McGregor's Warehouse are on the left. The R.C. Marshall Hardware is on the right. Note the dirt/mud streets and the oil derrick in the distance. This card was postmarked in 1912.

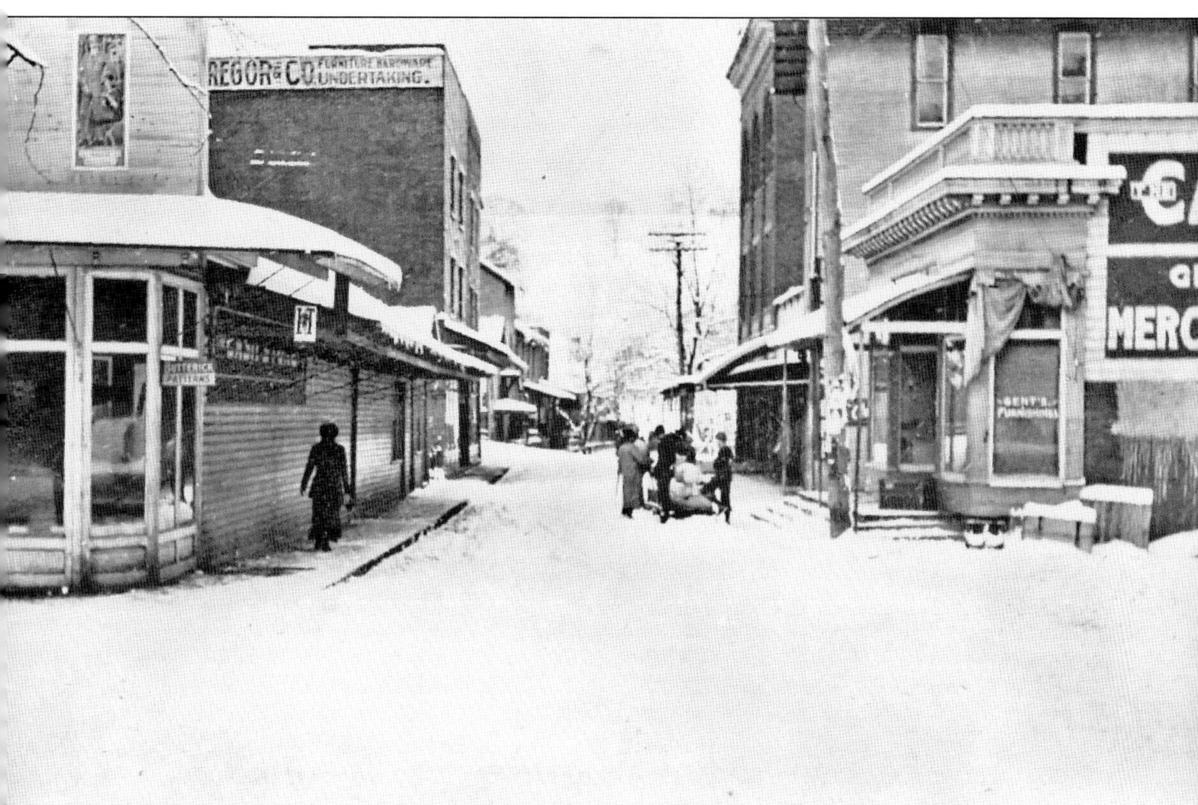

Shown in this *c.* 1908 postcard is a winter street scene of downtown Cairo, looking from the B&O mainline up Main Street. The Cash Store and McGregor and Company Hardware are located on the left, with the warehouse and the opera house just beyond. To the right are the Cairo Mercantile, the lodge building, Sharp's Restaurant, later the Cairo Theatre, and Greer Supply, later R.C. Marshall Hardware. Note the sled on the street.

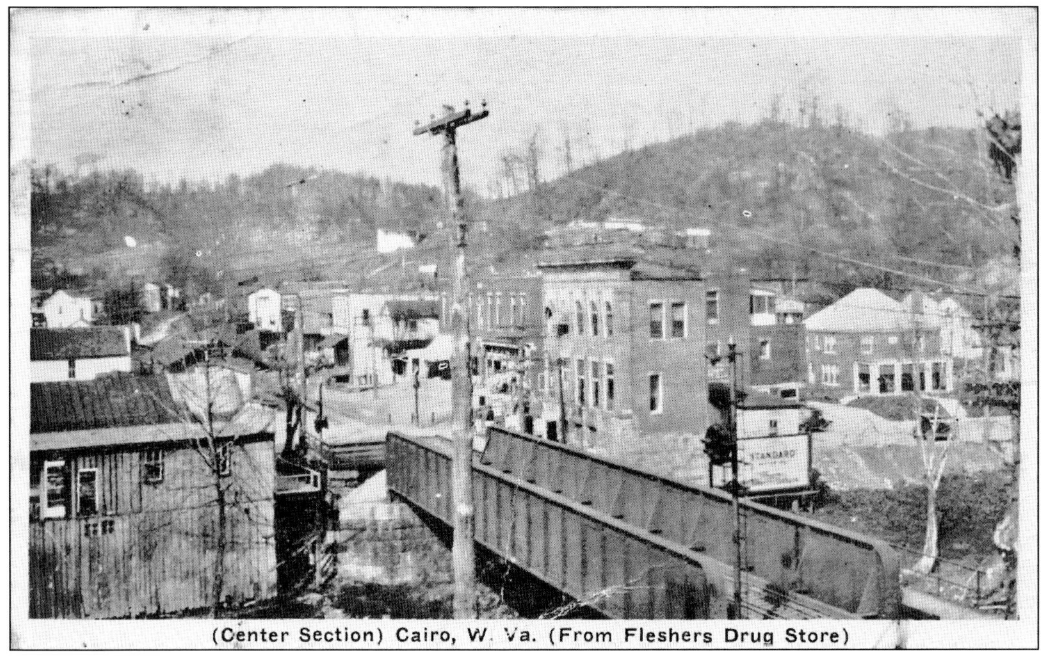

Downtown Cairo is shown looking from across the North Fork of the Hughes River in this 1931 image. The card was published by Auburn Greeting Card Company in Auburn, Indiana.

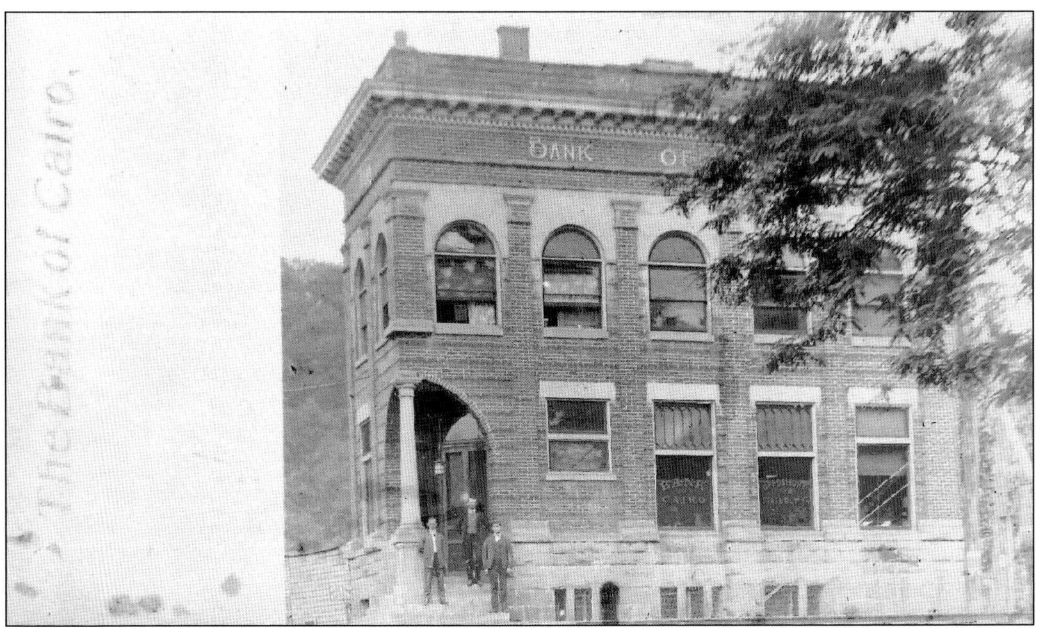

The building that once housed the Bank of Cairo was built in 1897 and is now on the National Register of Historic Places. The Bank of Cairo closed in the Great Depression. It is the current home of the Ritchie County Tourism and Visitors Bureau and the North Bend Rail Trail Foundation. This card was postmarked in 1910.

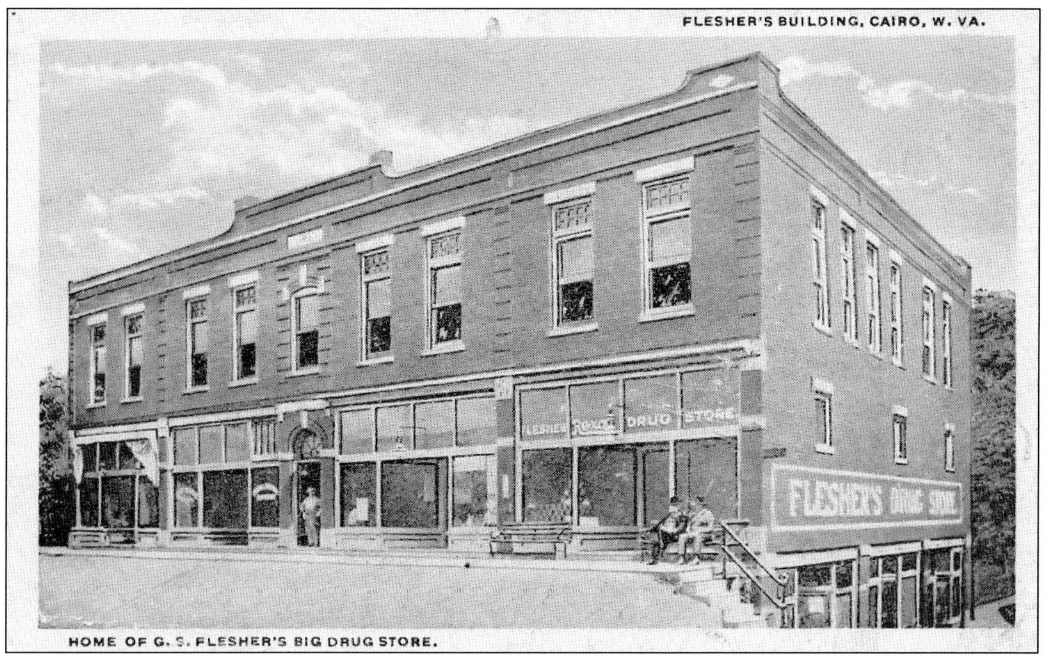

On this page is a color card of the Flesher Building and Flesher's Drug Store, which now houses the Hillbilly Gift Store, the U.S. Post Office, and the Senior Citizens hall. Flesher's Drug Store was in this location until the 1940s. The downstairs of this building housed several other businesses, including Sears Meat Market and the original R.C. Marshall Hardware. This card, postmarked in 1924, was published by I. Robbins and Son of Pittsburgh.

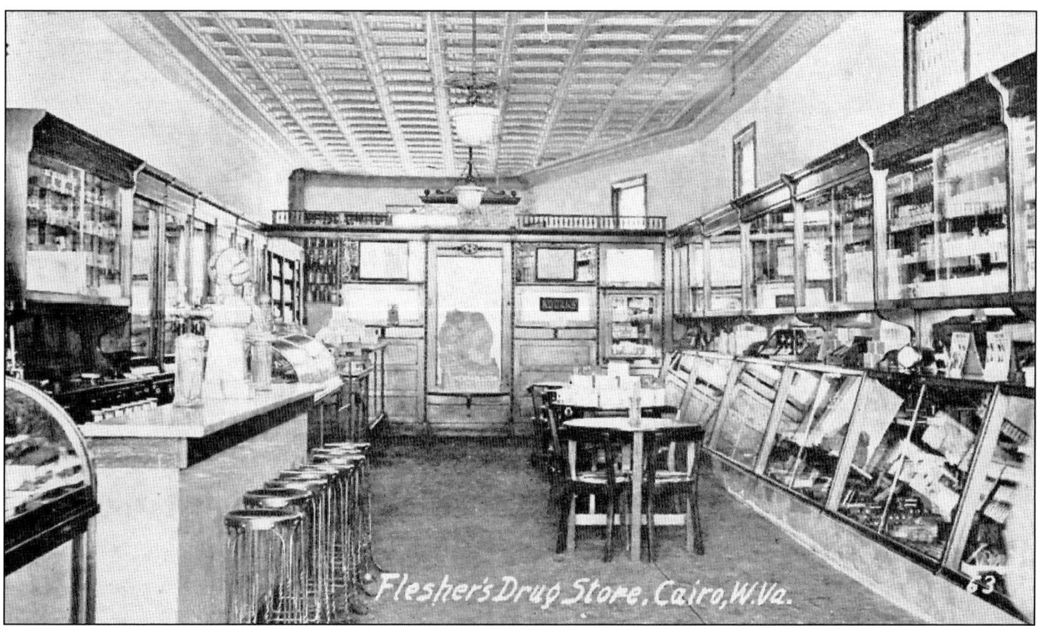

Postmarked in 1915, this card shows the interior of the original Flesher's Drug Store. Note the soda fountain and ice cream parlor to the left. Today, this is home to the Hillbilly Gift Shop.

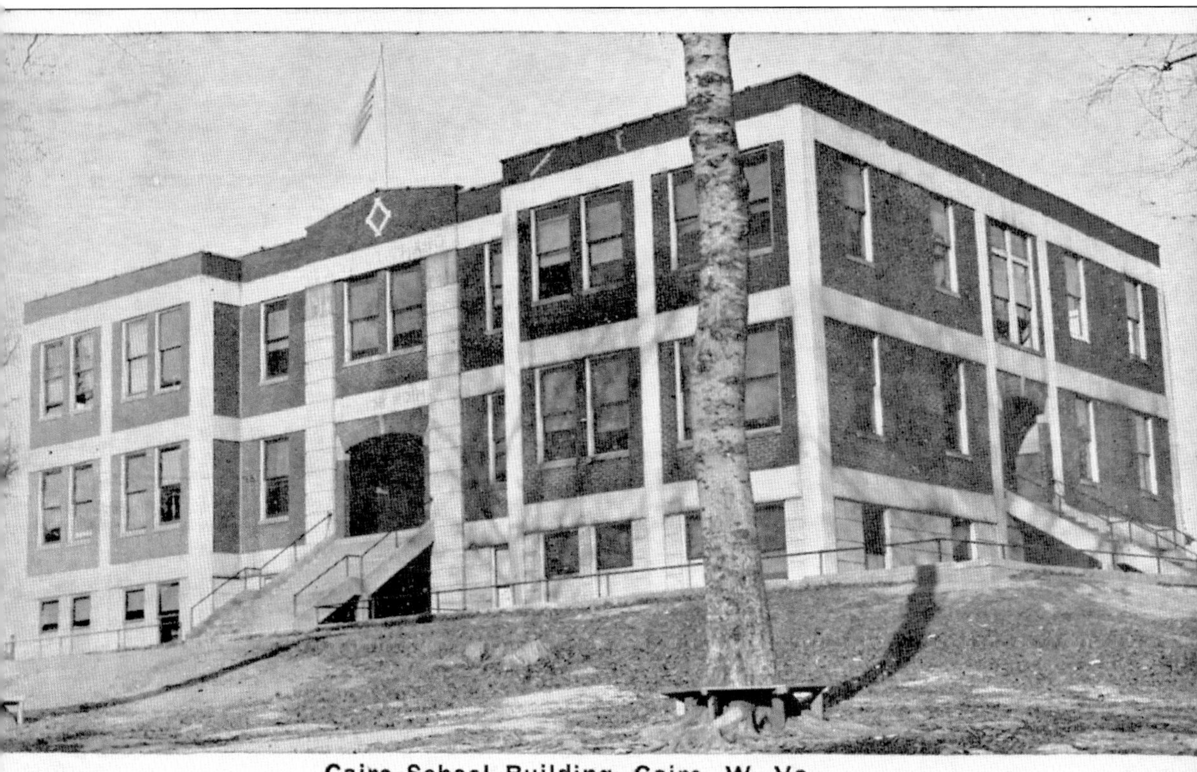

Cairo School Building, Cairo, W. Va.

The Cairo School building, constructed in 1913, was originally known as Grant District High School and only later became Cairo High School. The school was officially closed as a high school in 1971 and was used as a middle school until it was permanently closed in the mid-1990s. The building still exists, but it now sits empty. This card was postmarked in 1932 and was published by Auburn Greeting Card Company of Auburn, Indiana.

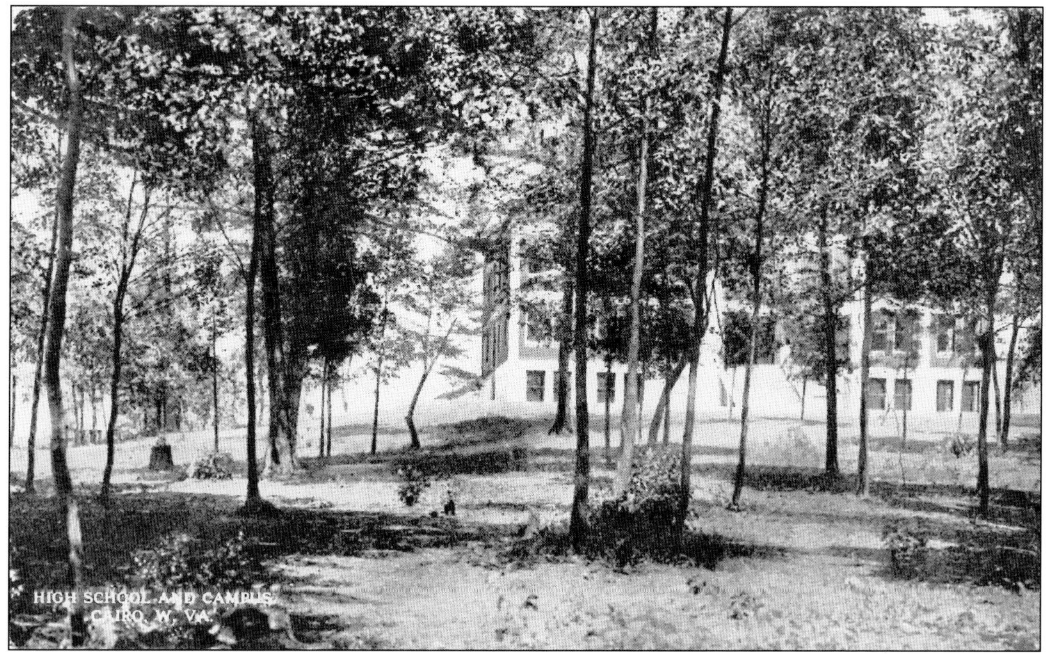

The front of this 1914 card calls this view the "High School and Campus." It is a strange view as the school is barely visible through the trees.

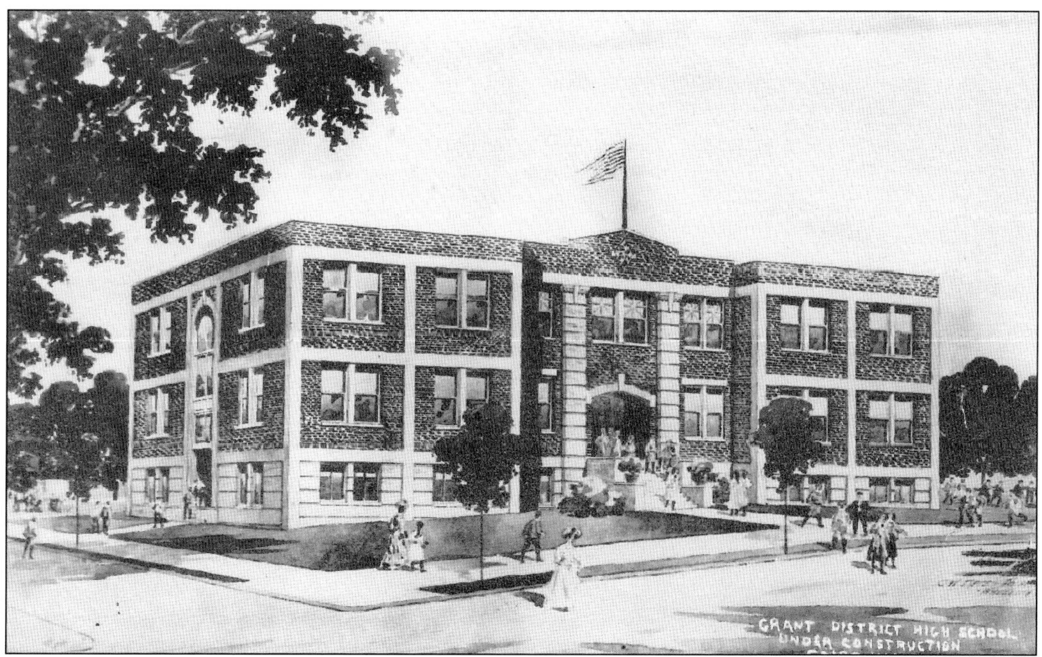

This card, which was postmarked in 1913, is an artist's rendering of the States Grant District High School while it was under construction.

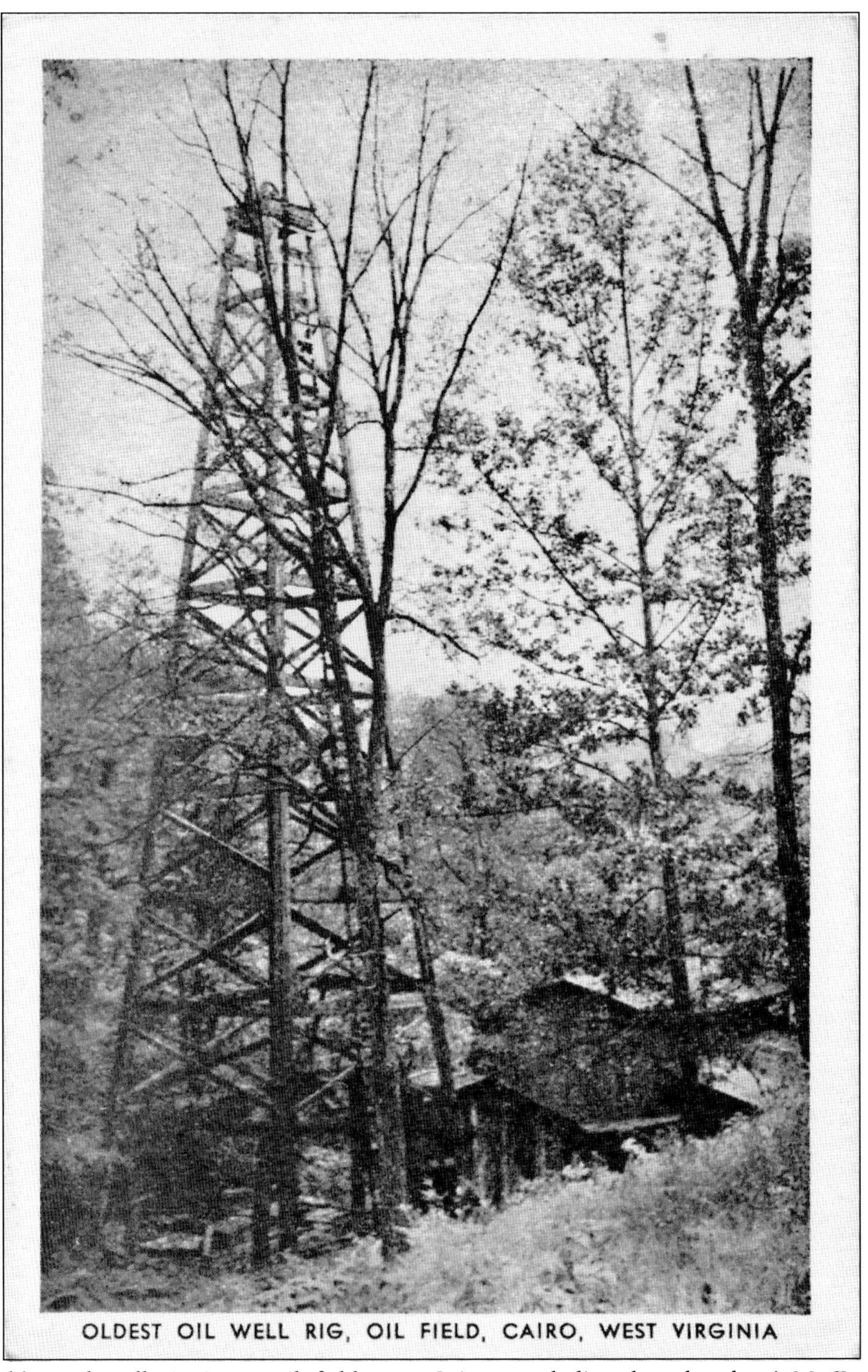

OLDEST OIL WELL RIG, OIL FIELD, CAIRO, WEST VIRGINIA

The oldest oil well rig in an oil field near Cairo was believed to be the A.M. Douglass well, drilled around 1890. Early pictures of Cairo show oil rigs all about town, but this was the first to be drilled. This undated card was published by Eagle Postcard View Company in New York City.

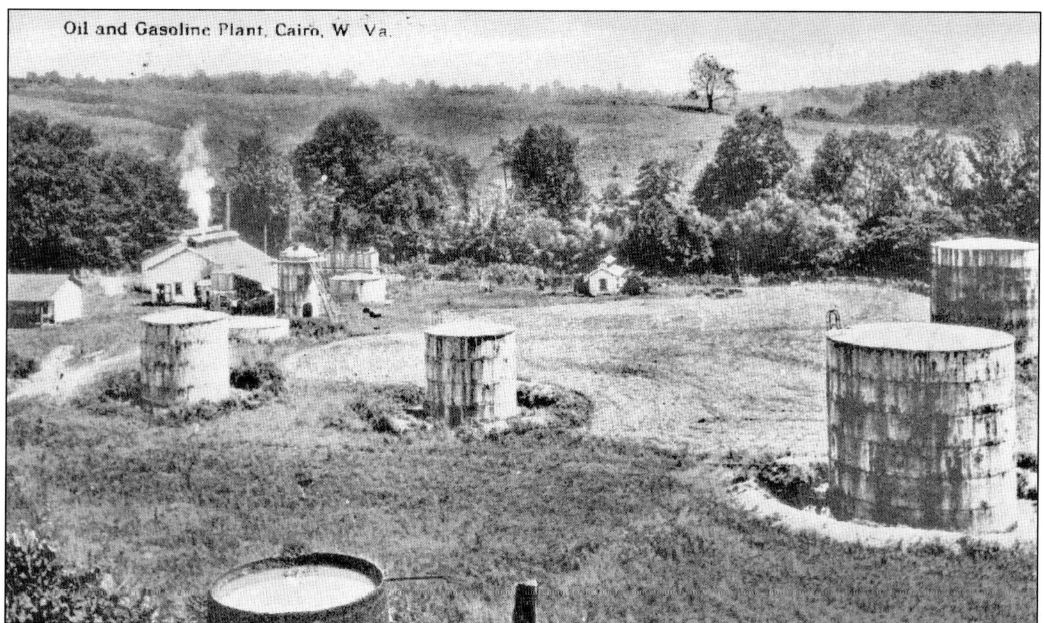

This *c.* 1920 card depicts the oil and gasoline plant that was near the mouth of Silver Run on the Hughes River, one mile west of Cairo and along the B&O. It was built in or about 1917 by Warner-Quinlain Asphalt Co. of New York. Valvoline Oil Co. acquired the plant in 1927, and it was later converted to a pumping-compressor station. The plant was abandoned in the 1960s.

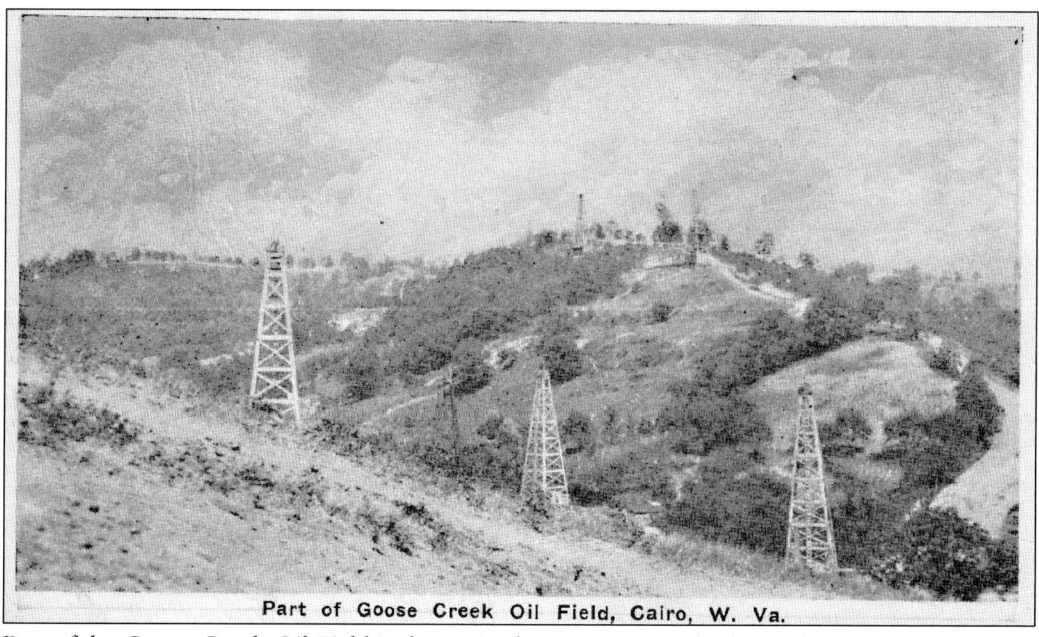

Part of the Goose Creek Oil Field is shown in this 1929 postcard. The card was published by the Auburn Postcard Manufacturer of Auburn, Indiana.

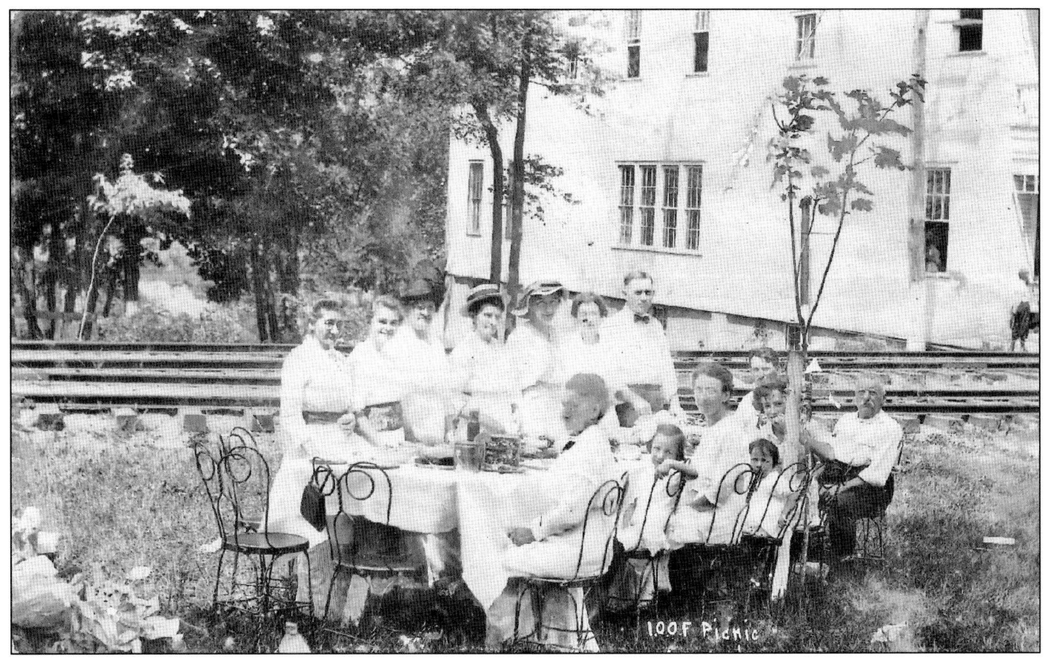

This card, dated August 20, 1914, depicts the IOOF picnic.

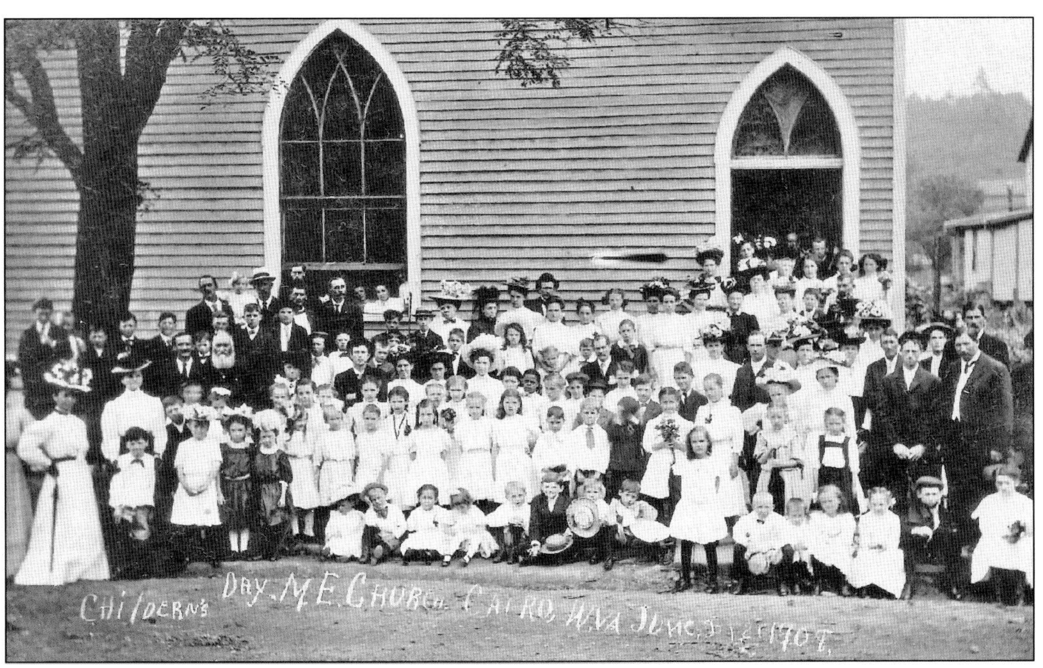

Children's Day at the Methodist Episcopal church on Main Street in Cairo was held in June of 1908.

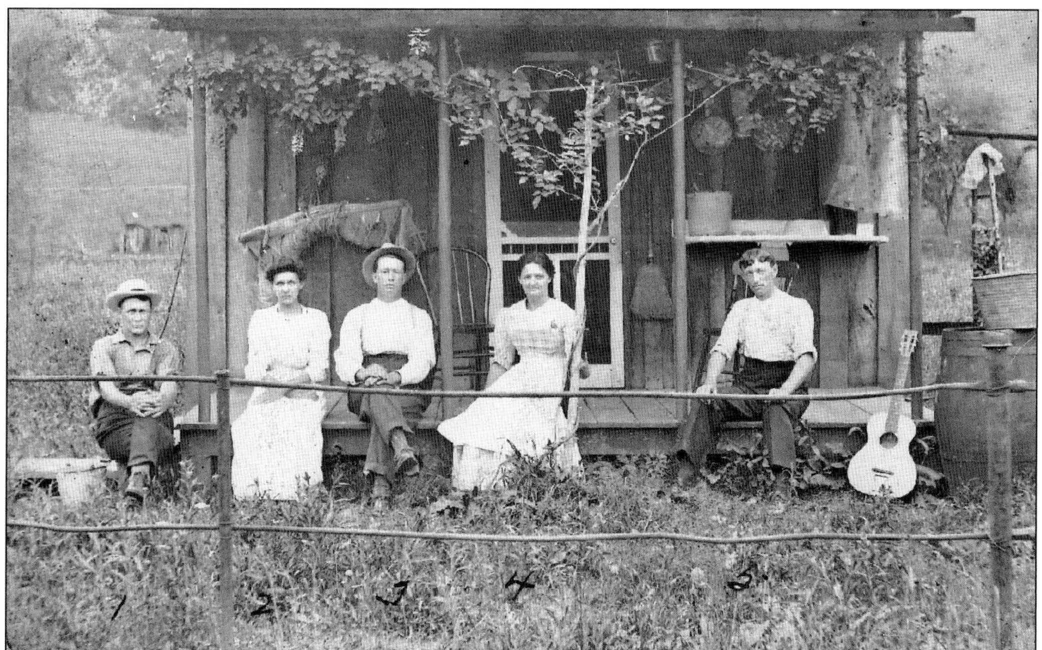

These folks are on the front porch of this house in Cairo. They are identified numerically as William Heron, Miss Greyfoulds?, William Snyder, Alyce, and Frank.

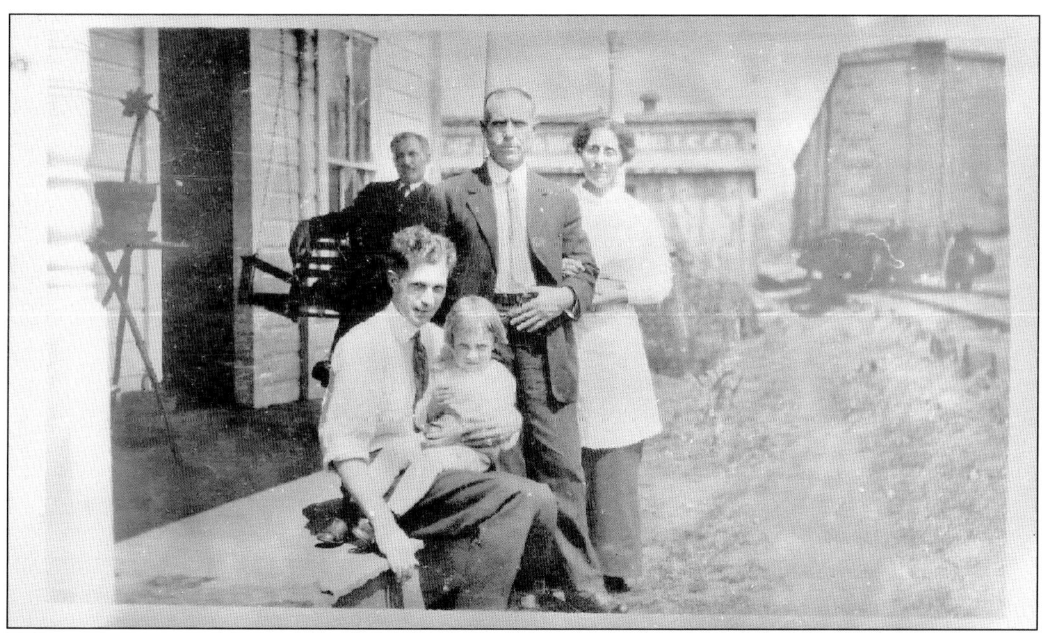

This postcard states that these people are in Cairo and identifies the people as John Winer, Jim Crarr?, Blanch and Lafayette Crarr?, and Frank Winer.

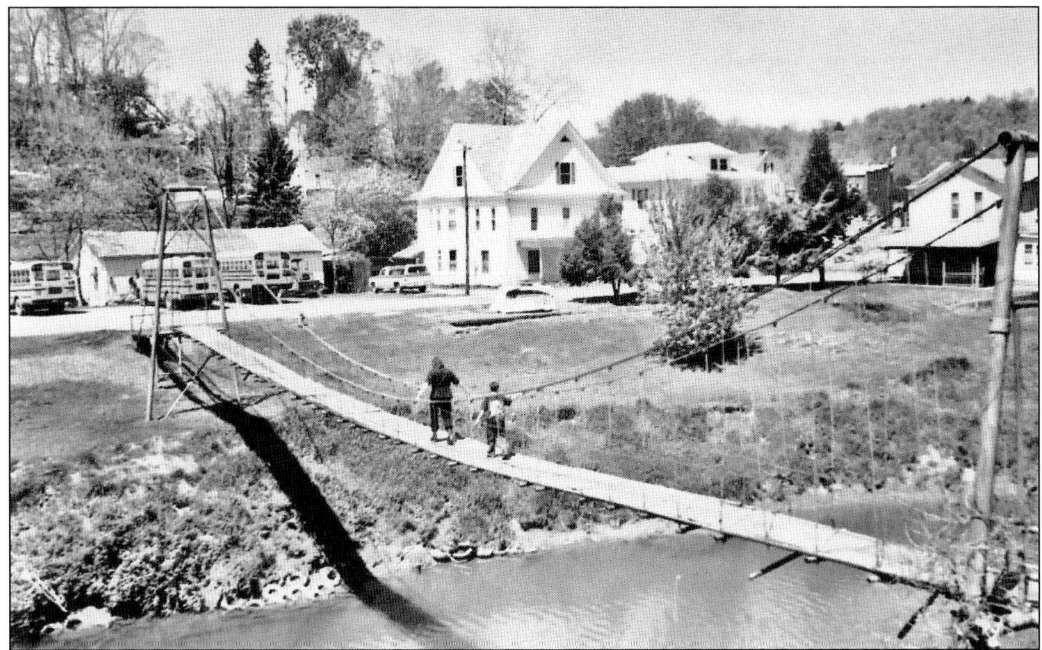

A swinging bridge spans 120 feet across the Hughes River in Cairo. The original bridge was a wooden structure built in the mid-1800s and was replaced in the early 1900s with a pipe structure. The bridge was reconstructed after incurring severe damage in the 1950 flood but was then completely destroyed by a flood in the late 1990s. (Card and photo courtesy of R. Daniel Simmons.)

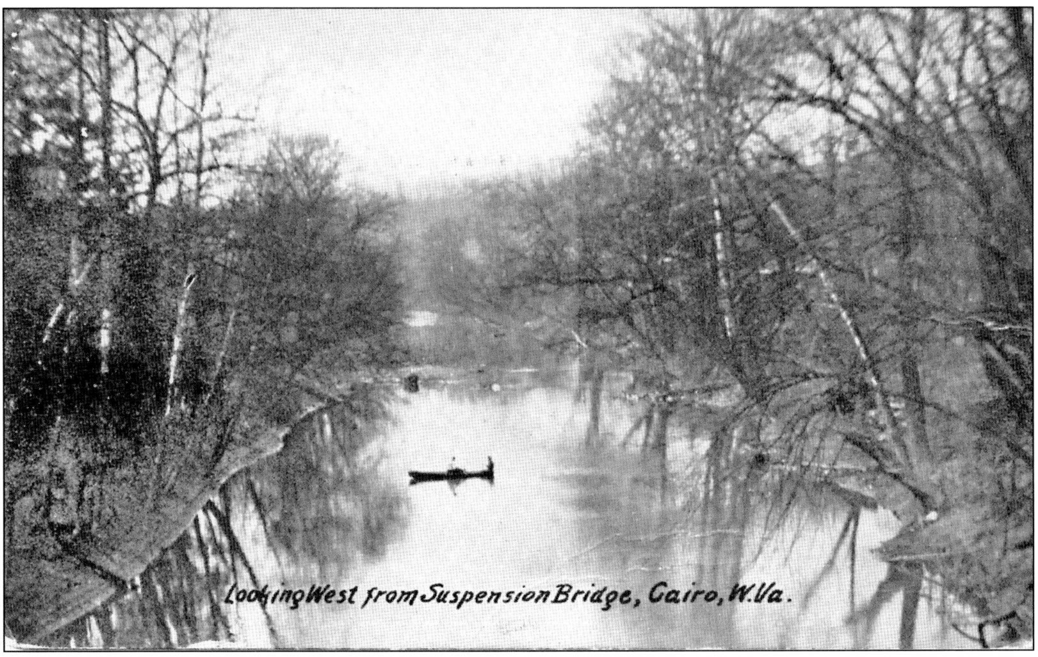

This card, postmarked in 1913, shows a view looking west from the Suspension Bridge.

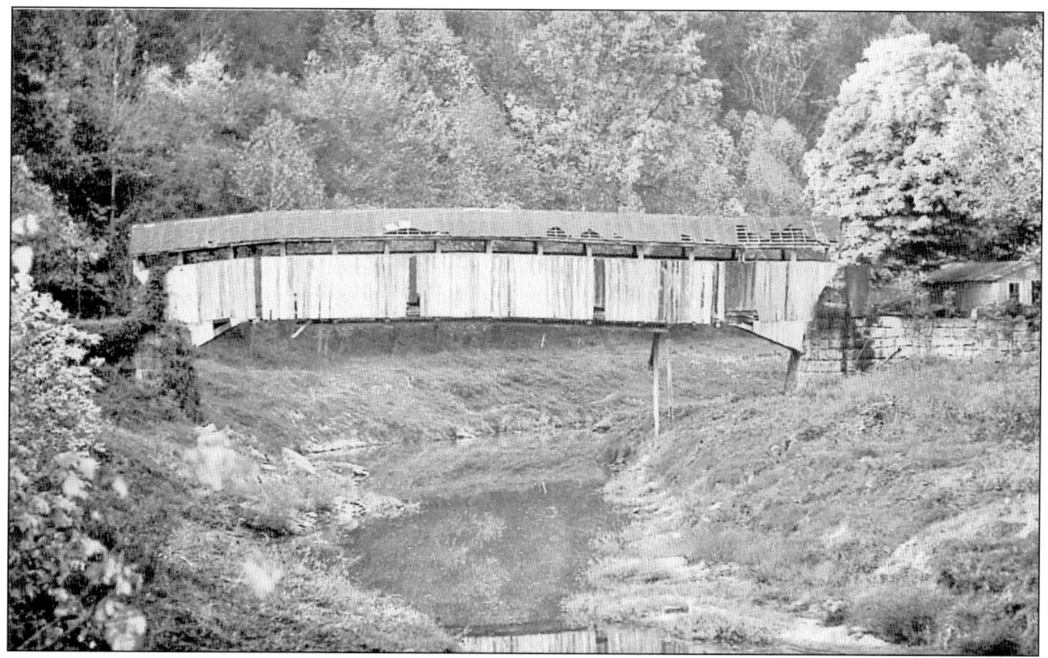

The McKinney Bridge was constructed in 1878 and was 110 feet in length. The bridge collapsed on September 3, 1970. (Courtesy of R. Daniel Simmons.)

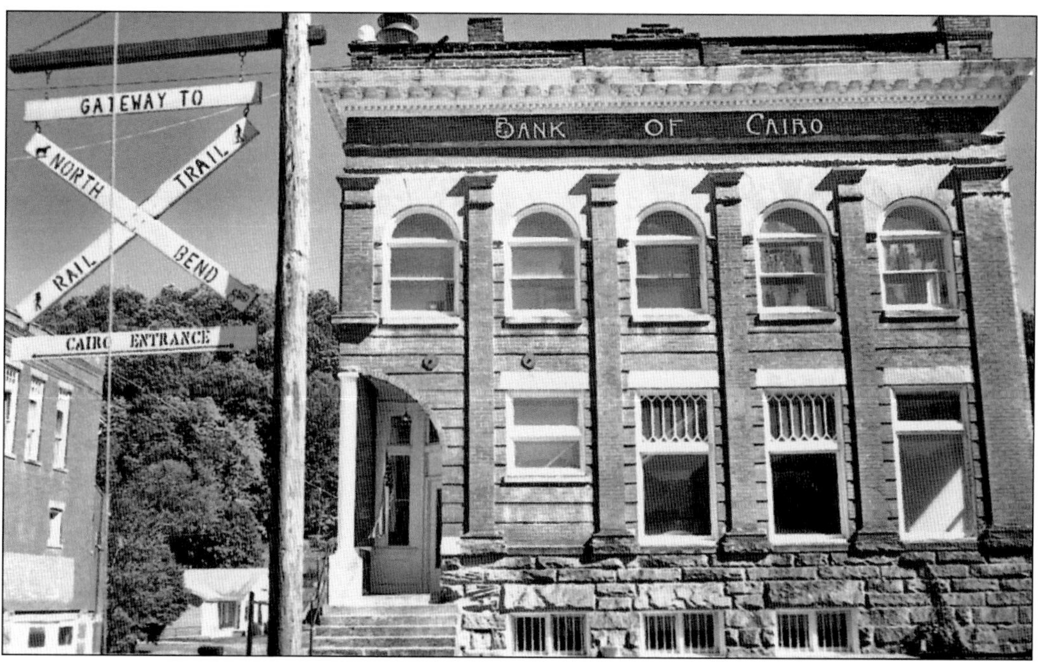

The Cairo Bank building, shown here in a recent image, was built in 1897 and is now on the National Register of Historic Places. This is the current home of the Ritchie County Tourism and Visitors Bureau and the North Bend Rail Trail Foundation. (Courtesy of R. Daniel Simmons.)

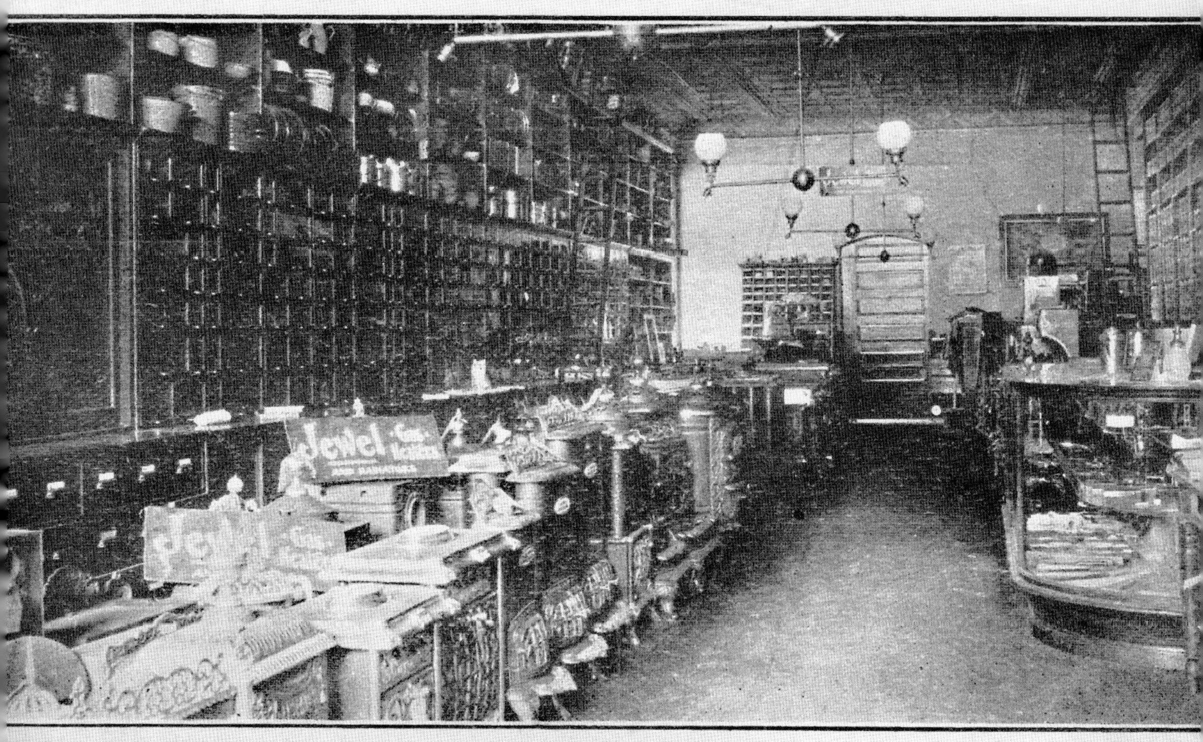

The interior of R.C. Marshall Hardware in Cairo is depicted in this image. This building is believed to have been built in or about 1902. All the original shelves and rolling ladders are still intact, and it still operates as an old-time hardware store.

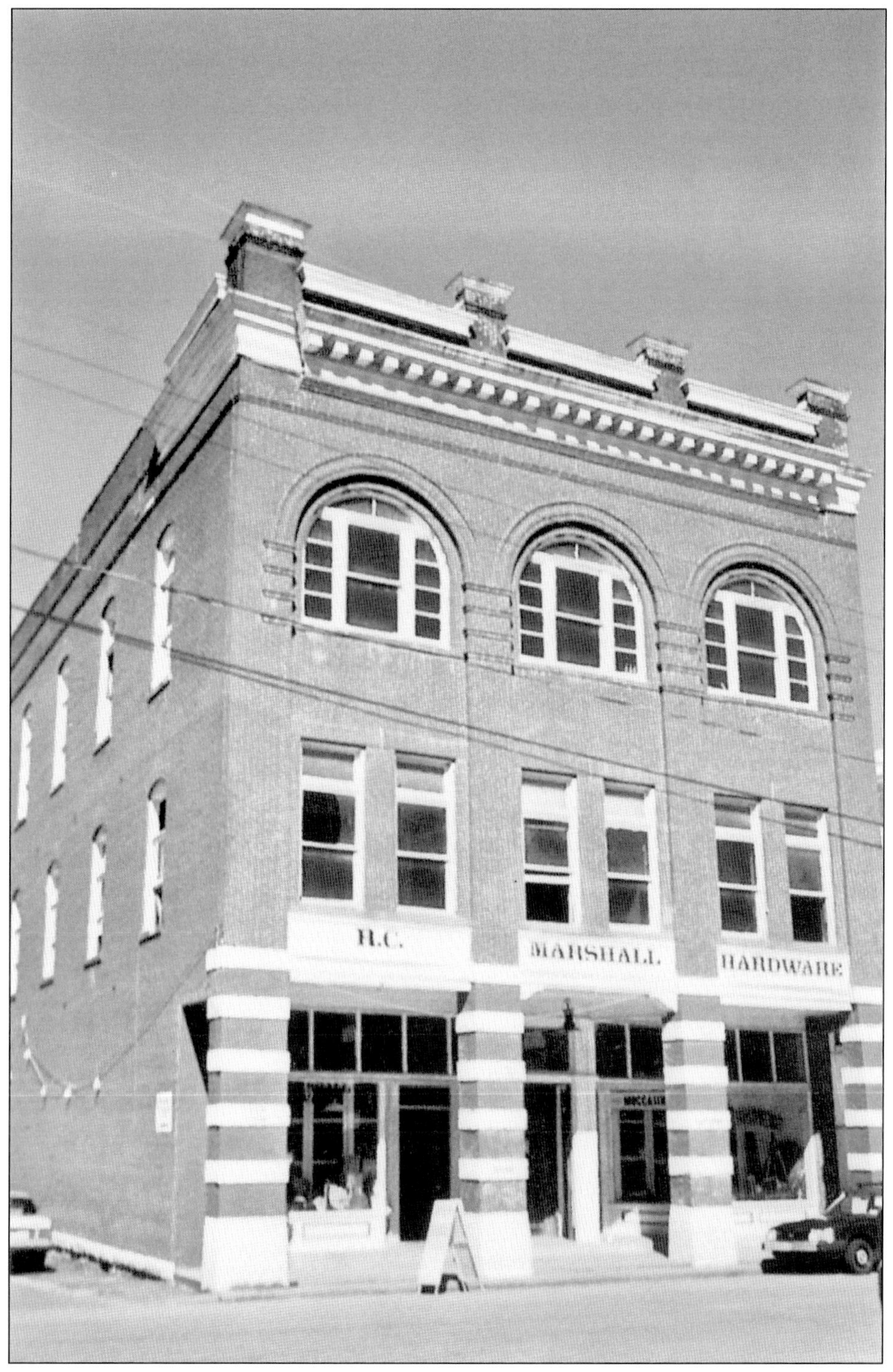

A recent card portrays the R.C. Marshall Hardware store, which is still in operation and partially owned by the author. This building was constructed in 1903 and is one of the historical mainstays of the Cairo community. (Courtesy of R. Daniel Simmons.)

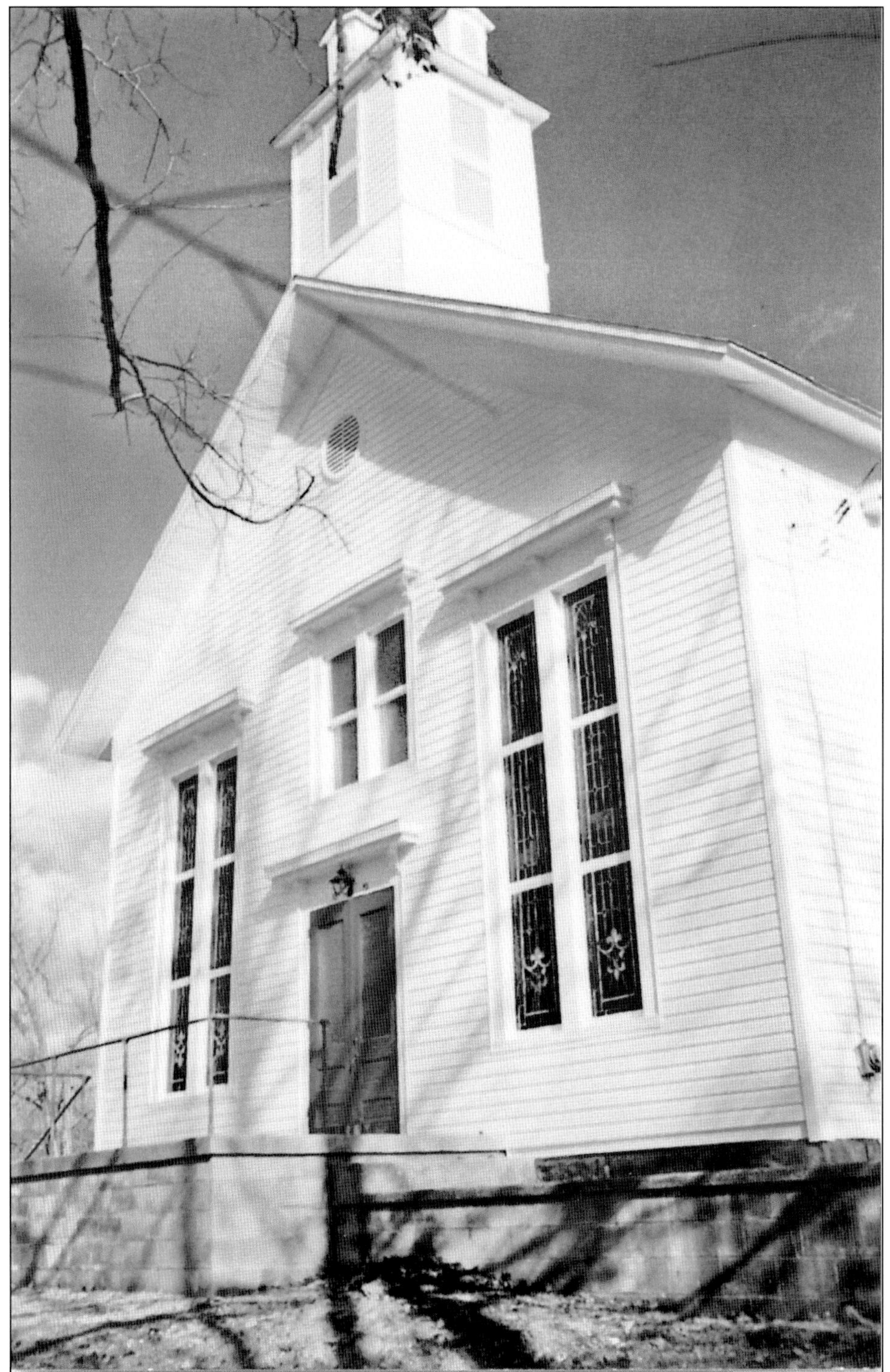

A recent card shows the Hughes River Presbyterian Church in Cairo. This church was built in 1870, and the stained-glass windows currently in the church are the original ones. (Courtesy of R. Daniel Simmons, pastor.)

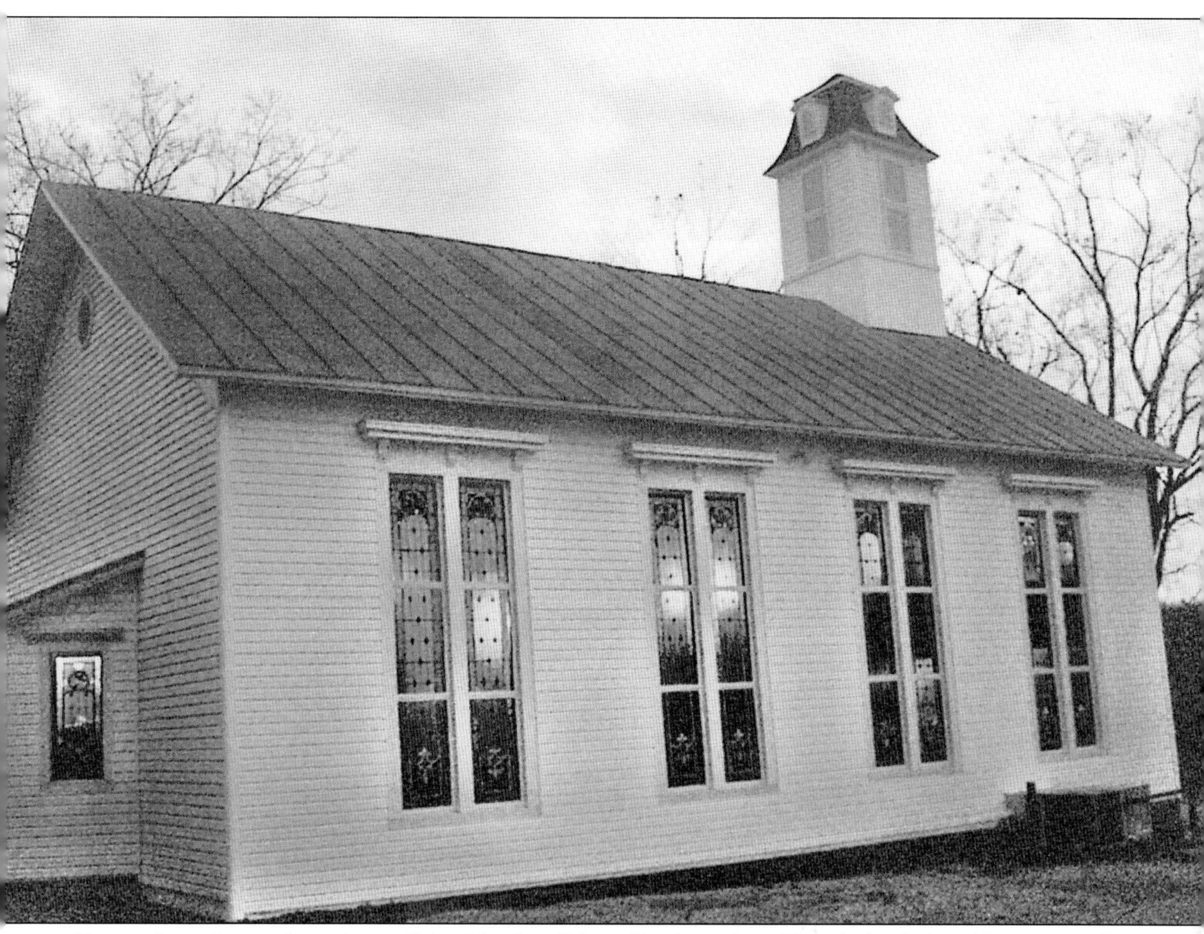

Shown here is another view of the Hughes River Presbyterian Church in Cairo. (Courtesy of R. Daniel Simmons.)

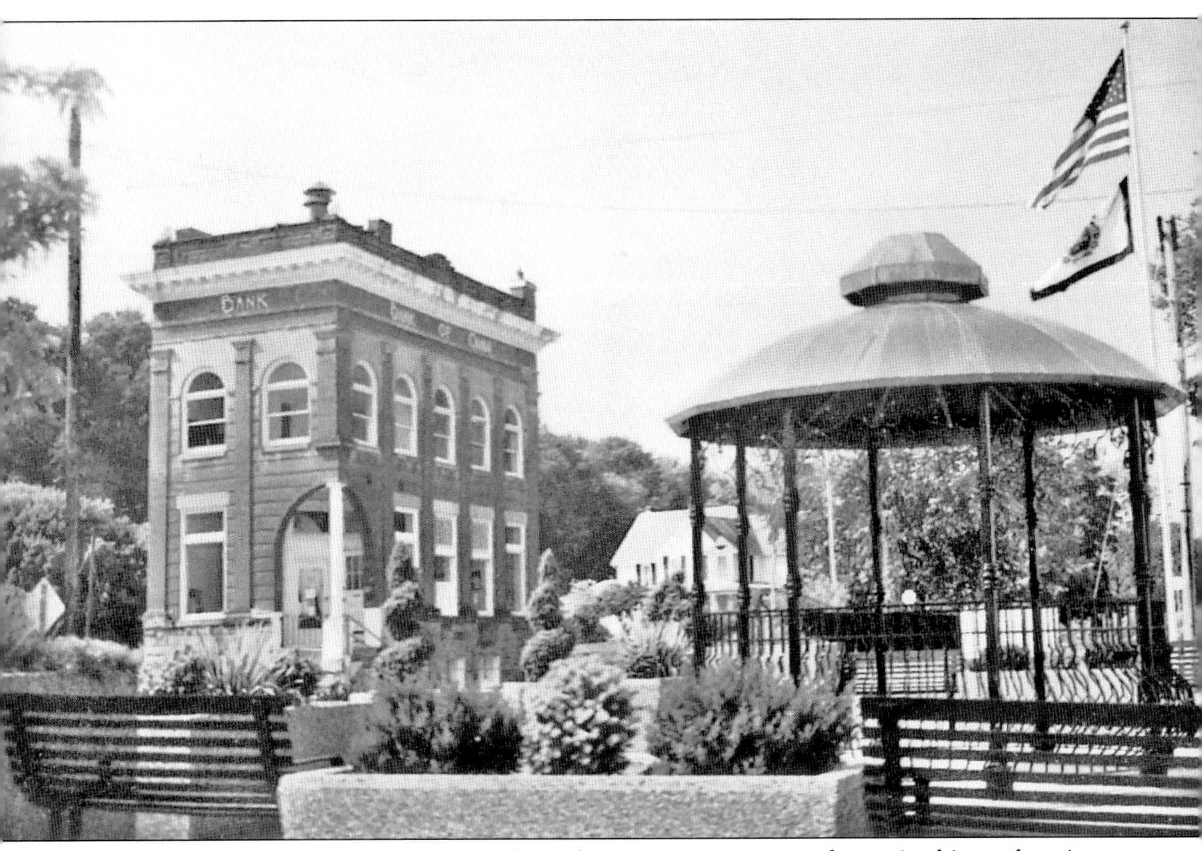

The Cairo Bank and the newly erected gazebo in town square are shown in this modern image. (Courtesy of R. Daniel Simmons).

Four

Other Communities and Points of Interest

The following cards are from various other small towns and outlying areas in and throughout Ritchie County, including some of the smaller communities such as Ellenboro, Petroleum, Pullman, Macfarlan, Smithville and Tollgate.

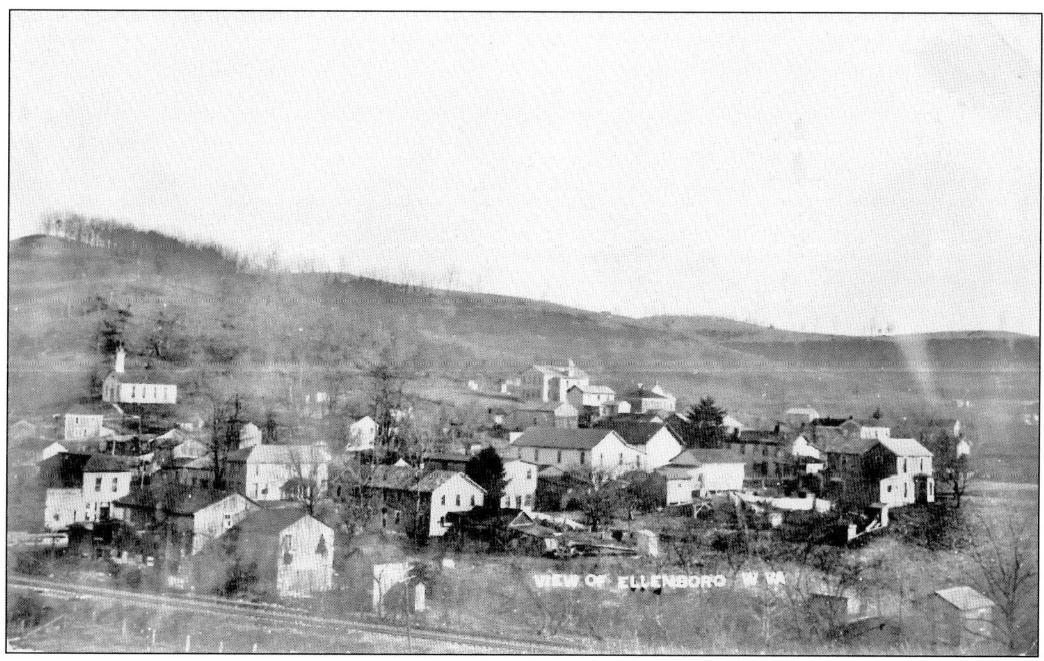

This *c.* 1905 card shows Ellenboro when looking across the B&O main line. Wilson Methodist Church is visible on the high left, and the old school house is in the center of the photo. Much of what can be seen in this photo was taken out when the new U.S. Route 50 was built.

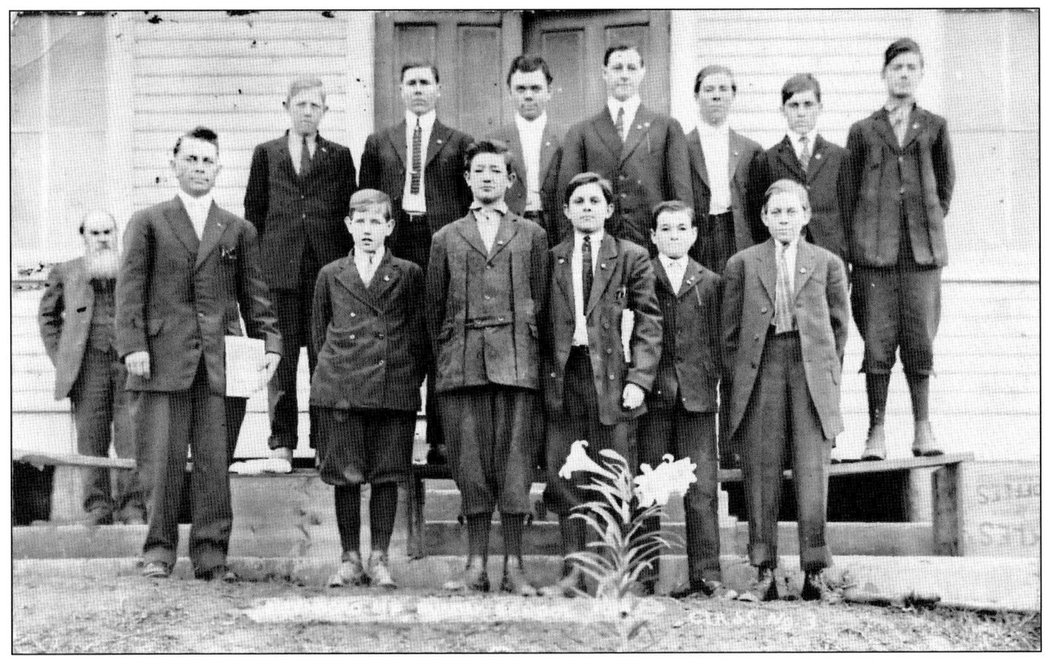

Shown is Ellenboro Methodist Protestant Sunday School Class Number Three. This particular card, postmarked in 1914, was written by Charles H. Cook and states that this is his Sunday school class.

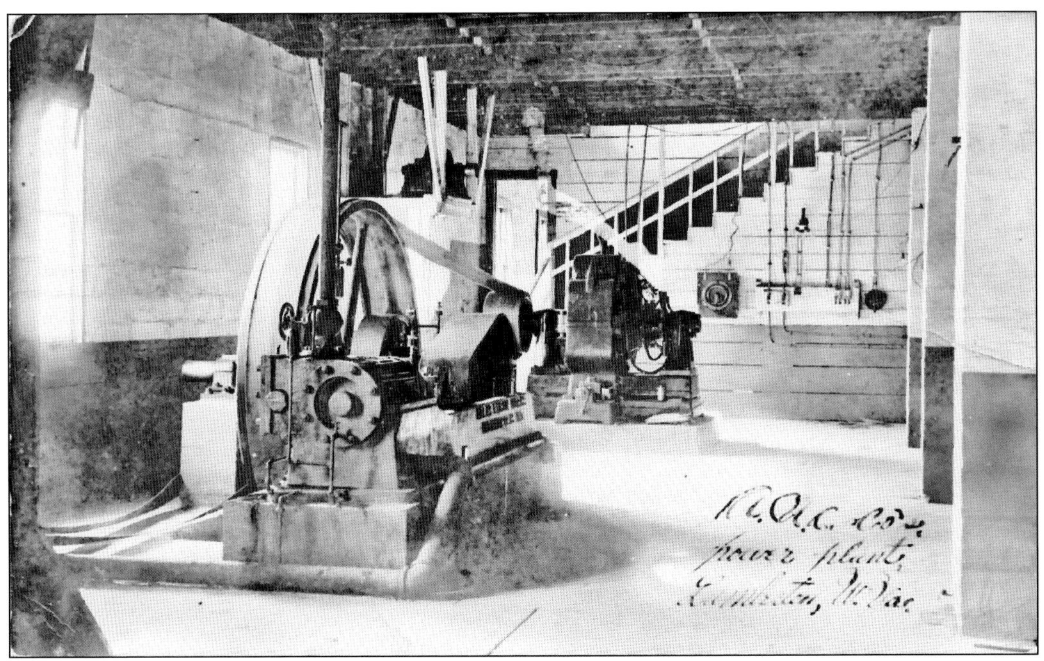

The interior of the power plant in Lamberton is shown in this 1913 card. The power plant, known as the Electric Undercurrent Company, was on the site of Mid-Atlantic Glass. The power plant was owned by Harry Lambert.

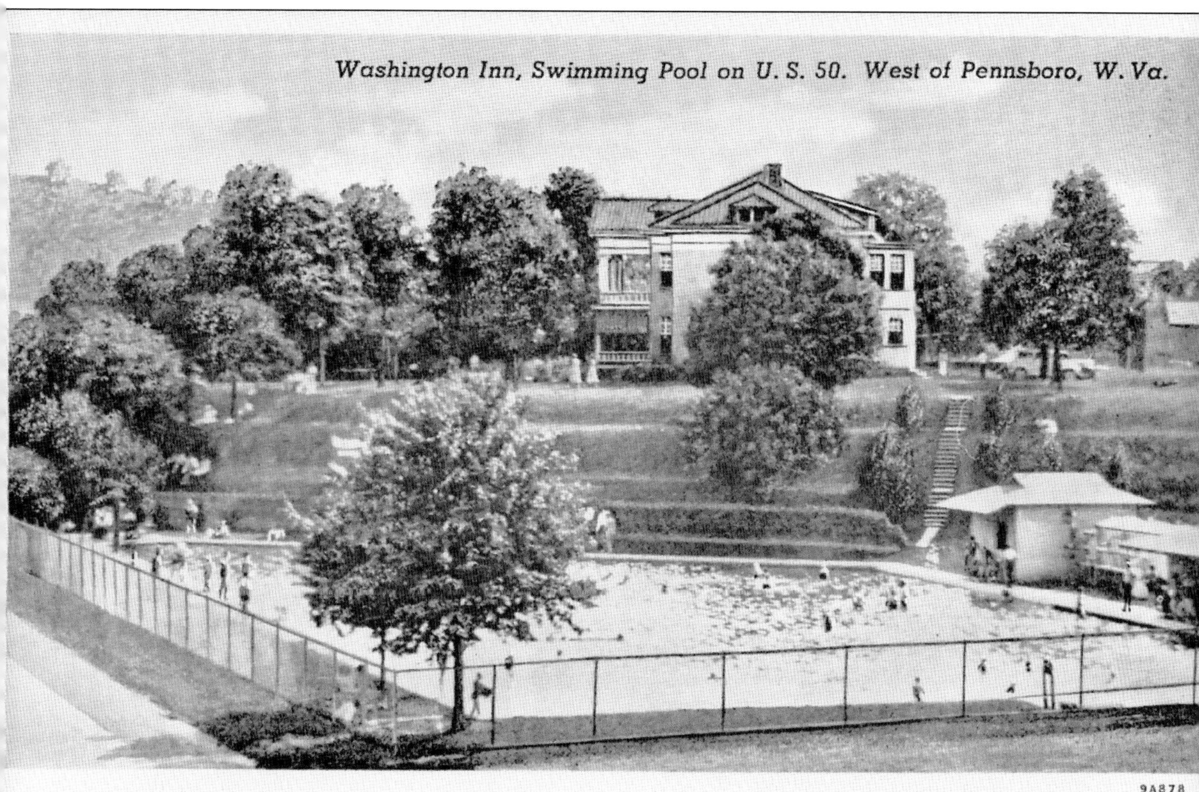

The Washington Inn established itself as a premier inn along the Washington Turnpike, or old U.S. 50. This *c.* 1940 card states that it is west of Pennsboro, although the inn sits in Lamberton. In its heyday, it boasted the largest swimming pool in the state of West Virginia. The pool is now filled in, but its outline can still be made out below the inn. This was the original home of Harry Lambert and boasted a golf course and airport. This card was published by Sigler's Pharmacy in Pennsboro.

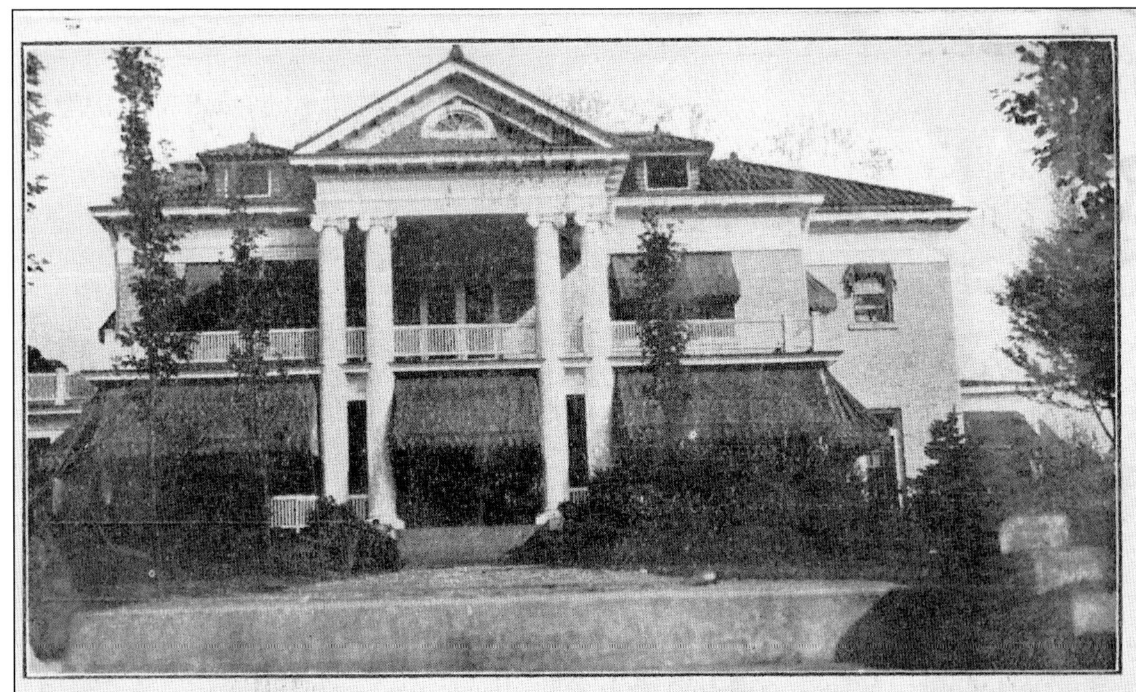

WASHINGTON INN. ROUTE 50. ELLENBORO. W. VA.

EASTWARD

Miles	
291	Washington, D. C.
318	Baltimore, Md.
210	Winchester, Va.
160	Romney, W. Va.
47	Clarksburg, W. Va.

WESTWARD

Miles	
16	St Marys, W. Va.
37	Marietta, Ohio
45	Parkersburg, W. Va.
166	Columbus, Ohio
224	Cleveland, Ohio

Depicted on these two pages is a *c.* 1910 fold-out advertising postcard of the Washington Inn. The four sides show a photo of the inn, a view of the inn looking across the pool, information about

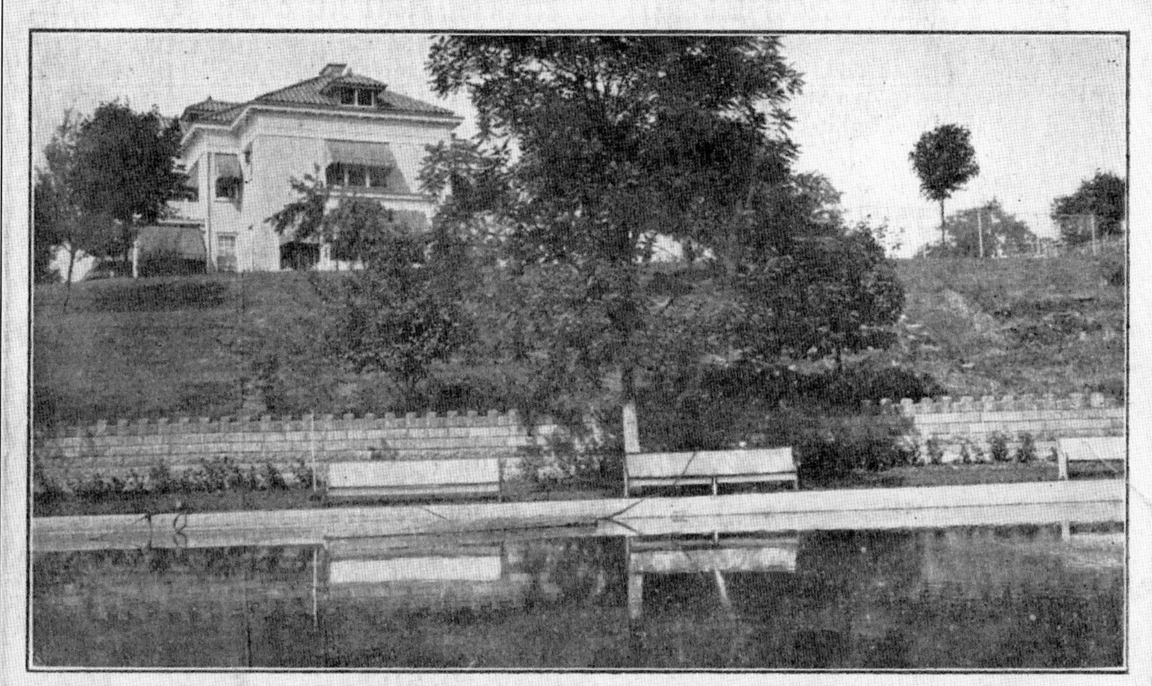

WASHINGTON INN

ELLENBORO, W. VA.

On Route 50, one-half mile east of Junction 50 N. and 50 S.

MEALS---ROOMS

Pure Well Water, Bath, Hot and Cold.

Many appreciate a realy fine place to rest over night in quiet and comfort. Washington Inn is one of the best you ever find. Good meals, bed and room. Cheap rates.

Once you are our guest, you are most sure to return.

Mr. and Mrs. S. M. Cunningham.

the inn, and the mileage to various cities (on the mailing side). Then owned and operated by Mr. and Mrs. S. M. Cunningham, it later housed Sheppard's Nursing home for decades.

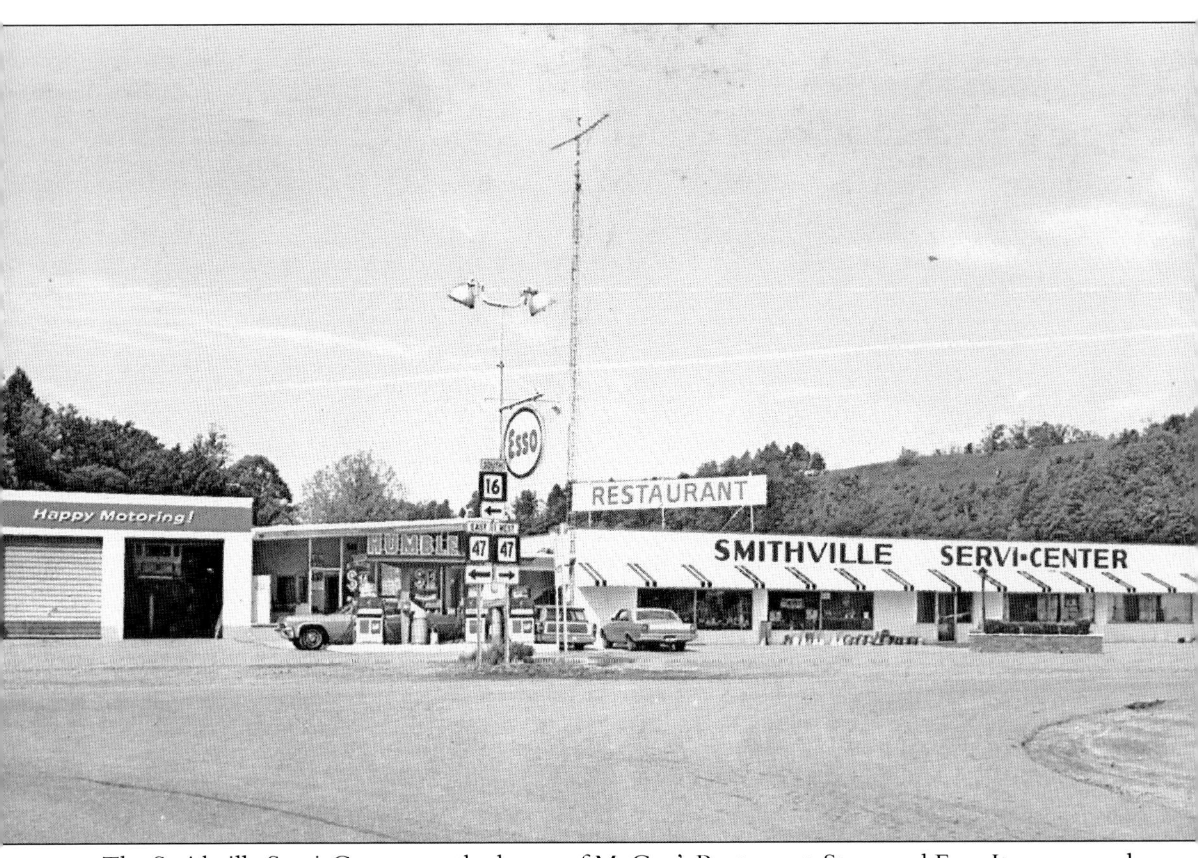

The Smithville Servi-Center was the home of McCoy's Restaurant, Store, and Esso. It was owned and operated by James, Paul, and Evelyn McCoy. This *c.* 1975 card was published by Luoma Photos in Weirton, West Virginia.

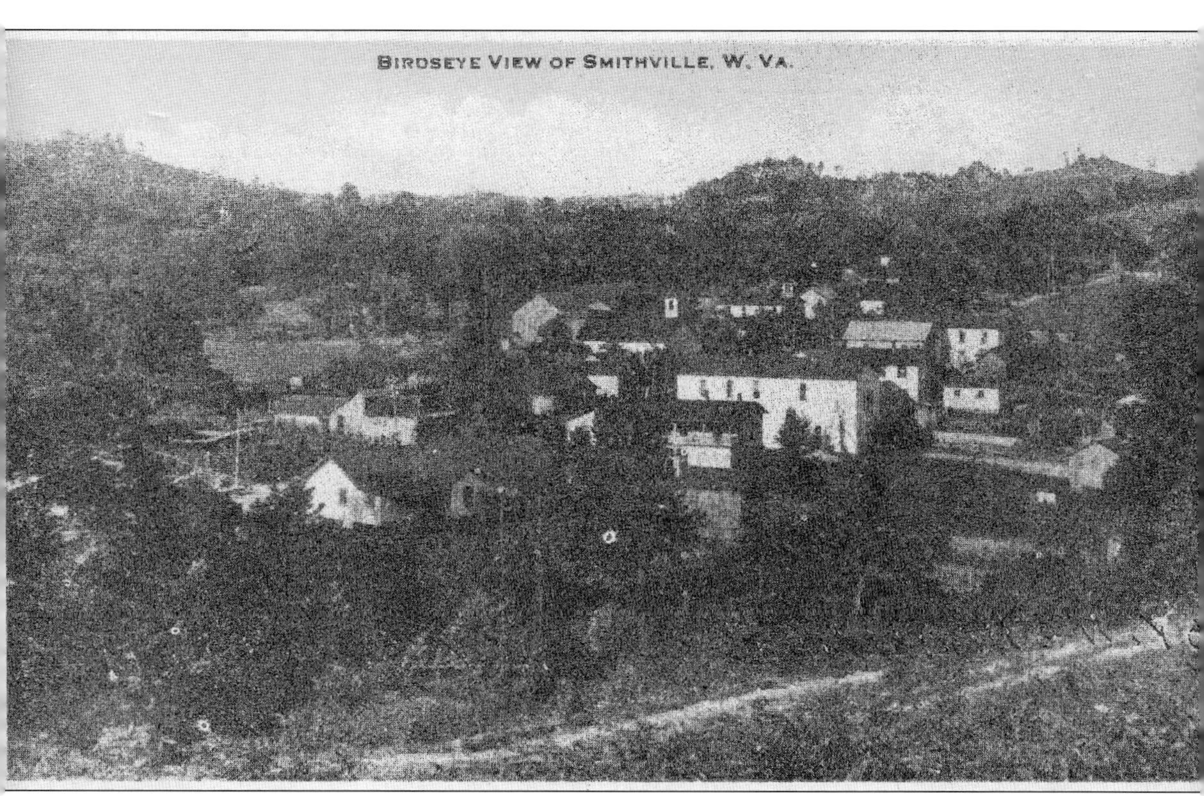

A bird's-eye view of Smithville is shown in this undated card.

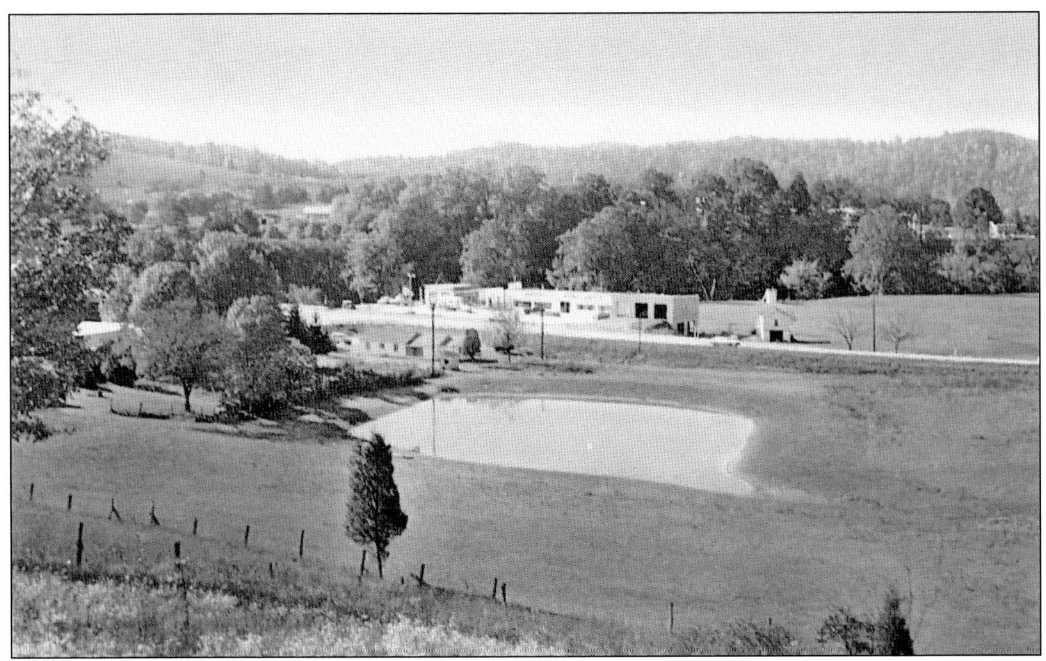

Shown in this *c.* 1975 series are four cards of Smithville and the surrounding area. The first card depicts the McCoy Servi-Center in the distance, which claims to be the only stop between Parkersburg and Weston that serves full-course, home-cooked meals. It references the "recreation lake" in the foreground. The second card claims to show a "typical mountain scene" overlooking Smithville to the west.

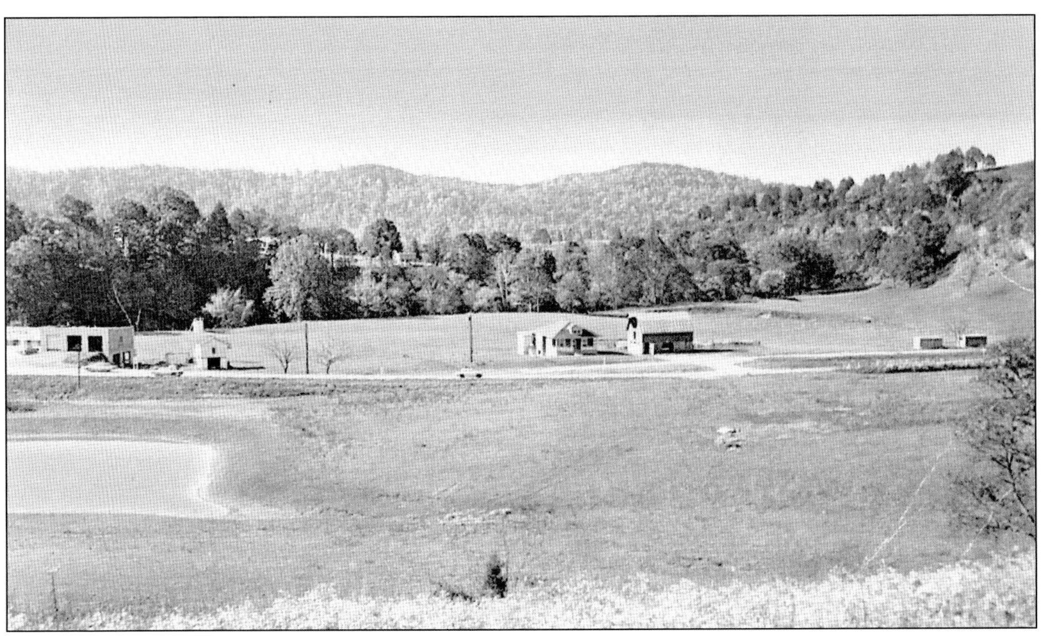

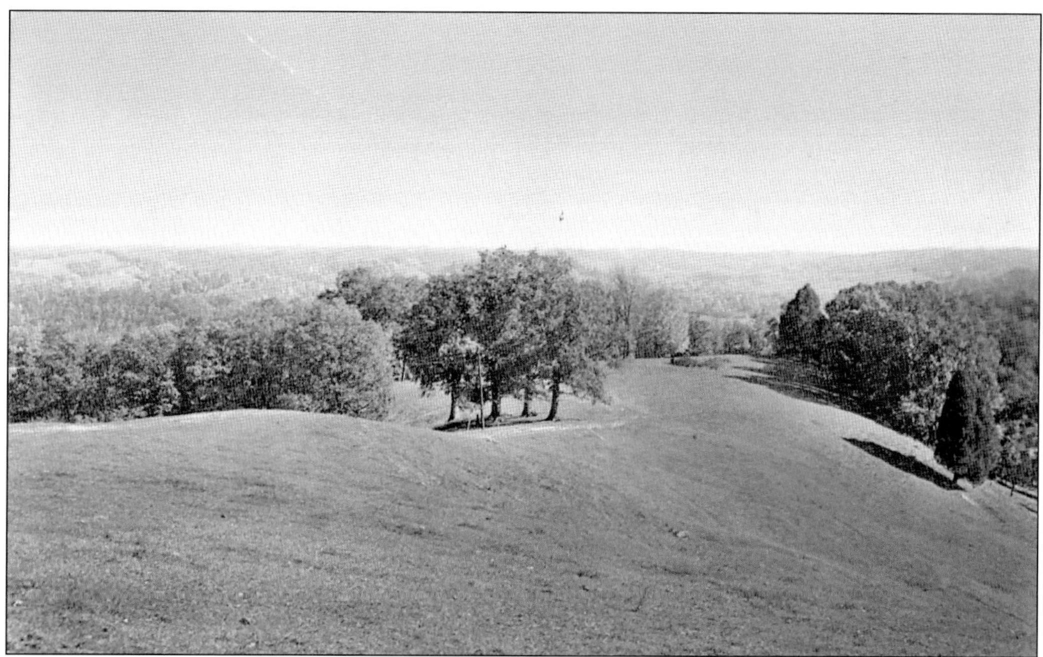

Above, the third card in this series is a scene looking north from U.S. Route 47, which is 3 miles east of Smithville and overlooks the historic Fonzo Valley. The home of A. Goff and Sons can be seen in the background. The fourth card, below, is the same area as the third but shot from a different angle. This series was published by Seneca Wholesale of Riverton, West Virginia.

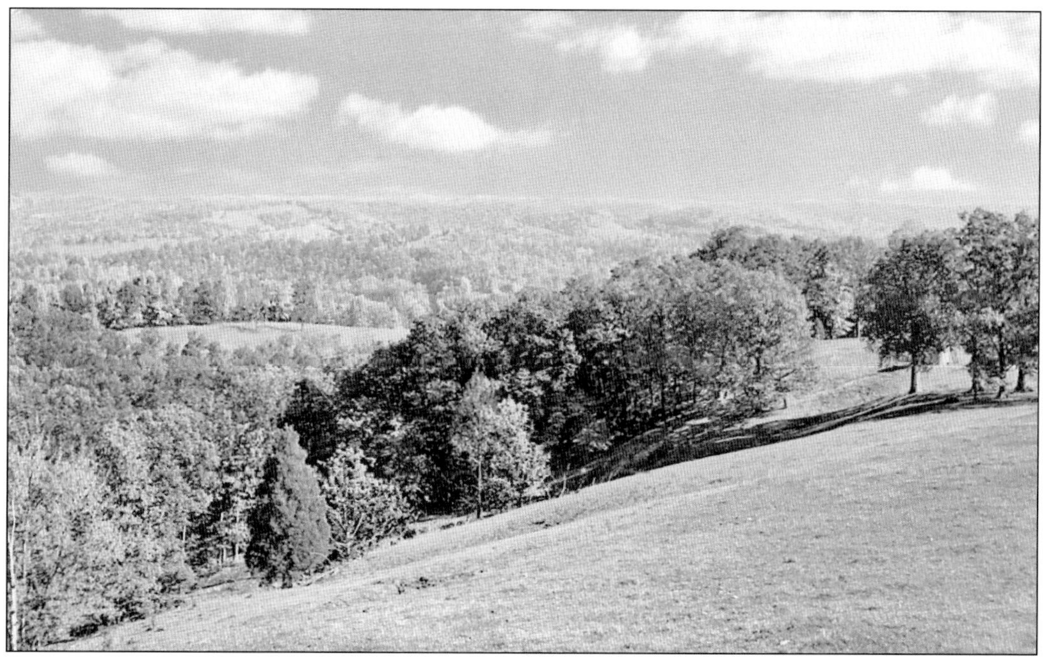

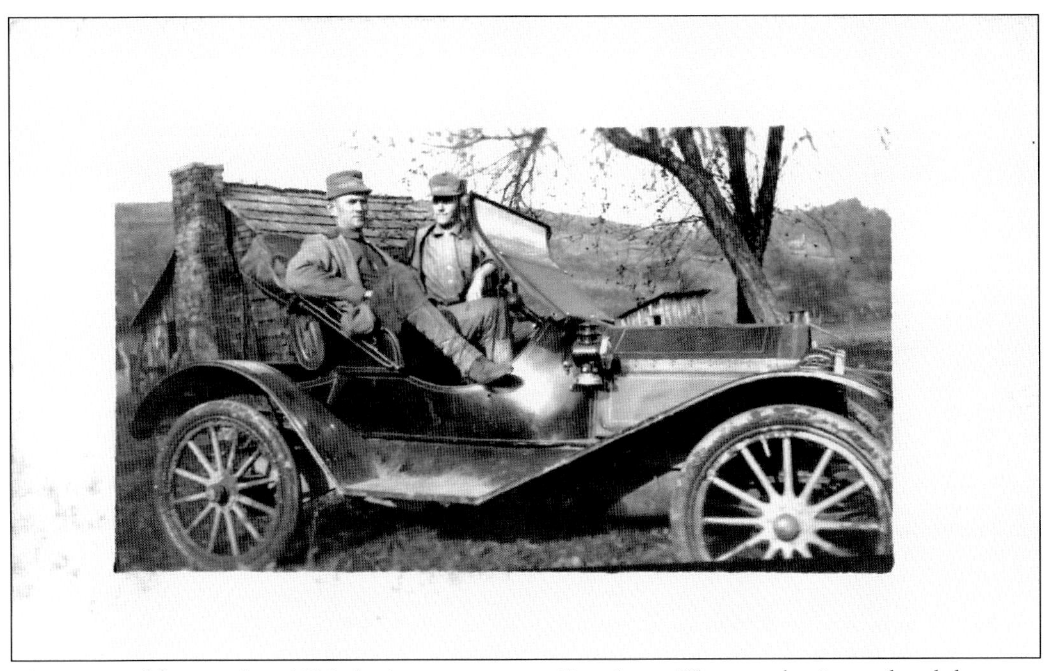

This series of four cards, *c.* 1925, depicts an area near Petroleum. The people pictured and the exact location are unknown.

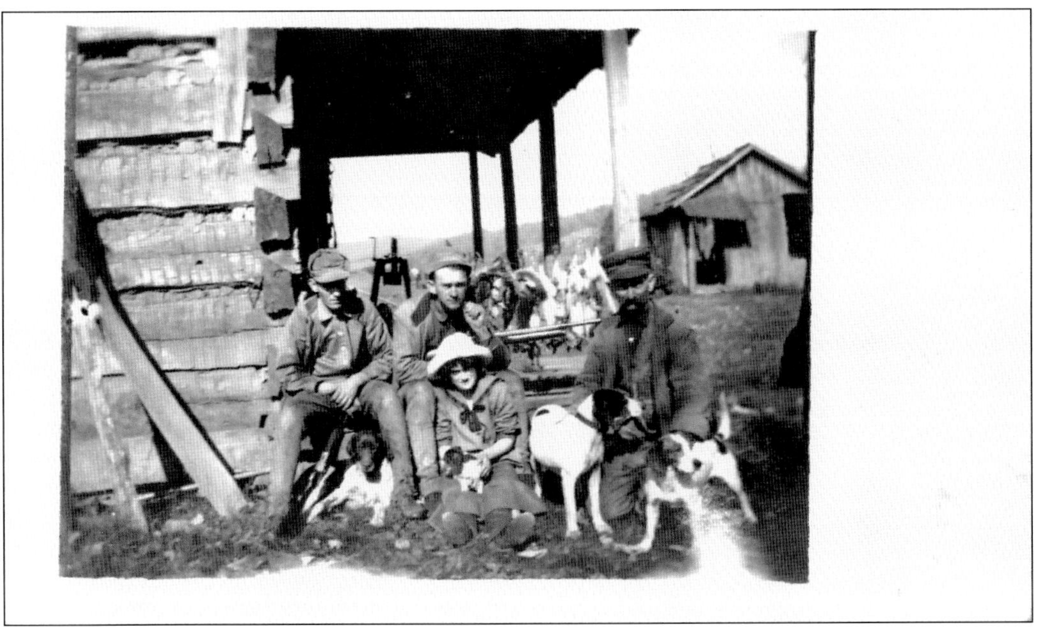

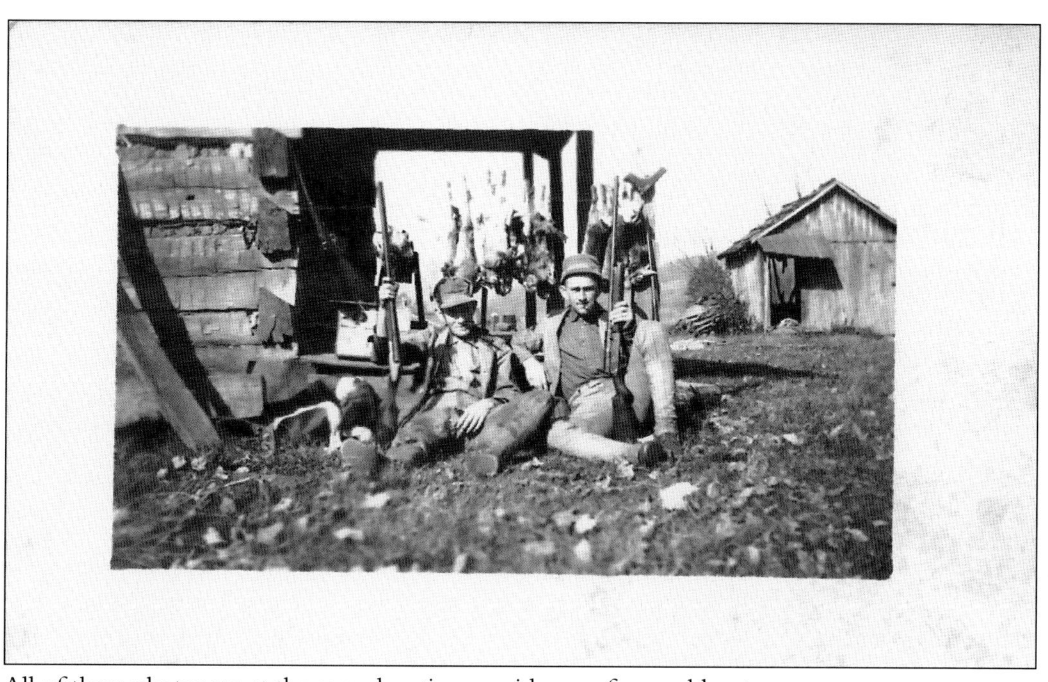

All of these photos are at the same location—evidence of a good hunt.

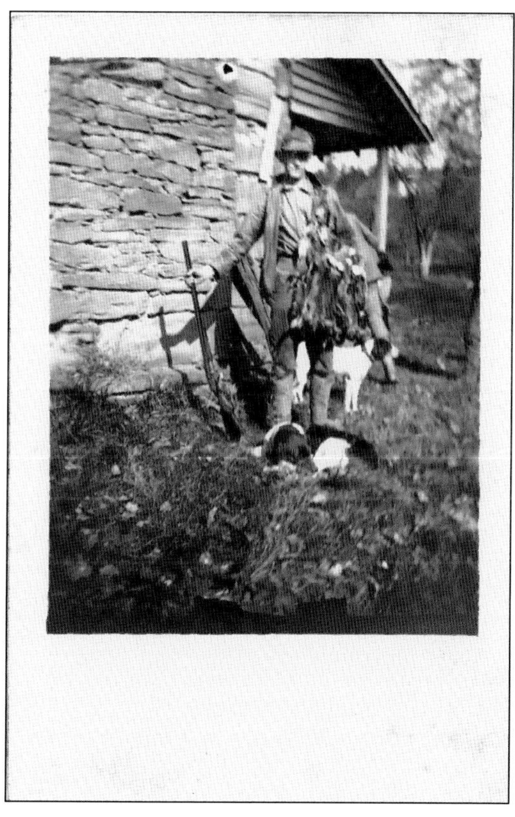

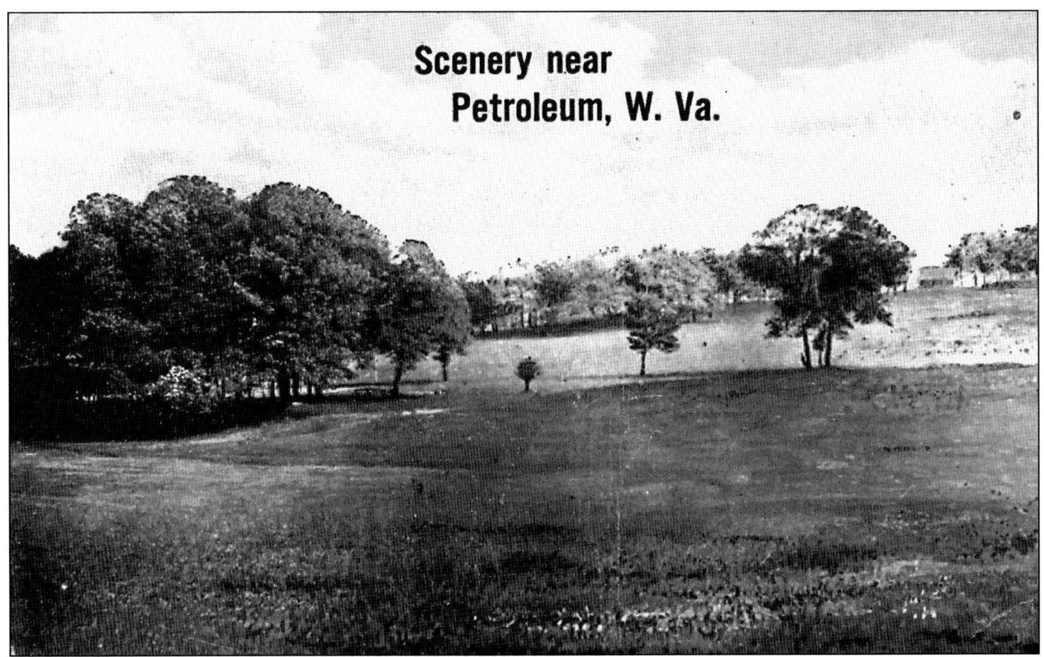

This undated card claims to show scenery near Petroleum. This assertion is questionable as many of these kinds of cards claimed to be of scenery in a particular area, but were in fact just random pictures chosen from images on hand by the postcard company. Therefore, the exact location is unknown.

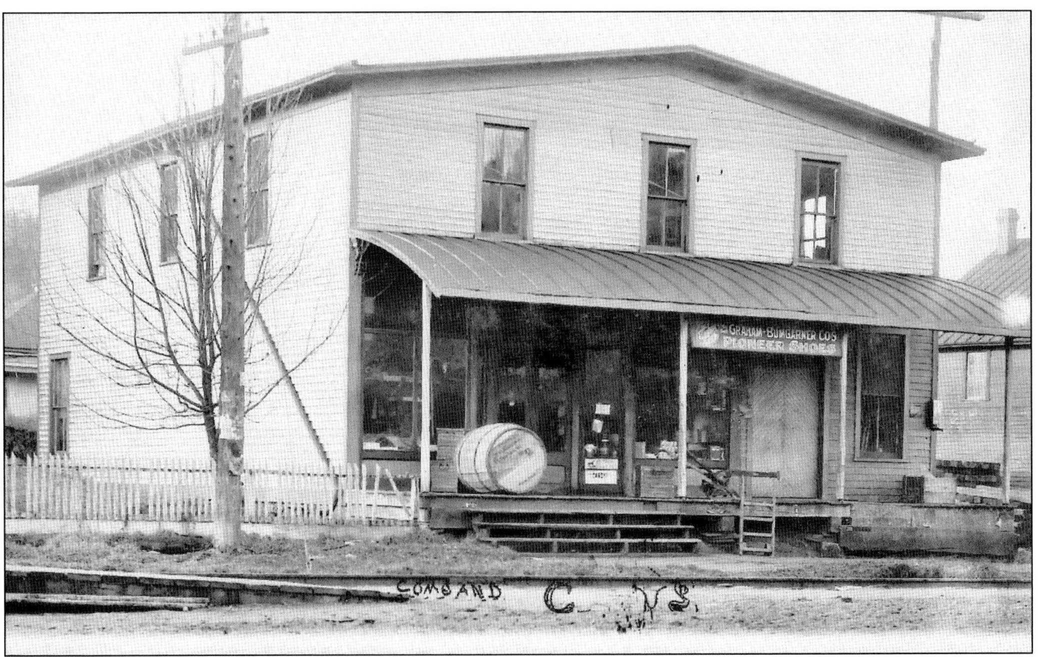

Graham and Bumgarner Company's Pioneer Shoes is shown in this *c.* 1910 card. This was last home to the Petroleum General Store and was destroyed by a wreck of the B&O in November 1982.

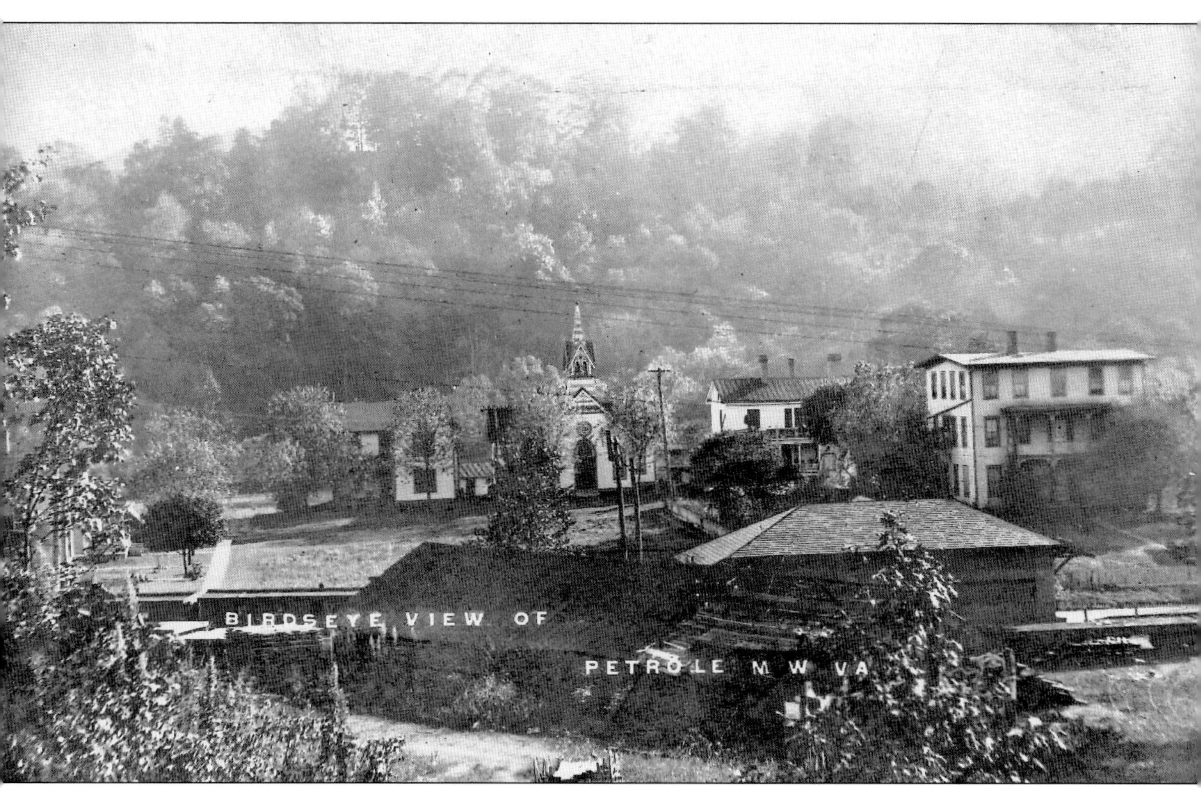

This undated card shows a bird's-eye view of Petroleum. The depot can be seen in the forefront, and the three-story hotel is located on the right. The Presbyterian church, which later became the Methodist church, is shown in the middle.

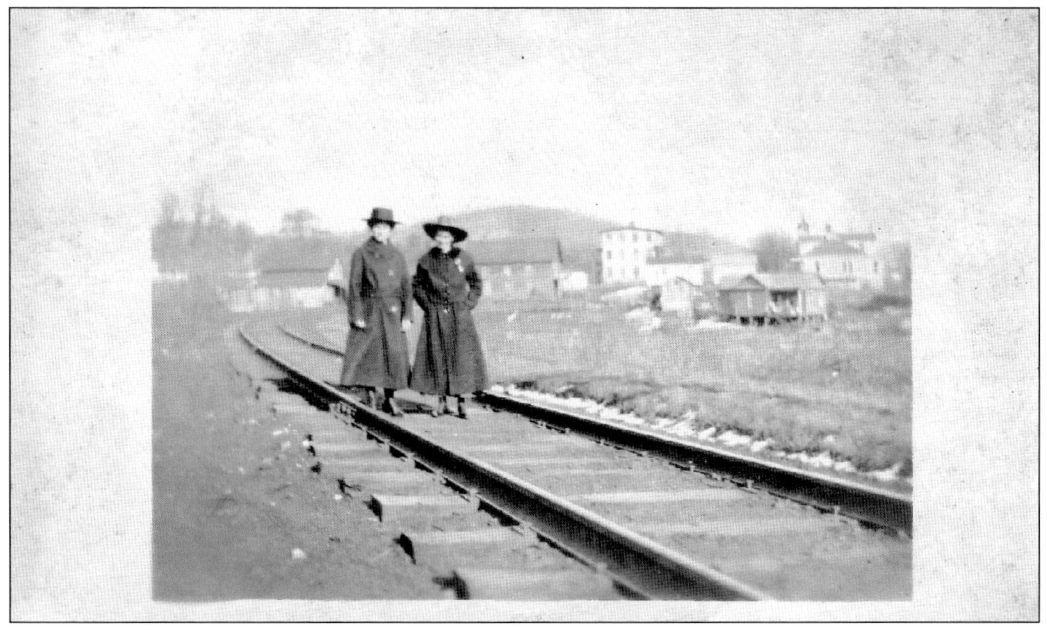

Two unidentified people walk along the B&O track just outside Petroleum. The hotel and church are visible in the background. This card was dated February 1, 1918.

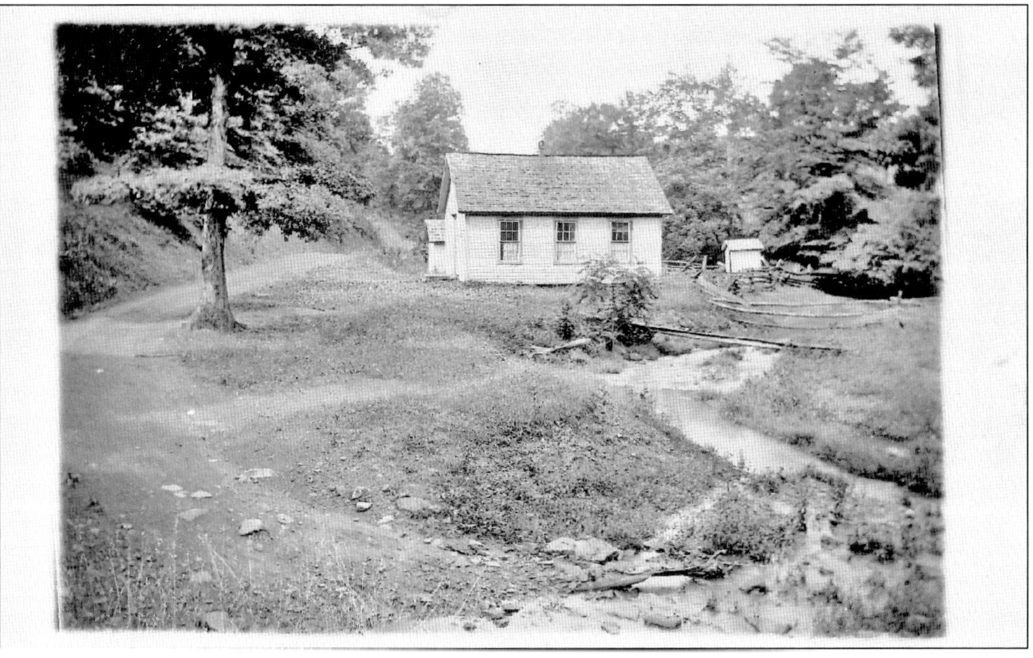

Myers Fork School was located between Nutter Farm and Petroleum. This photograph was taken on July 10, 1907.

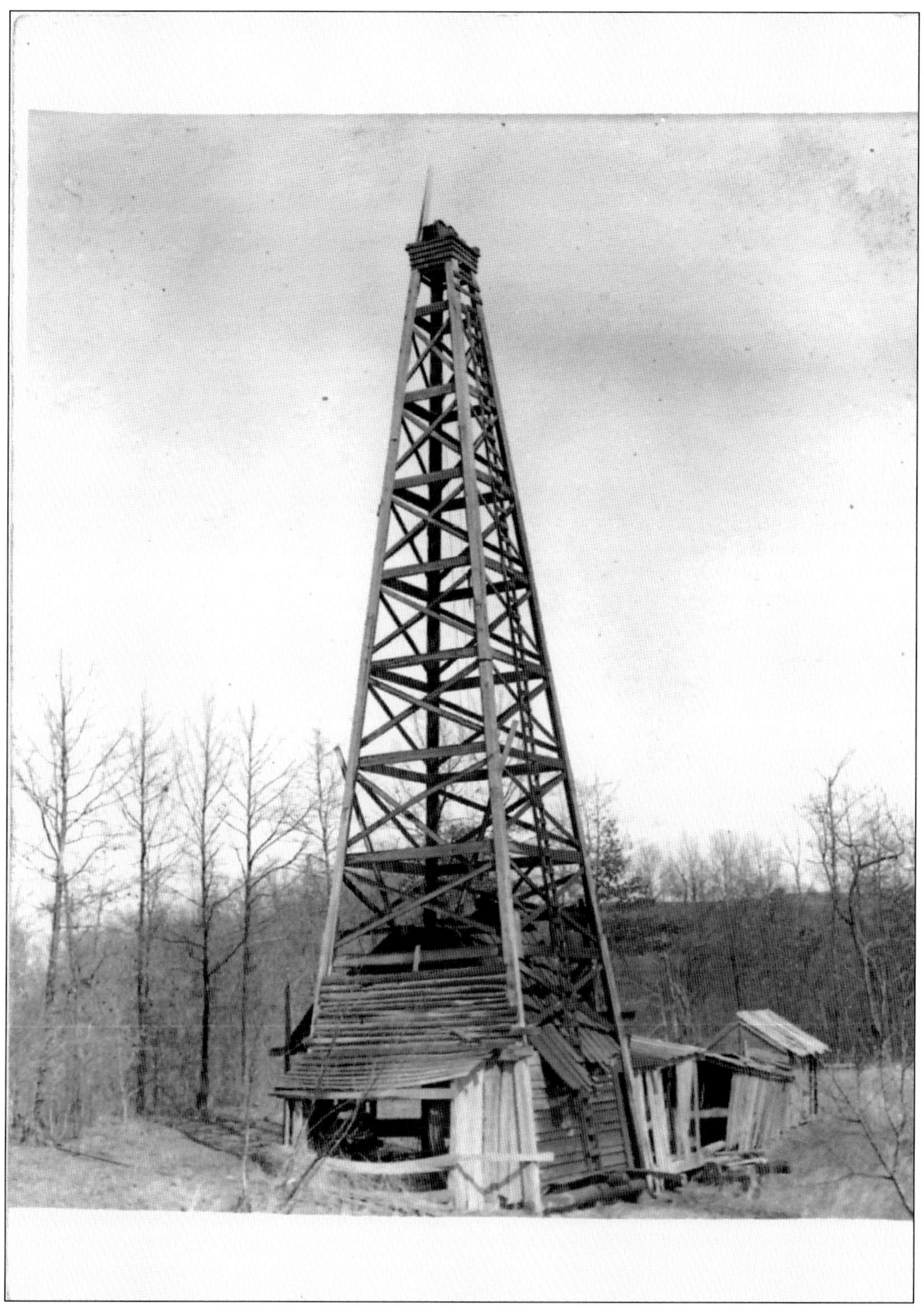

This image shows an oil rig located near Cornwallis. Although the card is undated, the state of disrepair would indicate this card could be dated no earlier than 1930.

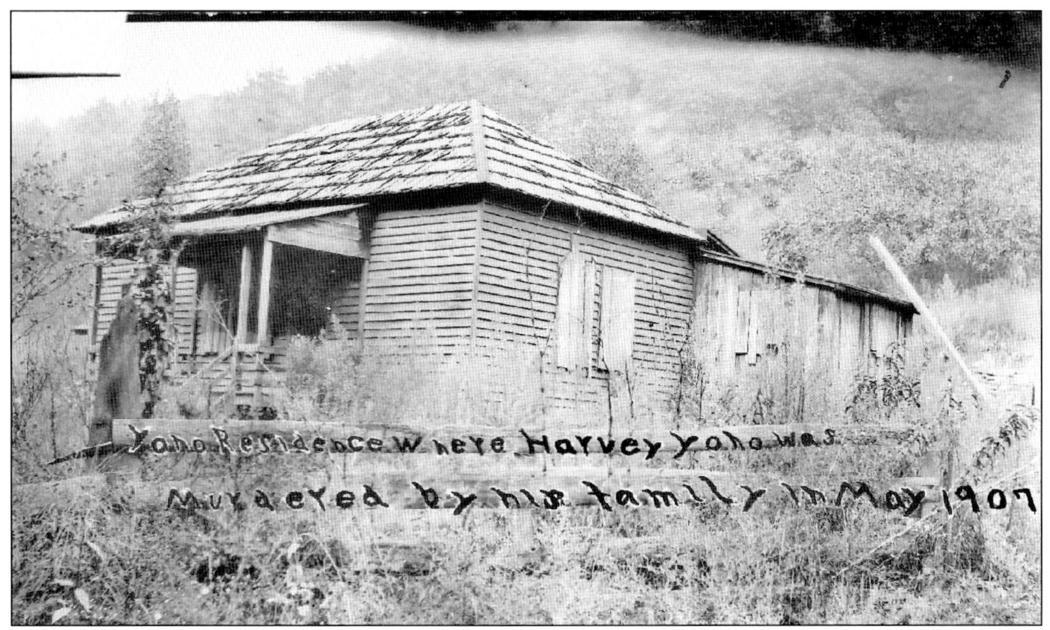

This card states that this is the "Yoho residence where Harvey Yoho was murdered by his family in May 1907." The newspaper account of this card states that he was shot in the head by his son after drinking and fighting, and he expired a short time later after he had been put into bed. This house was located in Beatrice.

THE PULLMAN STATE BANK.

PULLMAN, W. VA., Apr 21 1919

Yours of the .... inst. received with stated enclosures.

WE CREDIT		WE ENTER FOR COLLECTION
By J. J. Larue	40 00	
By M. McCroott	24 70	

plus the check I have been holding

Not responsible for lack of protest at points where there is no bank. All items (except checks on us) are credited subject to payment.

Respectfully,

F. A. HALL, CASHIER.

BUXTON & SKINNER PRINTERS, ST. LOUIS

This postcard from the Pullman State Bank is dated April 21, 1919.

This *c.* 1940 card shows the covered bridge at Tollgate.

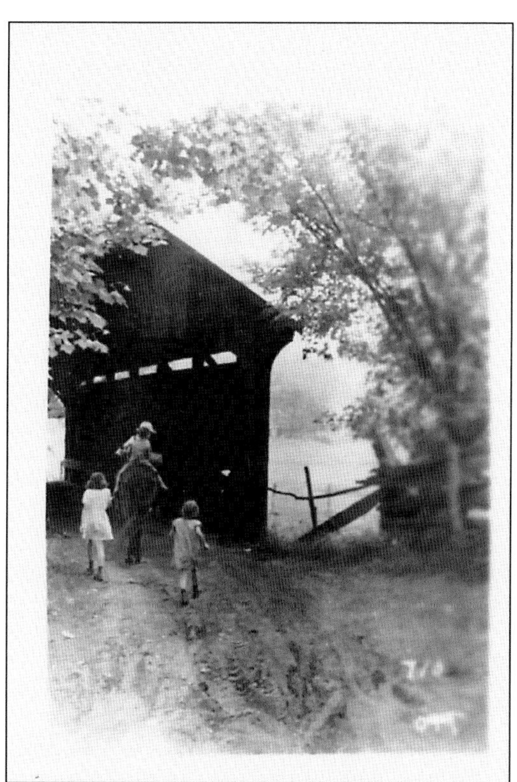

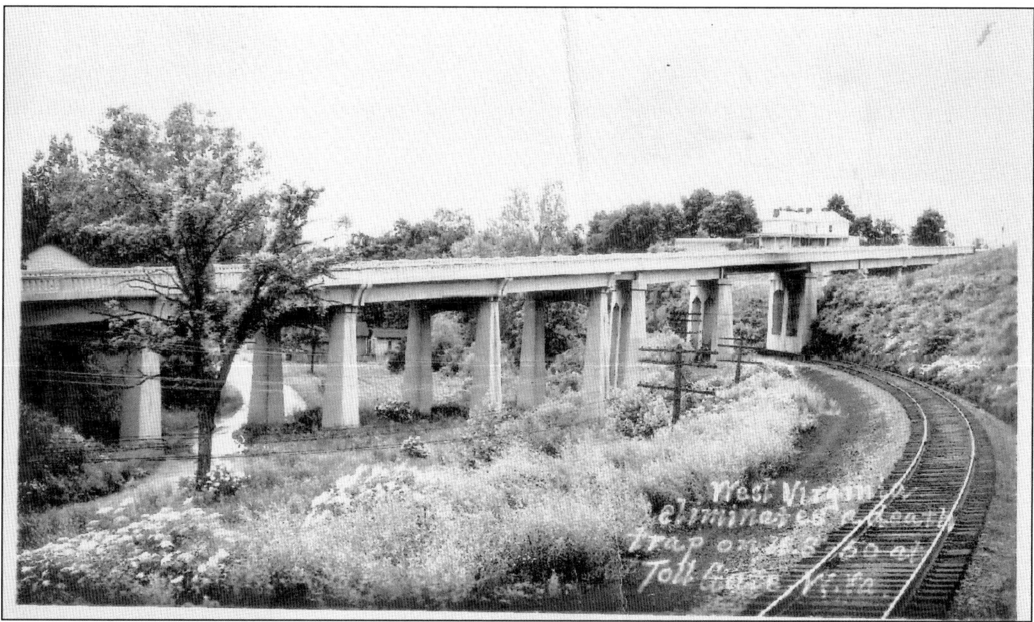

The large bridge in Tollgate was located on old U.S. Route 50. This undated card states, "West Virginia eliminates a death trap on U.S. 50 at Tollgate West Virginia." This statement is apparently a reference to people being hit by trains when the bridge did not exist. The bridge was removed in the 1990s, and the roadway was rerouted.

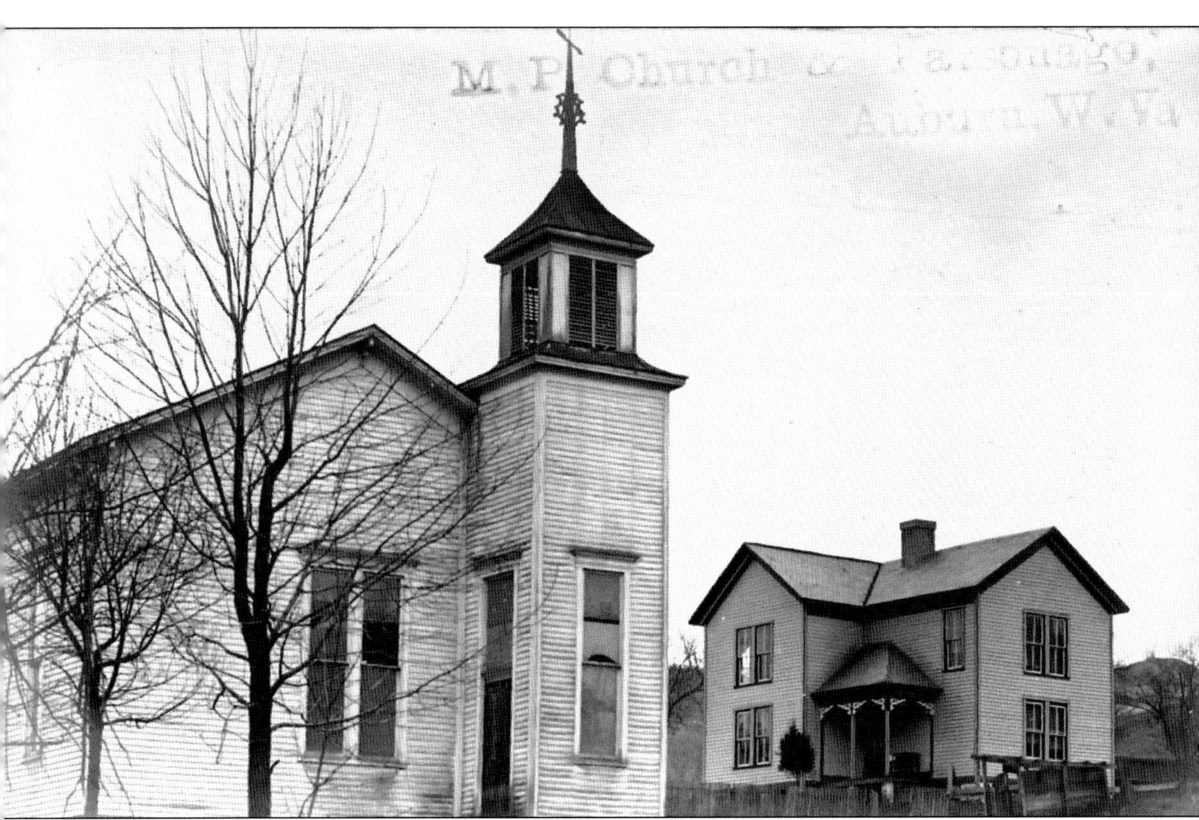

The Methodist Protestant church and its parsonage in Auburn are shown in this *c.* 1940 image. Neither of these structures are still standing.

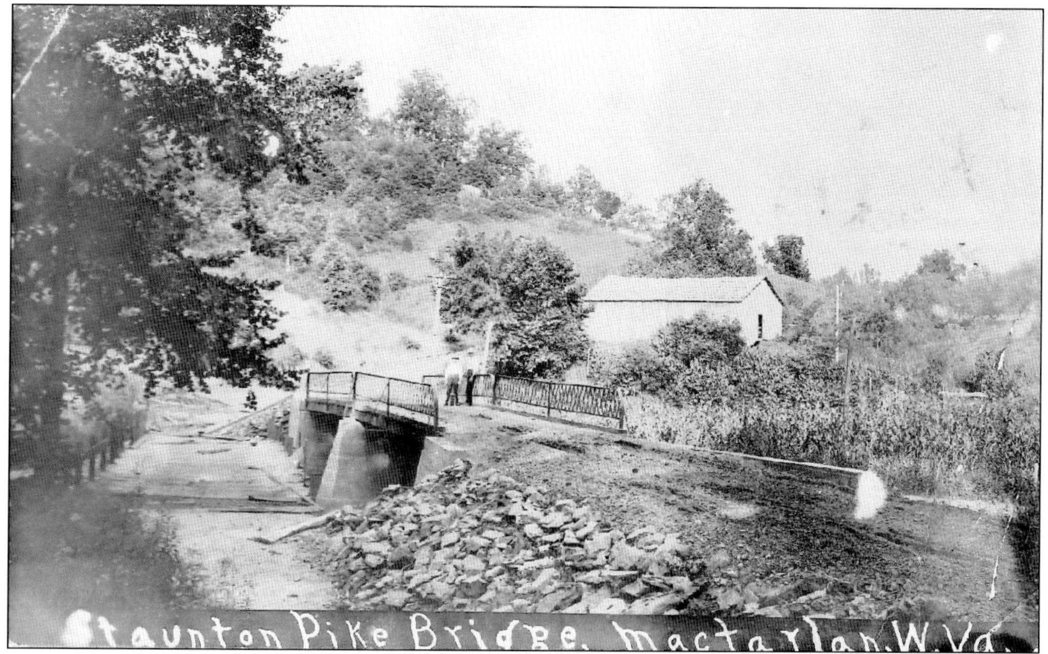

The Staunton Pike Bridge in Macfarlan is depicted in this 1908 card.

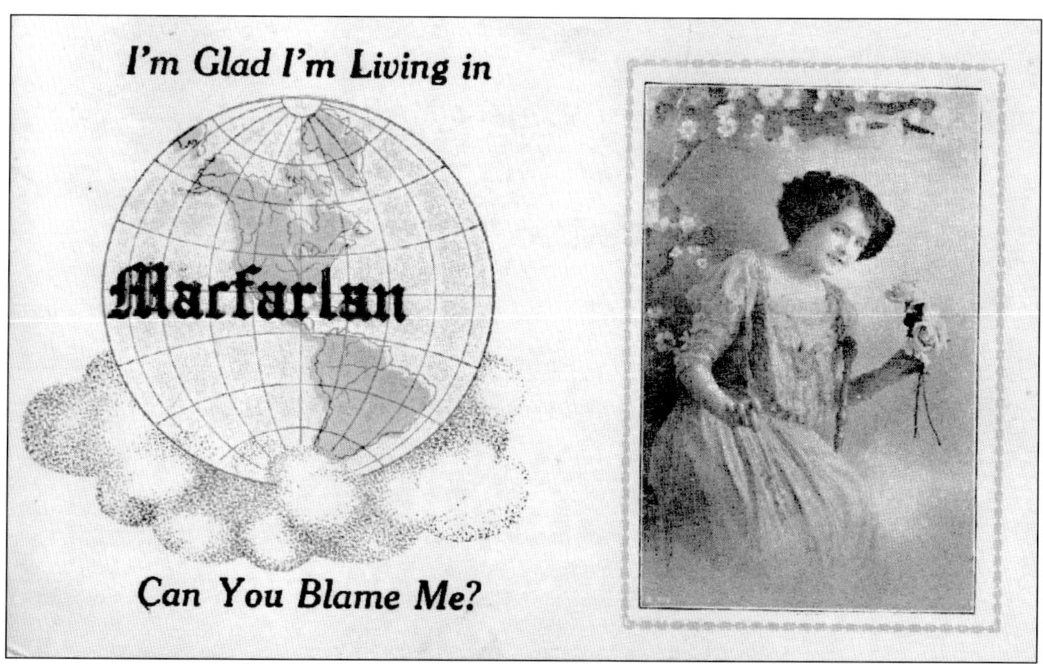

This Macfarlan card was postmarked in 1914.

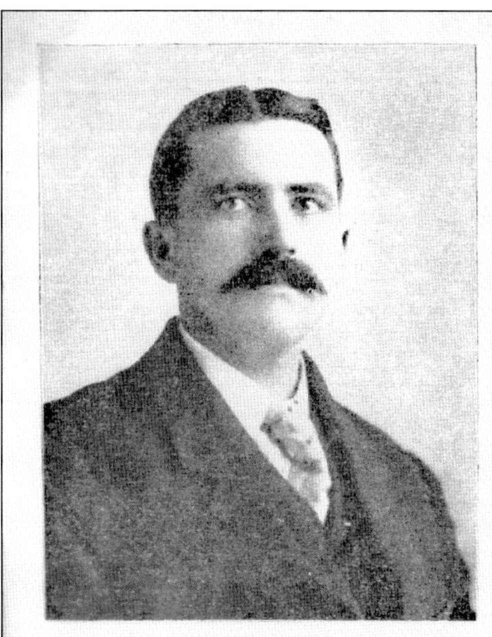

Shown here is a business advertising postcard for the W.R. Hays Trading Company in Macfarlan.

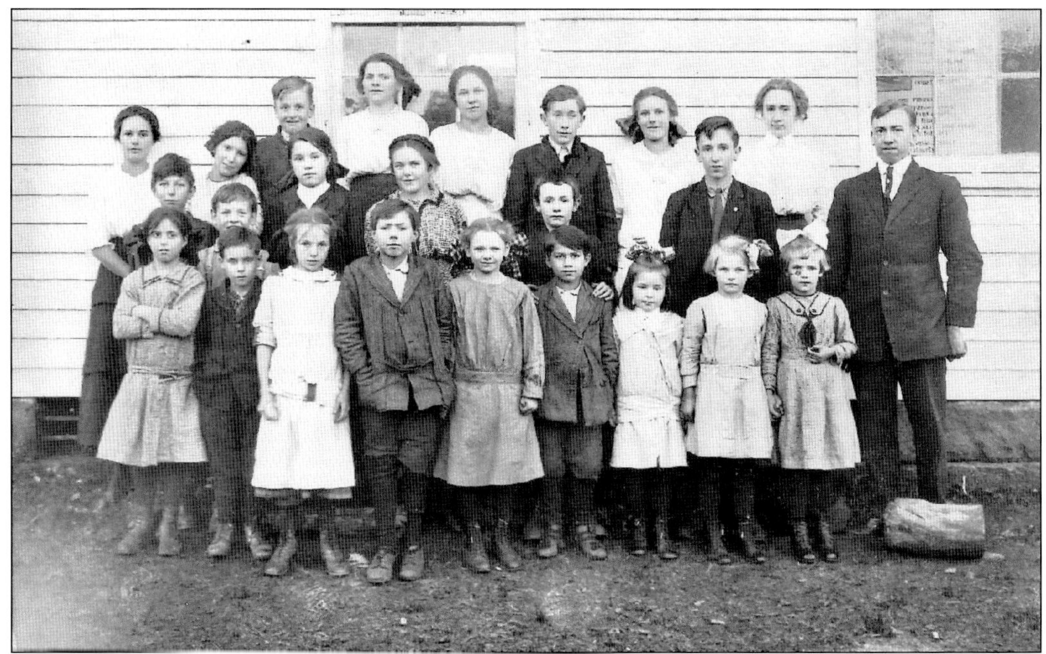

The Upper Addis Run School was located between Cairo and Harrisville just outside what is now North Bend State Park. This image dates between 1914 and 1915.

Five

TRAINS

As with many other areas of the country, Ritchie County lived and prospered because of its railroad systems, including the main line of the B&O. Other local railroads included the Ritchie Mines (also known as the Calico) which later became the C&K (Cairo & Kanawha), the P&H (Pennsboro & Harrisville), the Harrisville Southern, and the Laurel Fork and Sand Hill. The Ritchie Mines ran from Cairo to the Ritchie Mines and later to Macfarlan, where it became the C&K, a 17-mile line. The P&H ran from the B&O main line in Pennsboro to Harrisville. It later became known as the Lorama and also traveled to and through Pullman. The Harrisville Southern ran from Harrisville to Cornwallis. These railroads serviced Ritchie County as a way to send its natural resources and products to the world. The railways paved the way for an early boom in Ritchie County and brought many of its Irish immigrants here for the building of the railroads. Postcards of the trains are scarce, but these few will hopefully provide insight into Ritchie County's early railroads.

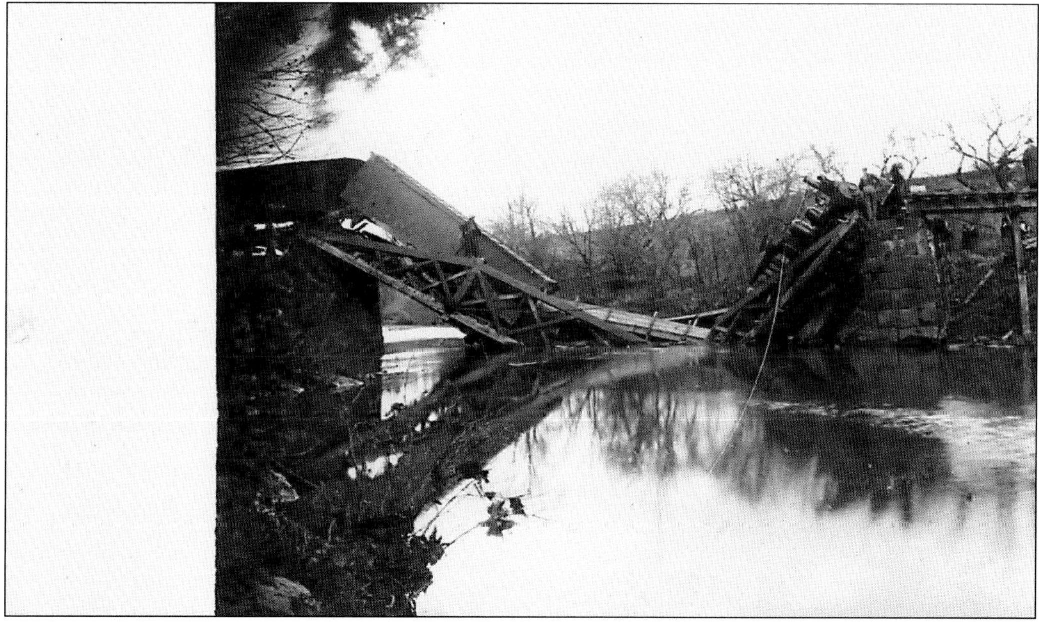

An early train wreck near Harrisville on the P&H Railroad is shown in this 1907 card. Several men can be seen in the picture. The message written on the back states that the writer was on the train, sitting in the car that is still up on the track, and that he almost received a "dunking." At the time of this mishap, 35 passengers were on board when the bridge was collapsing over the North Fork of the Hughes River at Hannadale. Train wrecks were plentiful on these smaller gauge railroads.

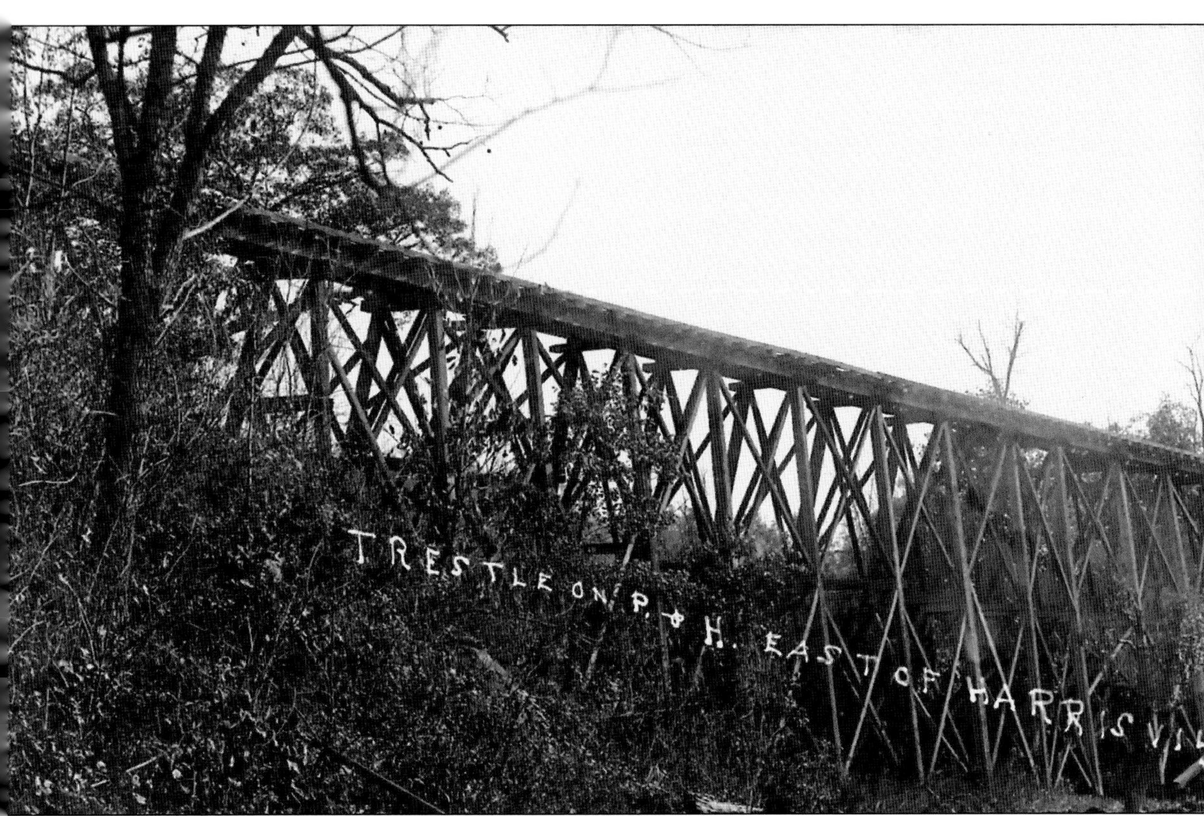

An undated card shows the trestle on the P&H Railway east of Harrisville as it crosses Happy Valley.

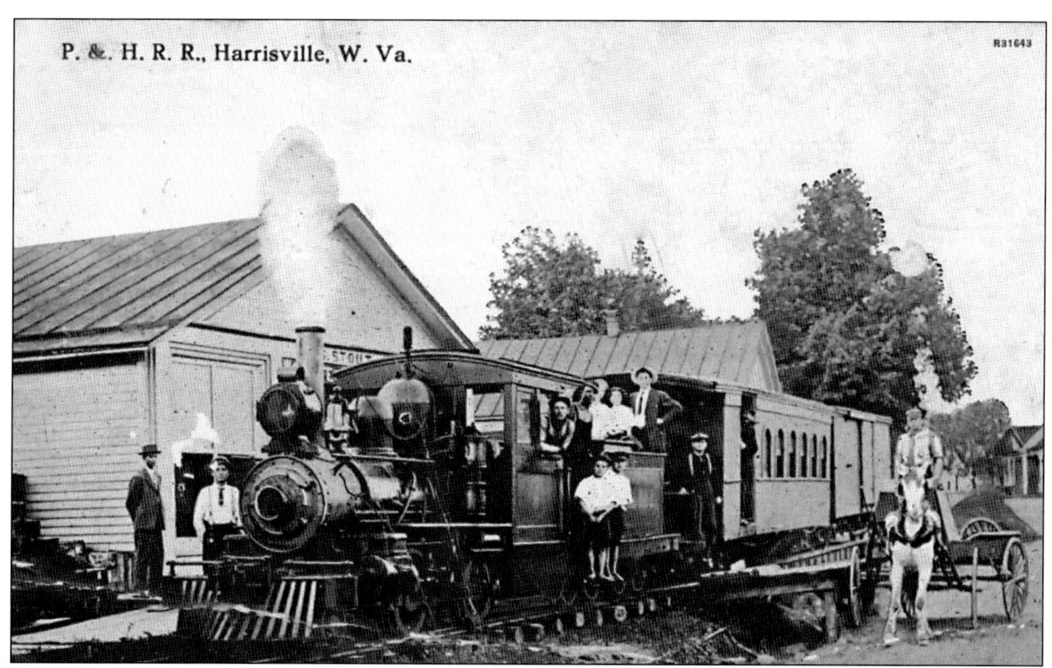

A P&H train sits in Harrisville in this undated card. The train is sitting at the corner of Main and Stout Street, facing west. The P&H made its first trip to Harrisville on Thanksgiving Day in 1875.

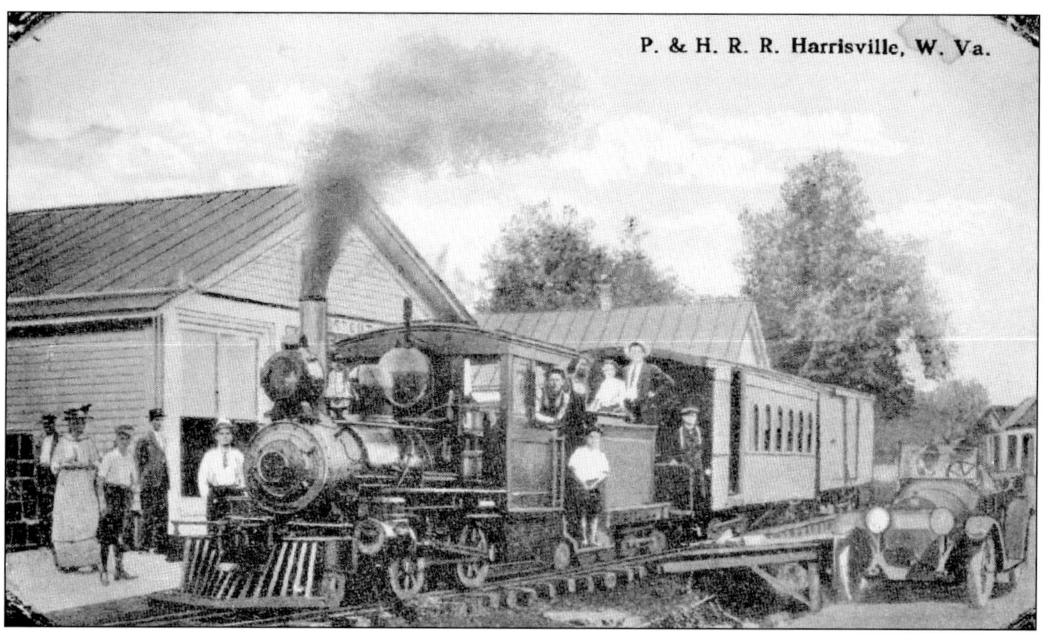

This card is the same as the one shown at the top of the page but with a few differences. It is an example of how cards were changed by artists' reconstructions. Note the people who were drawn in, as well as the second card having a car instead of a previous wagon.

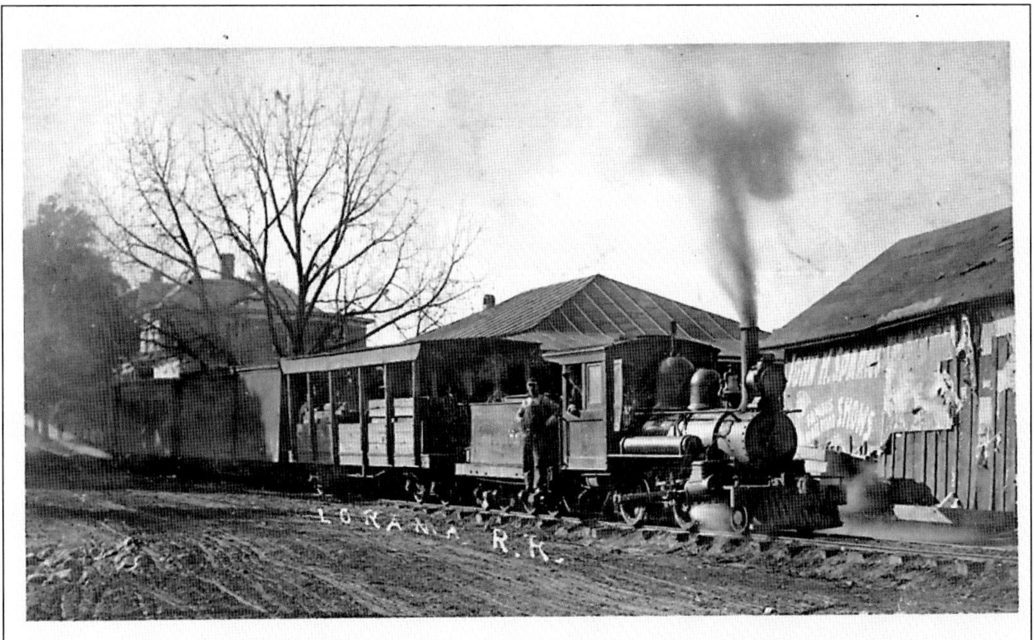

A Lorama (formerly the P&H) train sits at the depot in Harrisville in this undated card. The depot is still in use and is located on East Main Street beside the First Apostolic Church of Harrisville. It is used by the church as a youth center. The church now sits at the site of the building with the "John H. Sparks" sign on the front. On this side of the train is East Main Street looking west toward the middle of town.

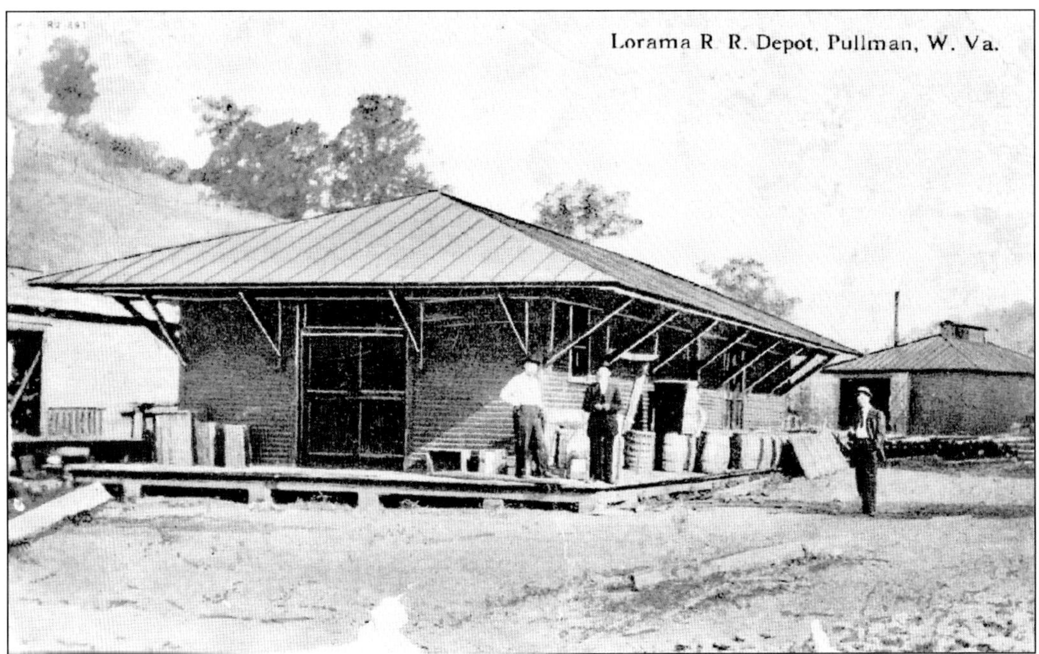

This undated card depicts the Lorama Railroad depot at Pullman. Pullman was a spur line between Harrisville and Pennsboro.

This undated postcard depicts a train on the Lorama Railroad.

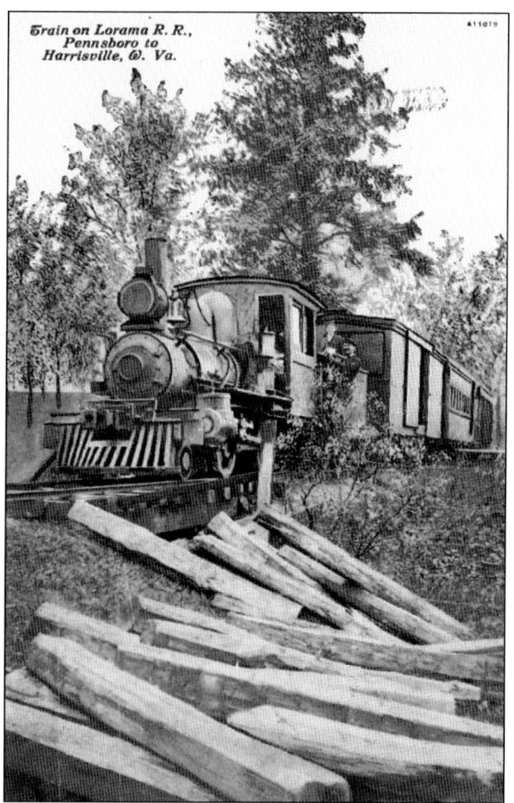

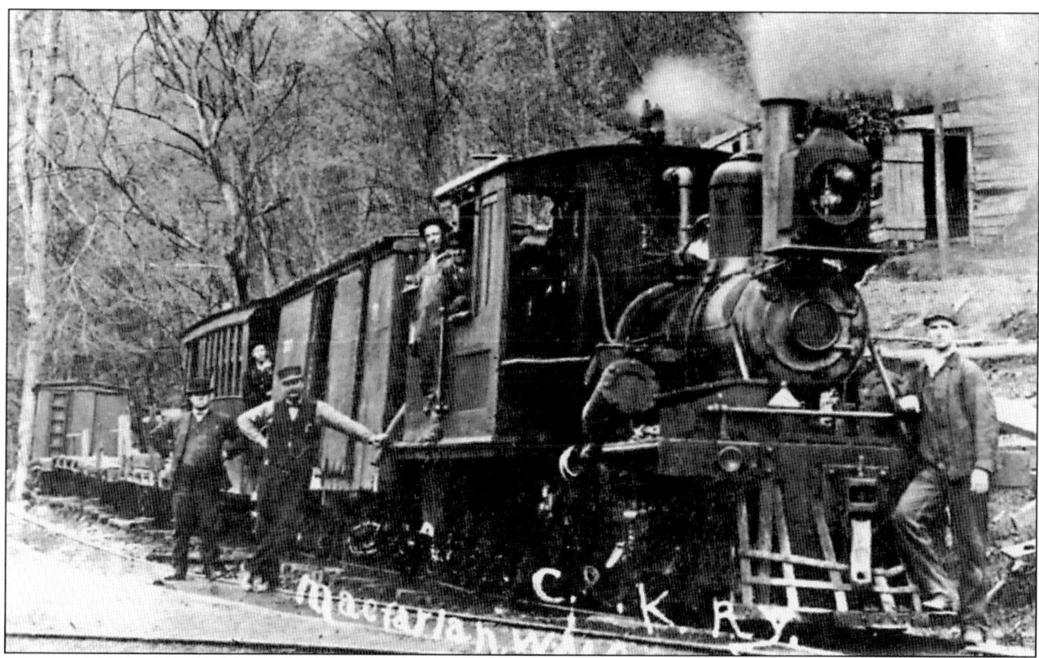

A C&K train sits in Macfarlan. This card is a reprint of a postcard that was issued by Berdine's Variety Store in 1993. The original date the photograph was taken is unknown.

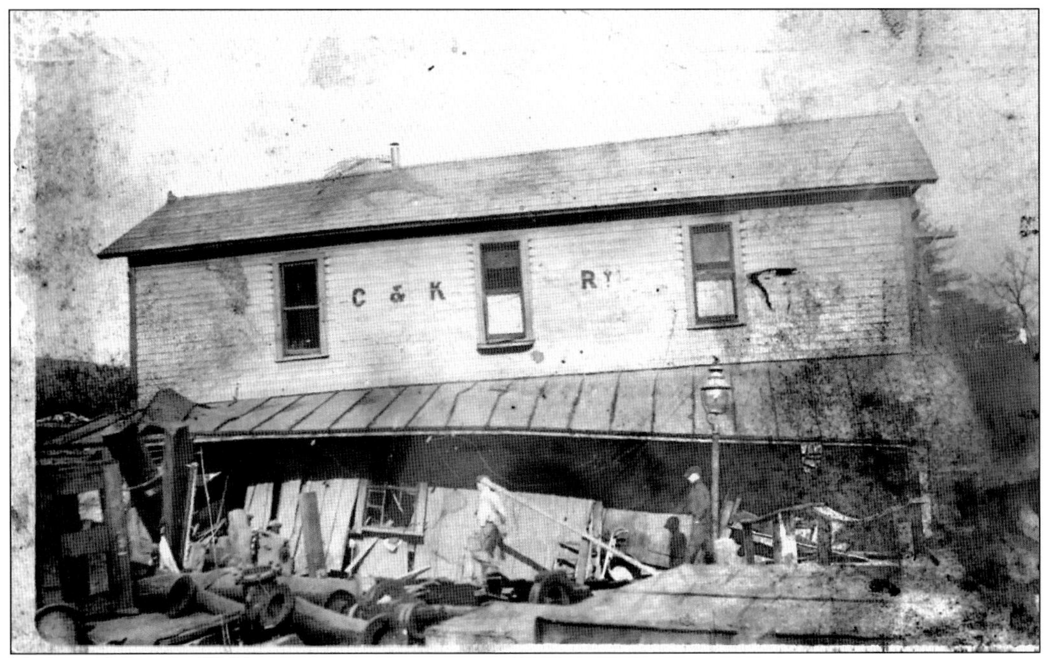

This card depicts another of the many train wrecks in Ritchie County. This wreck occurred when a B&O train ran into the C&K depot in Cairo and destroyed it. The card is undated, but the wreck was believed to have happened on November 8, 1913.

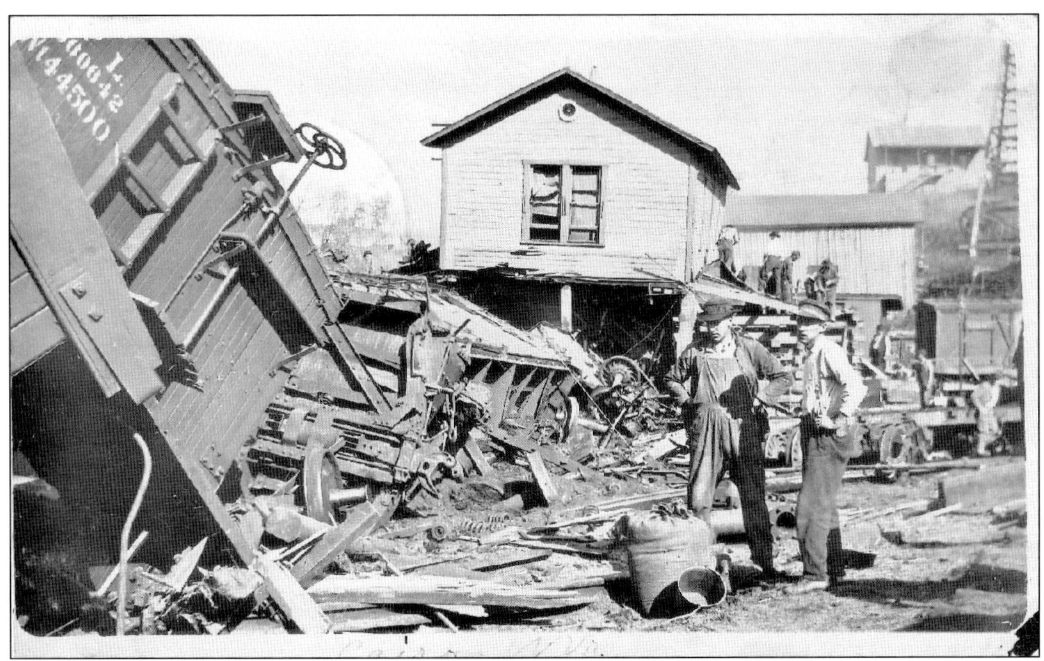

This undated card shows the same wreck as the above card.

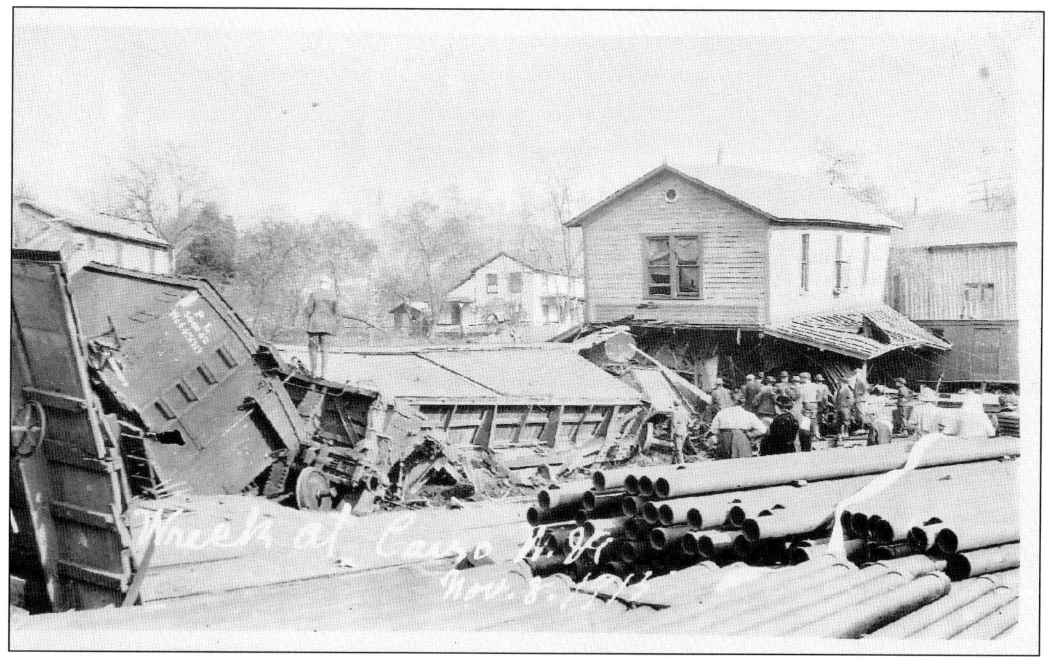

This undated card shows the same wreck as the card on the opposite page.

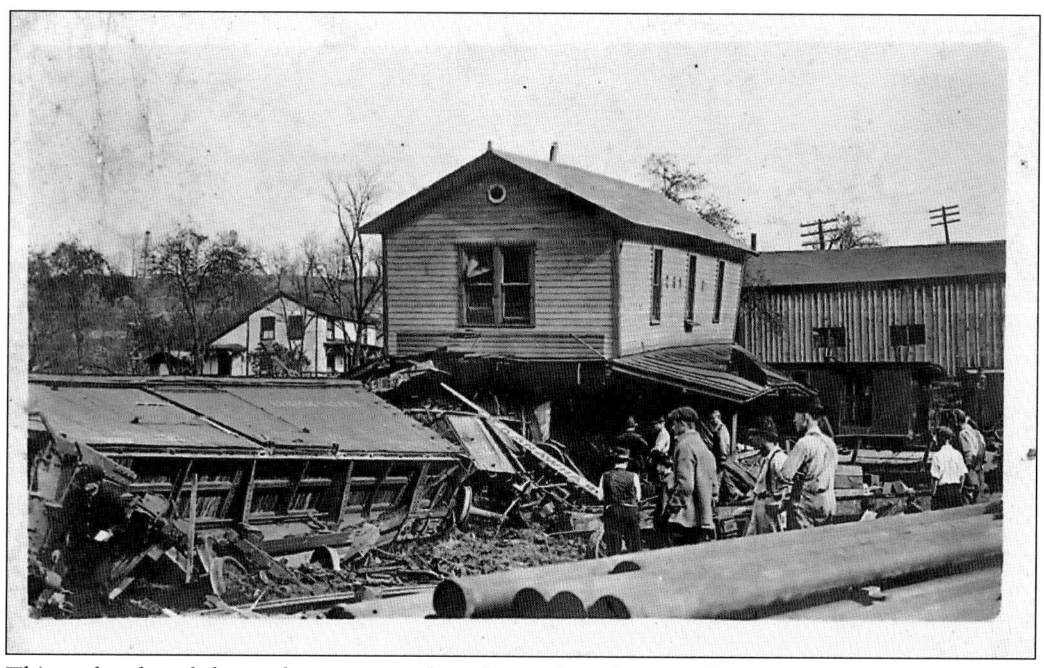

This undated card shows the same wreck as the card on the opposite page.

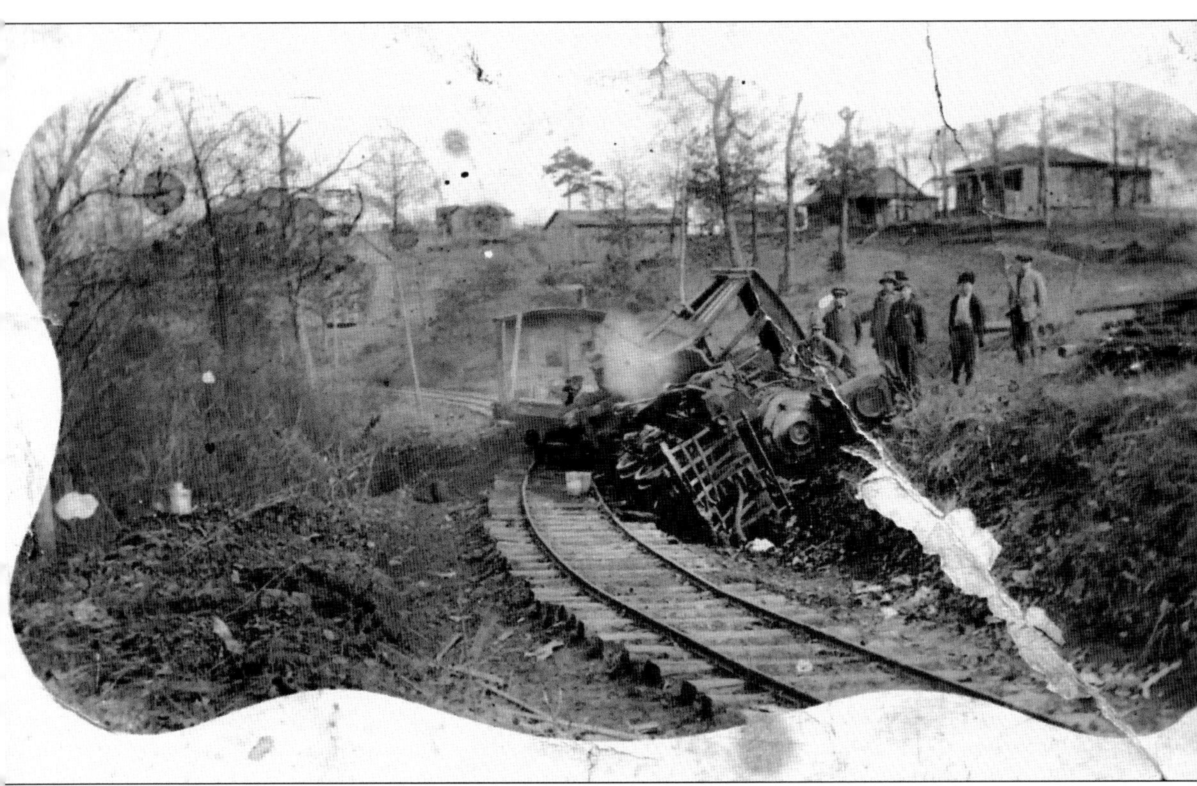

A wreck of the C&K occurred on February 14, 1918, near Mellin. From the message on the back of this card, we know this to be a wreck in which the engineer, George Cunningham, was badly scalded with steam. This card was postmarked in 1918.

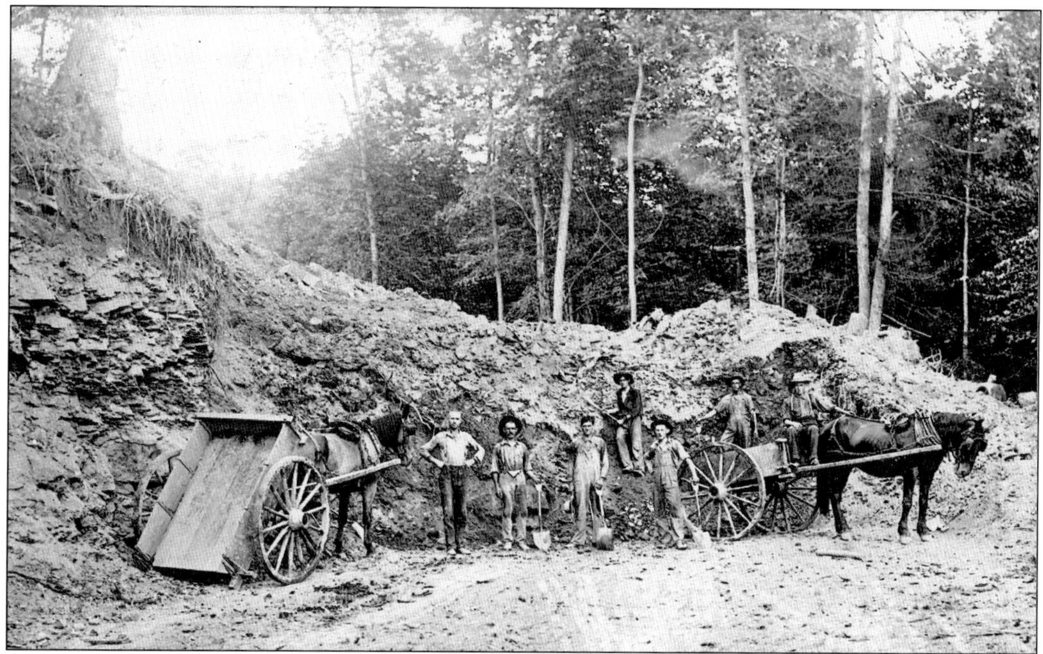

This card depicts workers on the Harrisville Southern Railroad. Although the card is undated, this is certainly the building of the railroad bed. This card reminds us of the labor intensive work that was involved in the building of the railroads. The exact location the card depicts is unknown.

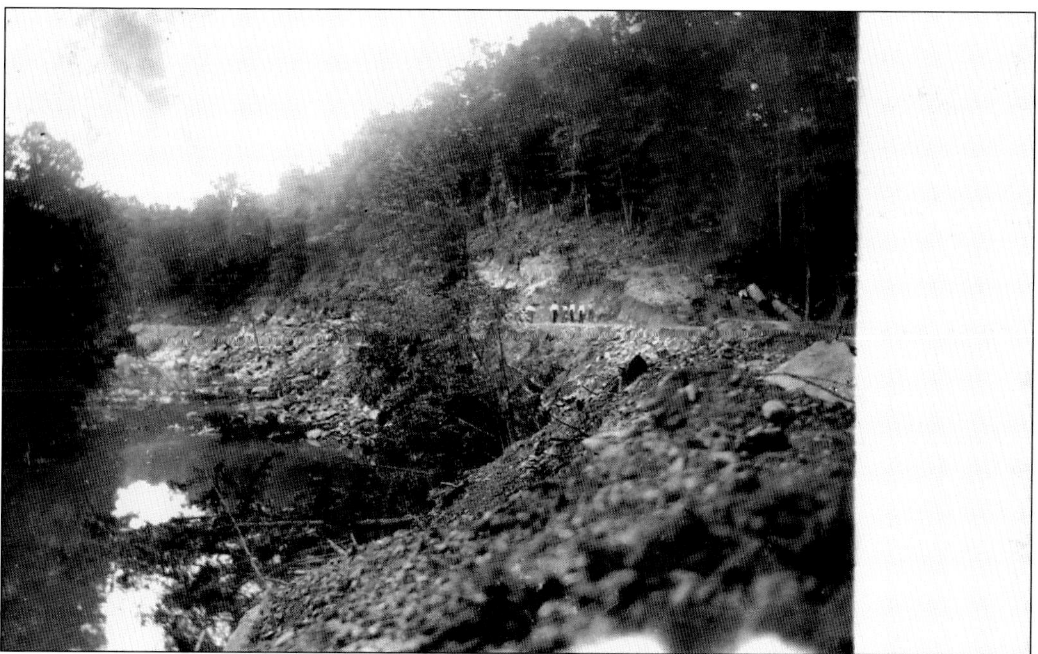

This card is another image believed to be of work on the railroad bed of the Harrisville Southern. The exact location and date are unknown.

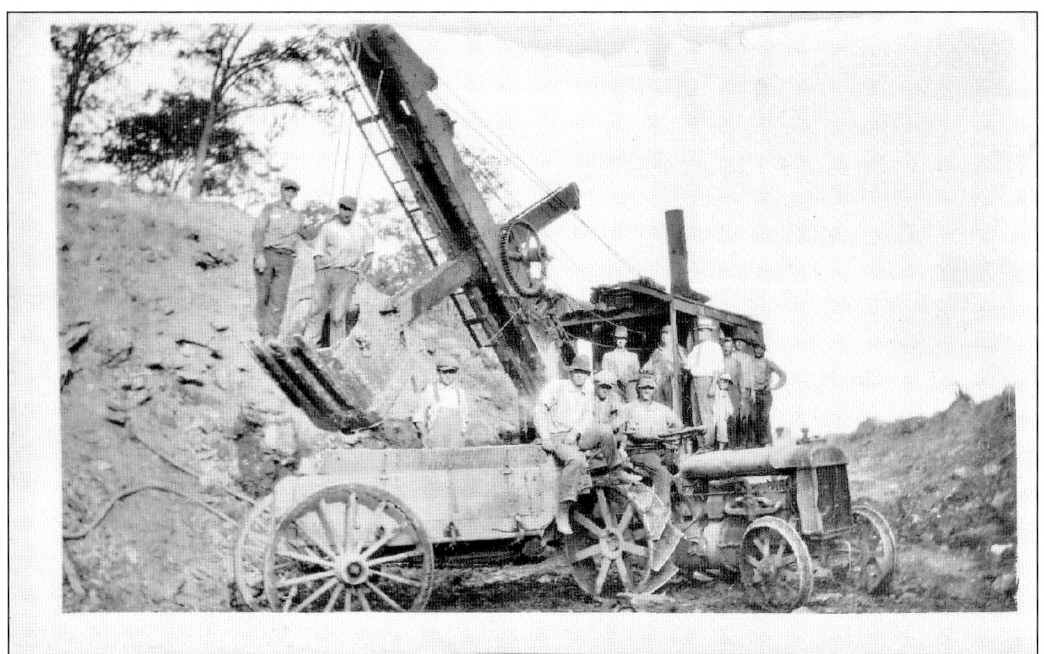

This undated card shows men and machinery. It is believed that the men are building roads somewhere in the county.

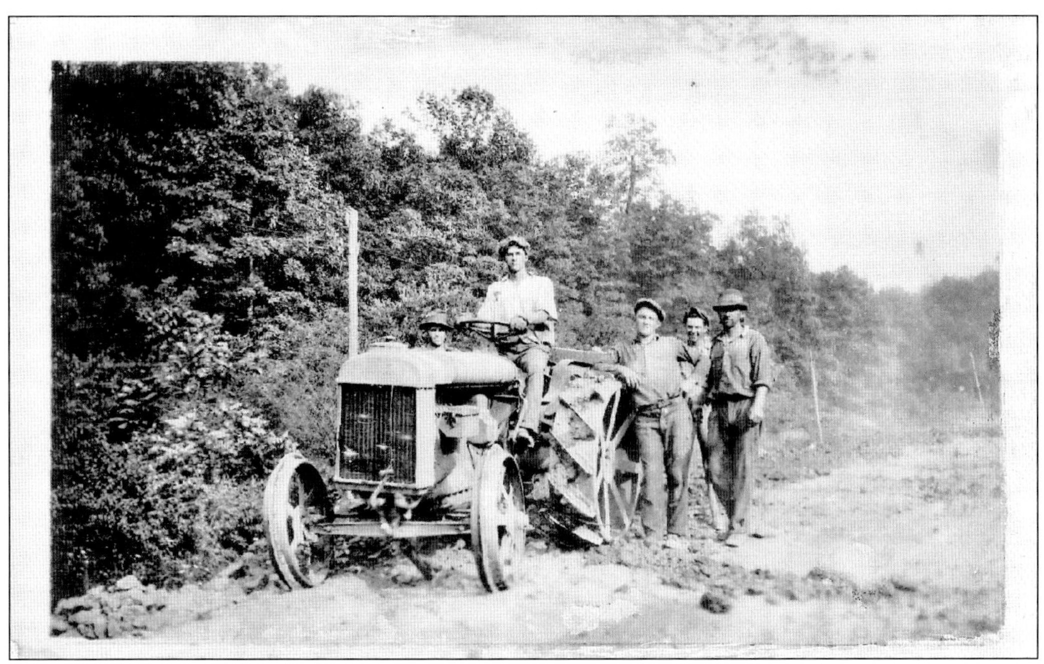

This card also shows the workers.

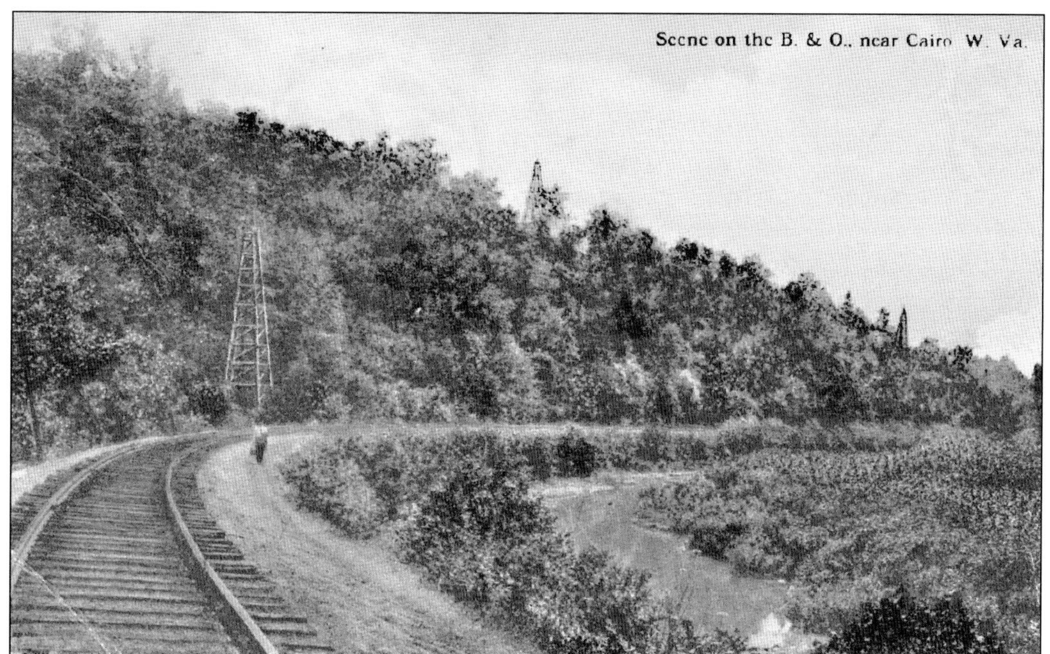

This undated card depicts a scene on the B&O line near Cairo.

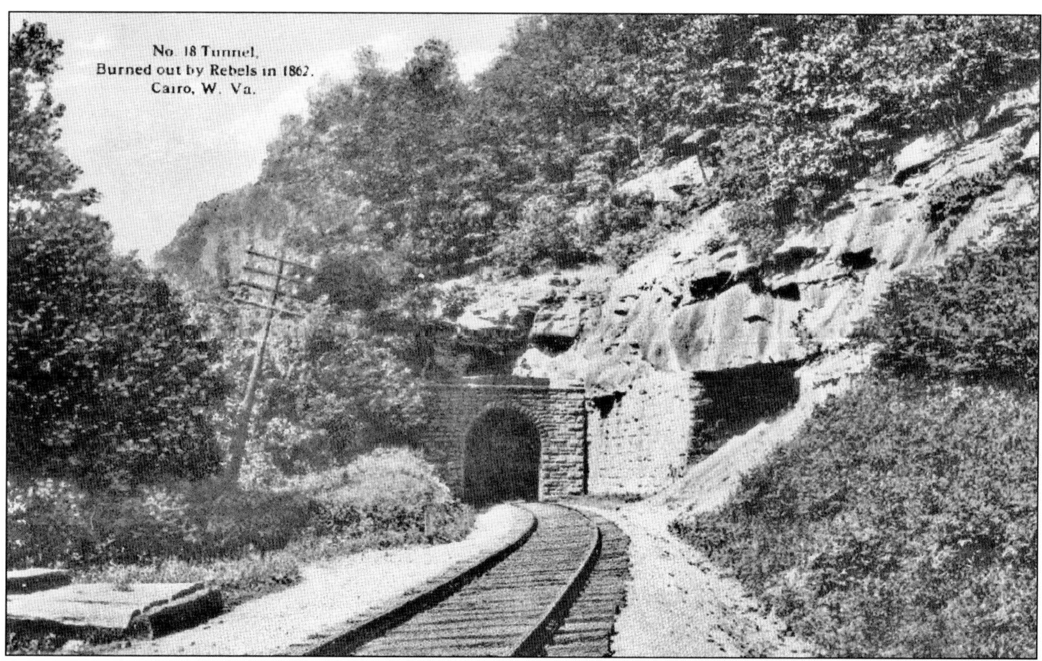

Tunnel No. 18 was removed in the 1960s, as shown in this undated card. Located near Cairo, this tunnel was burned out by rebels during the Civil War in 1862.

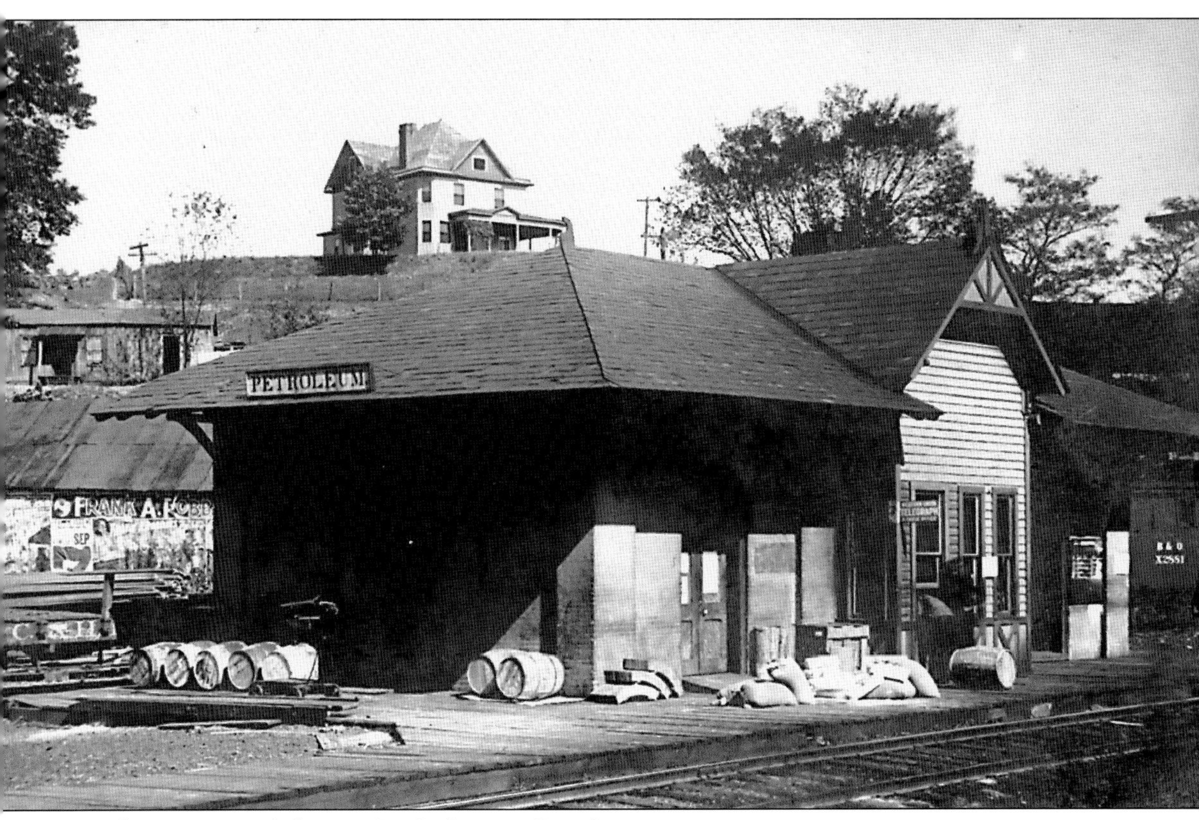

This *c.* 1915 card shows a B&O depot at Petroleum.